Sexual Paradox

Other books by the author:

Lay Voices in an Open Church
The Male-Female Church Staff:
    Celebrating the Gifts, Confronting the Challenges
      (with Anne Marie Nuechterlein)

Sexual Paradox

Creative Tensions
in Our Lives and
in Our Congregations

Celia Allison Hahn

The Pilgrim Press   New York

The scripture quotations, unless otherwise indicated, are from
the New Revised Standard Version of the Bible, copyright 1989,
Division of Christian Education of the National Council of the
Churches of Christ in the United States of America, and are used
by permission.

This book is printed on acid-free paper.

Library of Congress Cataloging-in-Publication Data

Hahn, Celia A.
　　Sexual paradox : creative tensions in our lives and in our
　congregations / by Celia Allison Hahn. — 1st ed.
　　　p.　cm.
　　ISBN 0-8298-0897-3 (pbk. : alk. paper)
　　　1. Interpersonal relations—Religious aspects—Christianity.
　2. Sex role—Religious aspects—Christianity.　3. Feminism—
　Religious aspects—Christianity.　4. Sociology, Christian.
　I. Title.
　BT708.H34　1991
　261.8'357—dc20　　　　　　　　　　　　　　　90-27105
　　　　　　　　　　　　　　　　　　　　　　　　　CIP

Printed in the United States of America.

10　9　8　7　6　5　4　3　2　1

The Pilgrim Press, 475 Riverside Drive, New York, NY 10115

Contents

Preface

We are now ready to enter a new stage of engagement between men and women in the church. The voices of feminists have brought women new awareness, new clarity, and a new sense of their own power. Women have worked hard to state their case quite independently of the male assumptions that have formerly been accepted as human assumptions. Now, having struggled to claim and proclaim their own reality, many women are beginning to see that they have an important new task: communicating effectively with men. How do women speak so that men may hear?

Only a handful of men have been listening to feminists. Many learned as little boys not to fight back at angry women. Instead, as adults, they politely refrain from rebuttal, and the conversation is stillborn. As dominant figures in society, they don't *have* to listen. It may not be clear to them what they will gain from hearing women calling them patriarchal oppressors. Aside from an ideological commitment to justice, is there anything in it for men, beyond the prospect of giving up more and more power, to look upon the human scene in a more inclusive way?

In the churches, women are being heard primarily by women, and a few men are beginning to discuss their male experience with other men. Can church people bring into one conversation these separate efforts to make sense out of women's experience and men's experience?

Throughout human history, people have seen in the encounter with the other sex a hint of the encounter with the Holy Other, and today people are displaying a renewed interest in the links between spirituality and sexuality. In our encounters with one another, transcendent hints point to paradox as a helpful approach.

Paradox affords a way for men and women to join their voices in conversation about their experience without compromising the integrity of either sex. Once we recognize that our realities as women and men may exist in tension or even contradict each other, we no longer have to deny or distort our own truth to achieve a false accommodation, which would be unacceptable to most women and many men today.

This book is about the tensions in our lives as men and women — how they break into contradictions that cause us pain, how they can serve as pointers to the Holy, and how they might enhance the richness, energy, and human wholeness of our life in the local church. In the pages that follow we will examine a series of tensions in our lives as men and women, in their physical, psychological, social, individual, and spiritual dimensions, and bring them into conversation with Christian symbols that address those human experiences. Where life and tradition intersect, gospel may happen. Out of the connections sparked by that intersection, we may draw some useful implications for our lives as individuals and as leaders and members of congregations.

This book is written for the generalist. As generalists, we all have to take the efforts of biblical scholars, psychologists, theologians, and experts in spiritual development and in congregational studies, integrate them, and put that united understanding to work in the local congregation. The book is addressed both to church professionals and to laity who are struggling to discern their ministries not only in the church but in families, at work, and in their communities. The book is about things that deeply concern all of us in our daily lives — our sense of self and our relationships, our struggles with work and leadership, our successes and our painful failures, the joy and heartache we encounter in love relationships.

I want to speak here both to women and men, both to feminists and those who haven't yet listened to them. I want to affirm the experience of men who, though they may not have greeted the present changes with enthusiasm, admit that justice demands some changes. I want to tell men that there is some promise for them in all these puzzling and distressing shifts, and point to some new ways of getting on with the practical challenges of working and living with women. And I want to suggest some alternative sources of energy to those who seek new vitality for mainline churches.

This book considers a series of issues or tensions that are part of the many-faceted reality of our lives as women and men, examining one facet at a time. These issues are human issues. We all experience them. While we can speak of ways men and women tend to lean to one or another side of an issue, these are generalizations that reflect only tendencies. Sometimes you may find yourself on the side of the issue that is presented as more typical of the other sex.

The spread of issues is designed to give breadth to the inquiry. The descent into each issue is a search for depth. What are the struggles of women and men in their own lives and in relation with each other? What relevant religious symbols might usefully be brought into their dialogue? Out of the encounter between experience and symbol, what implications spring forth for the spiritual lives of men and women and especially for their lives together in the local church?

The first two chapters lay "Foundations" for the work, presenting paradox as a way of talking about differences between the sexes and establishing our separate and connected postures as the foundational issue. In part I, "Women and Men in Tension," the next four chapters build on the foundations and raise implications for the life of the local church. Part II, "Work," explores issues related to work, the public and private spheres, and leadership. Part III, "Love," addresses aspects of love, including friendship, sexual ethics, and our relationships with mothers, fathers, and God. In "Conclusions" the final chapter proposes promises and challenges for men, women, and congregations as we move into a new future.

A note on the terms gender and sex: "Gender" has been defined as "a grammatical classification of nouns and pronouns into masculine, feminine, and neuter." Three definitions of "sex" from the Random House Dictionary read as follows: (1) "either the male or female divisions of a species, . . . (2) The fact or character of being male or female, (3) the attraction drawing one sex towards another." In this exploration I usually prefer to use the more ambiguous word sex, which includes many meanings and does not exclude the physical dimension, rather than the word gender, with its one-dimensional, grammatical meaning.

I would not have been able to complete this task without the support and critique of colleagues and friends. James R. Adams read the whole manuscript twice and offered a careful and candid critique, for which I am more grateful than I can say. Malcolm C. Burson also read the entire work and provided me with support, ideas, and useful criticism. Jim and Malcolm taught me important lessons about men's experience and response to women. I am also grateful to the following people who read parts of the manuscript and gave helpful feedback: Barbara Potter, Marianne Micks, Ruth Tiffany Barnhouse, Nancy Van Scoyoc, Loren B. Mead, Lesley M. Adams, and Mary Sudman Donovan. I want also to acknowledge my thanks for the editorial help of Barbara Withers and Susan C. Winslow of The Pilgrim Press. I owe a profound debt, as well, to two corporate teachers. The functional education program at St. Mark's Church, Capitol Hill, in Washington, D.C., has informed and challenged my thinking in basic ways for decades. And the ecumenical breadth, systems perspective, and wealth of congregational data available in my work at the Alban Institute has made important contributions to this exploration.

FOUNDATIONS

1

"Male and Female" or "All One"?

When I visited the Australian Museum in Sydney, I found myself captivated by the exhibit of great red kangaroos. The sign next to those six-foot-tall stuffed animals informed me that the males are distinctly red in color, while the females have a bluish tinge and are in fact called "blue flyers." But not always. About 30 percent of the females are reddish, and about 20 percent of the males are bluish gray. Here, I thought, is a helpful metaphor for other male-female differences. We seem to find it so hard to affirm that women and men tend to be different in some ways (it *does* make sense to call male kangaroos red and female kangaroos blue) and also to acknowledge that no differences are absolute (females can be red, and males can be blue).

A brief review of our struggles to clarify or deny male-female differences may help us move ahead to explore some new possibilities. In recent years many people have been reluctant to admit any differences between men and women, encouraged by anthropologists and psychologists who tell us that we have been clearer about the differences between the sexes than the facts warrant. Many of us seek to find liberty and equality in stressing, instead, our common human nature.

We now understand all too well that differentiating too clearly between men and women distorts reality and causes us many kinds of pain. Stereotypical thinking leads us to caricature one another with labels such as "macho," "wimp," "fluff," "bitch." It limits our freedom: little boys would rather die than do anything that might provoke the taunt "Sissy!" Being a girl may take on a similarly narrow and negative meaning. When we try to be "a real man" or "a real woman" we turn *de*scriptions of a gift that is ours — by virtue of creation — into burdensome *pre*scriptions that are likely to leave us feeling like losers.

Distinguishing too clearly the differences between men and women can lead us to project what we wish we weren't, and what we wish we *were*, onto the other person. This tendency leads us either to hate or to idolize the one carrying our unclaimed baggage. The result may be idolatry and the death of our own self-esteem, or it may be violence — ranging from verbal violence to death by stoning. And of course dividing the world into "real men" and "real women" reflects and exacerbates the split *within* each of us, as well.

People would not be tempted to resort to stereotypes unless they had some attractive features. Either/or thinking makes us feel more firmly in control of our world. But the benefits — the comfort that structured souls find in familiar patterns and the opportunity to simplify life by relating to "people like that" instead of the bewildering variety of unique human beings we in fact encounter — do not stack up very well against all the painful problems we cause ourselves by being inappropriately clear about gender differences.

The Denial of Differences

When a male colleague and I taught a class in our church titled "Women and Men: a Biblical Perspective," we found ourselves confronted by fourteen women and thirteen men — all of whom refused to agree on any gender-specific characteristics they hoped their children would carry into the future. They did acknowledge some physical differences, but many speculated that scientific advances might render even those obsolete.

This group of people insisted that differences between men and women are "only physical" or "only cultural." These women and men had reasons for their inclination to dismiss differences by placing them in those two categories. Differences that are "only cultural," it is implied, can be readily unlearned by a more enlightened generation. It is not surprising that they wanted to minimize physical differences; biology has too often been used as a club by reactionaries. If anatomy is destiny, our future threatens to be a carbon copy of our past.

While I was filled with admiration for this group's dedication to equal rights and their concern to open the whole range of human experiences to women and men, I couldn't help noting some problems in their passion for human uniformity. Dismissing the differences between men and women, like carving them in stone, seemed to result in a seductively simple picture of human life.

One major problem I saw in the "only physical" and "only cultural" approach was its underlying assumption that essential humanity is *not* physical and *not* cultural but, presumably, some form of disembodied solitary spirit. This assumption is not congruent with a faith centered on the incarnation or with the Hebraic appreciation of the unity of our bodies, minds, and spirits, and of our oneness with the rest of humanity. Nor is this isolated and abstract view of human nature hospitable to convictions many women hold dear: that our bodily life is real and valuable and very *much* a part of us, that part and parcel of our identity is being connected with the web of human society, which is real (and often agonizingly resistant to change).

This passion for homogenization catches us in a second problem: dismissing gender differences does not secure equality between men and women. A sole emphasis on "human" nature runs the risk of judging women's realities by "man, the measure of all things," making women look inferior when in fact they are just different. The tragic and unintended result of the unisex movement is that women's reality remains hidden. The tendency to overlook women's special contribution to human life is exacerbated because the English language defines women as derived from men: *man*kind, wo*man*, fe*male*, Miss *father's name*, Mrs. *husband's name*, Ms. *father's name or husband's name*. To protest that "Women are *not* inferior; they are just like men" is a contradiction in terms. And when men say there are no differences, they may be avoiding dealing with inequality while subtly assuming it. When dominants say, "There is no difference between you and us"; "You are just as good as we are"; "You measure up...to *us*!" men and women are invited to collude in maintaining the status quo, to our common human detriment.

An illogical assumption commonly goes unexamined: that we must deny differences, because if two things are different one has to be better than the other. The notion that differences can only be ranked hierarchically is imported unthinkingly from the conceptual world of the dominants.[1] Here again the denial of differences reflects a dominant-subordinate universe rather than the equality its adherents hoped to support.

Denying differences reduces the richness of our human experience. Inclusive language and equal opportunities for women are keys with which we can begin to unlock the hidden and rich contributions of women — *and men, too*. Not only the oppressed but the oppressors suffer, as systems thinking teaches us. When men are freed from the necessity of representing and encompassing all that is human, their distinctly male reality will shine forth more clearly. And we will recapture the human energy that is always generated when differences are held in tension.

Still another problem with a homogenized view of humanity is that it can lead us to treat other people in hurtful ways. Unfortunately, some women are now taking Henry Higgins' outraged complaint in *My Fair Lady* and turning it around: "Why can't a man be more like a woman?" The assumption that the other's reality is like mine does not lead to respectful and loving behavior toward others — or toward ourselves. When we assume that we are all the same, we may try hard to obtain things we really do not want. Some women today are finding themselves disappointed by the sexual freedom traditionally considered male for which they once longed.

Finally, denying differences impoverishes our lives spiritually, for the mystery of the other sex points to the rich mystery of the Holy Other. Uniformity may be a characteristic of technology, but it does not seem to be a principle of creation's rich and intricate and surprising variety. "In the image of God he created them; male and female he created them." Our created differences point toward a richer realm of the spirit, with more warmth and sparkle, than we could know as undifferentiated earth creatures.

In Search of a Balance

How can we avoid the difficulties that arise both from over-emphasizing the differences between women and men and from denying that there are any differences? How can we find a balance between both realities: that we are created "male and female" and also that we are "all one"?

Your story, my story, and the stories in the Bible are rich in tension, concreteness, and embodied character, as well as a hint of mystery. The stories in Genesis 1 and 2 explore the tensive and enfleshed mystery of the tales of our beginnings. Here are stories in which male and female are clearly one — and two, in which their equality is clear, and in which their relationship with God is hinted at in their sexuality.[2]

Human sexuality is the crown of creation. The first words spoken are a beautiful erotic poem ("This at last is bone of my bones and flesh of my flesh."), and the new creatures move toward each other to become one flesh. How paradoxical that the point of the operation is to create "one flesh"! From one, to two, to one.

Like the story in Genesis 2, the creation story in the first chapter presents male and female as created simultaneously. Their freedom and equality are evident in that *both* are to share equally in two responsibilities: dominion over creation (a task shared with God) and procreation (a task shared with other creatures). The words chosen to point to "image of God" are "male and female" — very biological and sexual words. As Philip Turner points out, "The Priestly writer...insists, first of all, that being male and female is not something we seek to transcend on our way to becoming individual 'persons.' The distinction between male and female is written into the order of the cosmos and it is good."[3] Not only humankind but Deity is referred to by singular and plural pronouns: "Let *us* make humankind....Behold *I* have given you..."

Unity and differentiation appear to be not only inherent in human nature but shared with divine nature. The finger pointing from the human nature we know to the divine nature we do not know is seen most clearly in the placing of "in the image of God" and "male and female" in parallel positions in verse 27. The story speaks of unity and equality and also of the energy and mystery that come only from interaction with the *other*. Human beings have always seen our relationship with the mysterious other sex as a metaphor for the Holy, a way of participating in the creative energy of God.

Standing in the Tension

These creation stories pointing to the mystery of human and divine life may suggest a way to stand in the tension between two certainties that deny reality's richness and that, ultimately, let us down: the certainty that we know the differences between men and women precisely and the certainty that no significant differences exist.

Standing in the tension embraces four intertwined but distinguishable elements: ambiguity, contradiction, energy, and paradox.

Ambiguity

The word ambiguity speaks of the muddled quality of life, its refusal to fall into neat distinctions or to be encapsulated in any monolithic statement. We can't tidy things up by deciding to exclude the physical, social, or psychological dimensions of life — or by reducing all of life to one dimension. We have to give up the illusion that truth is linear and simple. We have to accept that there is no easy way to climb on top of life's complexities. When we give up those illusions, we claim the freedom to live with reality as it is, and we open ourselves to mystery.

Contradiction

The word contradiction points to the hurtful opposition in which we often find ourselves caught. Women often find encounters with men painful. And men speak of the pain they experience in their relationships with women. Our individual pain is compounded by the systemic dimension, the oppressive structures that feel out of our control but that hurt us all. An awareness of the contradictions in our lives makes us know we need healing and peace.

Energy

Tension also suggests exciting possibilities. When we talk about "creative tension" we express our hope for energy and creativity in spite of the muddle and the struggle. Those who have convinced themselves that differences between women and men are set in concrete, or that there are no differences, hope to make the relationships between men and women simple and controllable. In fact, they remove the life from them. Now we may find that if we hold our differences together, not leaving either out, energy is generated, as with a positive and negative charge of electricity. Certainly energy is generated between men and women! Tension as energy also points to risk and adventure. We find we are making a choice for life when we are willing to venture ahead in spite of the tension.

Because my capacity for embracing opposing realities is so limited, I may need to do this by moving from one pole of a tension to another as I journey through life. During periods such as adolescence, I find that separating myself from others is a prerequisite for defining my boundaries. Having made some discoveries about who I am, I am freer to embrace the other. Mature men and women seem to be on friendly terms with characteristics of the other sex that once seemed alien. Not only individuals but cultures seem to propel themselves into the future by this kind of "tacking" back and forth in the tension. Now that mainline Christians have spent a decade or two emphasizing our common humanity, we will probably see a renewed ability to look at the differences between men and women, at a deeper and more complex level.

Paradox

The word paradox points to a transcendent resolution that cannot be explained logically. I can open myself to this possibility when I no longer take a fragment and make it *the whole truth*, when I do not reduce reality artificially through false saviors. False saviors might be found within me or in others (especially the other sex), or in ideologies, literal acceptance of texts, or stereotypical thought patterns. When I do not reject part of myself, part of reality, or the truth about other people's lives, I may consent to receive the reality that is given to me by the Creator. When the half-gods go, the gods arrive. When I give up my simple answers, I consent to fall between the poles of the tension. This consent is a free fall in space where I must trust in God.

Through paradox, I acknowledge mystery — the mystery that lies in the otherness-in-which-I-find-what-is-closest-to-my-heart. I acknowledge the immensity of life and my finite inability to climb on top of it. Paradox points beyond us to the One who can "contradict the contradictions"[4] and transform them into abundant possibilities. "In the image of God he created them, male and female he created them." "In Christ . . . neither male nor female."

I see many kinds of promise in "sexual paradox" as a way of religiously understanding men and women.

It offers a way to recognize differences without splitting and polarizing them or ranking differences hierarchically. Unlike stereotypical, polarizing ways of looking at difference, sexual paradox means holding two ambiguously different realities in tension. A paradoxical approach, unlike some dualistic ones, is hospitable to women's way of thinking. When we are able to acknowledge differences without saying one is better than the other, we may be able to move beyond the contempt and revenge that commonly alienate men and women today. Instead, we can celebrate our different gifts as mutual offerings. To be "one in Christ Jesus" doesn't mean denying our differences. To say that we are "neither male nor female" is a statement about *value*, not *sameness*. The Galatians 3:28 passage says that dominant-subordinate arrangements, like those between masters and slaves, have now lost their power.

Sexual paradox offers us a way to hold different dimensions of our lives together, and it therefore implies a sacramental and incarnational approach, a way of seeing our enfleshed lives as a gift that is not irrelevant to the spiritual, social, psychological, or communal dimensions of our existence. We *are* our male and female bodies, and they are metaphors of many of our life postures. Physical sexuality is more appropriately seen as pointing beyond itself to God and to the wholeness of our lives than as a restriction that separates us from God or confines the scope of our life work to prescribed biological functions.

Sexual paradox suggests ways to live ethically as sexual persons. People have often been unwilling to stay in the tension when it comes to sexual behavior; instead they have denied or ignored sexual realities on one hand or acted them out in unreflective and inappropriate ways on the other. Surely we can live more faithfully if we consent to live in the tension between two realities: awareness of our feelings and drives and also of the call to behave in responsible ways.

Sexual paradox invites us to live where the currents of energy spark back and forth. People discover new sources of vitality when they hold opposites together in tension. And there is a lot of good energy for ministry in male-female collaboration — energy that is one of the most precious gifts of God for the people of God!

Sexual paradox points beyond human realities to the mystery of the divine life. By opening the hands with which we clutch partial certainties, we let go, and swing into the space between the truths signified by those two biblical texts: "male and female he created them" and "neither male nor female...in Christ Jesus." It is an ambiguous space, a contradictory space, a space full of energy, a paradoxical space. But that fragile space may be the best place for frail creatures of dust to stand, hanging on the breath of God, in "holy insecurity."[5]

2

Connected
and Separate

Are we all one? Or are we separate? In the church course on women and men that I and my colleague taught, the participants who said there were no significant differences between the sexes behaved very differently when they signed up for the class. Since we wanted a balanced group, we put equal numbers of spaces for women and men on the sign-up sheet. Women filled all their spaces before more than a couple of men had registered, and rumors spread that the teachers "had a bounty out on men." Serious recruiting efforts during the coffee hour finally induced an equal number of men to join. As the class got underway, women asked eager questions about men's experience; men betrayed no curiosity about what it was like to be a woman.

Church classes with "a bounty out on men" are not news. But what's the meaning of this commonplace situation? Why are women eager and men reluctant to talk about the relationships between them?

Why Do Women Connect?
Why Do Men Separate?

Within us and between us, we often discover a conflict between two basic human needs: the need to be me, to be free, to stake out my boundaries, and the need to be related, to be intimate, to commit myself to another.

With the snipping of the umbilical cord, my warmly dim, cozily engulfed existence within another ends abruptly. I am no longer afloat in an environment with automatic catering and climate control but suddenly separate from all that is not-me. Others may try in vain to silence my wails. Any illusions that I control the not-me are shattered by the occasional empty belly and soggy diaper. The garden gates have closed. I become a vulnerable adventurer. The myths of the Fall dramatize the loss of primal oneness with the All — a loss that brings to birth both anticipation and grief.

The conflict between our need to be separate and our need to be connected is waged not only within every human heart but between women, with a leaning toward connectedness, and men, with a bent toward separation. Of course these are *tendencies*, not clear categories that distinguish men and women. With that caveat firmly in mind, let us search for the sources of these pervasive proclivities.

On the one hand, the growing male human being confirms his masculine identity by separating from that original other who is *not like him*. Because he certified his being-as-male by breaking away from his beginnings, he finds it natural to continue taking things apart, noticing distinctions, analyzing components.

On the other hand, the growing female has found source and solace in a relationship with one who is *like her*. Because her feminine identity unfolds alongside this intimate connection with mother, she will continue to know herself in and through her relationships with other people. She approaches life with a preference for *putting things together* over taking them apart.

Masculinity: Defined by Distinction

When asked "Who are you?" men are likely to tell about what sets them apart, what distinguishes them from others. A little boy hears the message "Don't be like your mother, and don't be like girls — that's 'sissy.'" He may learn to tune out womantalk ("Put your bike away"..."Stand in line"..."No fighting!") He is interested in things and takes them apart to see how they work. Tall figures stride out of Wild West stories into a boy's imagination. The hero of a boy's tales and dreams might have a sidekick, like the Lone Ranger's Tonto, but he was more likely to travel alone. "The hero was always right.... Nothing made him cry."[1] Significantly, the Lone Ranger's early nurture in Tonto's tribe has disappeared from the legend.

The separate stance holds promise. It offers freedom and adventure, the joy of exploring a world full of possibilities. It beckons toward a quest, an unencumbered journey. Though it involves painful losses, letting go of attachments is one of life's most necessary skills; it builds personal strength and presses a man to speak in his own distinctive voice. There is high energy in being one's own self, freely questioning time-worn assumptions, choosing a personal direction uncompromised by others' agendas. An ad for masculine scent suggests this allure: "Chaps is for men who are strong and proud and living with a feeling of independence." In personal as well as geographical boundaries, good fences can make good neighbors.

Yet the disconnected state is not without its costs. It's cold out there. One must be prepared for loneliness and isolation, conflict and alienation. When we are cut off from community, we may miss the warnings that could keep us off destructive paths. We will leave things out of our lives. Many men discover in midlife that they are strangers to the territory of the human heart.

The posture of a separate life generates its own brand of fear: the specter of losing one's hard-earned freedom. As one man put it, "To me, getting married means giving up a lot of things." Tying the knot spells bondage. One study found that the more successful men were, the more they feared women as all-powerful.[2] The fear of being swallowed up by the feminine may even be enfleshed in impotence.

As he tries to find his way between these promises and costs, the man confronts a dual task. First he must wrench himself free and claim his manhood. He has to say goodbye to mother before he can ride out to seek his fortune. He has to leave the world of women and learn from men how to be a man. Only then can he relax his boundaries enough to reconnect, reclaiming the parts of his experience that he has until now assigned to women. Moving toward one side of a tension often calls forth the other. That haunting Civil War song, "Just before the battle, Mother, I am thinking most of you" evokes predawn fear in a cold, muddy trench, where perhaps the soldier's memories of mother's warm arms and fragrant kitchen signaled all that made life good.

It is the completion of this sequence — separation and reconnection — that gives a man's life wholeness, grace, and authentic freedom. Paradoxically, if his life continues to be determined by separation and opposition to women, he betrays his continuing bondage. His freedom eludes him.

Femininity: Defined Through Connection

"Who are you?" Women don't answer that question by pointing out what distinguishes them from others; they define themselves through their ties to others. They will tell you they are wives, daughters, sisters, lovers, mothers. The pattern continues unbroken from childhood. The "latency" period notwithstanding, a little girl never stops wanting to be friends with boys. Her concern about interacting with people shows up in precocious verbal fluency. She'll stand around the edge of the playground with her friends and talk about relationships. In her games she is concerned that nobody be left out. In art class, while her brother's complicated battle scene features jet planes shooting each other down, her pictures are likely to show a family in a house.

As adults, even highly successful women do not describe themselves by telling about academic and professional distinctions.[3] Recent interviews with young people found that in spite of two decades of liberation, women's love relationships are crucially important to them. "Ask a young woman to tell you about herself and she will give you a history of her love affairs."[4] Because she does not have to claim her being as a woman by saying, "I am *not like mother*," her identity is not separate from intimacy, and she discovers more sameness than difference as she meets her world. Stages and sequences are not built into her soul.

Connections in many ways enhance the life of a woman and those with whom she is linked. Her concern for interdependent relationships teaches her how to give and how to care. Because under the best of circumstances she feels safe in the universe, a woman often conveys a restful sense of centeredness within herself, providing a warm, nurturing environment in which not only her own children but others can grow.

But there are costs in not being more fully differentiated; they can take three major forms. First, her sense of self may be shaky if it is too enmeshed in relationships with others. If she acts like the grout that holds together her mosaic of relationships, she may accurately perceive that she herself is "bent out of shape." She may find that her focus on relationships is self-defeating when she takes such good care of a relationship with a man that he remains quite oblivious of it. The death of a relationship may feel like the loss of her very self; it may lead to depression and a total loss of self-determination: "I will do anything if only you will let me stay in this relationship with you." A life rooted in connections with others evokes fears of abandonment.

Second, a woman who is insufficiently separate won't achieve as much as she otherwise could. A woman whose life is determined by relationships may not know what she herself really wants to do. Lacking the struggles of a separate self that give birth to self-confidence, a woman may subordinate herself and her work to her relationships, settling for derivative kinds of tasks. When others' agendas direct her work, her efforts generate less energy, more stress and fatigue.

A third cost of an overly connected stance may lie in the ambiguous character of "love" that binds others rather than respecting their freedom. Love includes willingness to let go when one's own and the other's well-being requires some distance, as with grown children who must break away and build independent lives. Binding love makes them feel oppressively engulfed by her care.

The promise and cost of her connected stance make woman's life task less complicated than a man's — but no easier. She needs to learn to balance her connected stance, with all its positive gifts to herself and others, with appropriate self-definition. In contrast to the man, who must learn to reconnect, she needs to clarify her own boundaries, make her own choices, including the choice to be alone when solitude is what she needs.

Connected and Separate

We can detect tendencies toward a connected or separate stance in a broad range of human experiences, from thinking to work to worship.

Thinking

Some research indicates that the two hemispheres of the human brain are more integrated in women, more separated in men.[5] This means that there is a small but consistent tendency for men to be more self-reliant and nonconforming, while women as a group tend to be more affectionate and considerate.[6] It's not surprising, then, that little boys like taking things apart, while little girls hold them together.

Men tend to compartmentalize their experience so that it does not compromise the objectivity of their thinking. In contrast, women tend to allow their experiences to inform their perceptions and their analysis of the world around them. Professors of preaching observed in their women students a tendency to weave personal examples through their sermons, integrating them with their biblical and theological points.[7]

Work

Men tend to identify themselves by the work they do. If they succeed in becoming "distinguished" practitioners of their calling, we use that separating word to say they've done their work well. In a life that revolves around self and work, rather than around connections with others, work is more likely to have a high profile, a visibility that may outlive the man. But work that is centered around relationships will probably be less visible. Women are more often found in service occupations, in which interdependence is more important than distinction.

Church Life

In religious organizations, too, research persistently points to gender-related patterns of connection and separation. Women are more likely to belong to churches and attend regularly than men. In one study, clergy couples (both pastors) were asked how they attended to their need for spiritual nourishment. Only women reported "relational" disciplines, such as praying with their husbands or families, or listed among their spiritual disciplines having friends and forgiving them when necessary.[8] Research also indicates that women clergy support one another more than clergymen do. Clergymen, by contrast, "may use ministry to get in touch with people without having to get close."[9]

After years of advising women married to clergymen to get their fingers out of their husbands' churches and busy themselves with their own concerns, Laura Deming discovered that men married to clergywomen were much clearer about their own separate identity. These husbands are glad their wives are doing what they want to do, and want to support them, but they are not enmeshed in their wives' churches.[10]

In general, then, we see more women exhibiting social religious behavior, more men walking a solitary spiritual path.

A Recipe for Trouble

Women who want to connect and men who want to separate certainly spell trouble. If a woman is so eager for intimacy that she downplays her own requirements or sits on her angry feelings, her life becomes distorted. In this new age of sexual freedom, a woman's eagerness to connect may paradoxically isolate her. She may have unwittingly colluded in creating arrangements whereby men maintain their autonomy and women maintain their loneliness. If a woman is too willing to suffer in the service of her bonds with others, she may be unable to leave a destructive relationship. Led by her guilt and the primacy of marriage vows in her value system, Diane returned again and again to a husband who beat her. When children were born, the pain to which she had become accustomed escalated to terror.

> "I had to hear my babies screaming in fear as he threw dinner to the floor and went after me. I had to watch as he threw my son's toys in the wood stove, and as he threw my daughter's little kitten against a wall and broke its nose. When I was on the floor with my back injured so that I couldn't move, I watched him rip the phone out of the wall so that I couldn't get help, while my children cried." Diane went to a church for help, "and the pastor preached about the evils of divorce and the damage done by broken homes." And so she went home.[11]

Women themselves are not the only victims of a one-sided need to connect. Too much eagerness to be close to another, without respect for the other's centered selfhood, core of integrity, and personal boundaries feels like love to the woman but may be experienced as invasion by a man.

All we can be sure of having is our own experience. If it is coopted by others, we feel violated. At a women's conference, Mary was trying to tell her story. Martha kept interrupting with "helpful" parallels: "Oh, I know just what you mean. The exact same thing happened to me..." After the conference, Mary reflected, "But that was not helpful. When people tell their stories, they need listeners, not necessarily fellow travelers. I needed her to listen, to say 'yes, that's your story,' and leave it at that. I didn't appreciate Martha invading my story." If someone else is suffering, we need enough separation to let that person have his or her suffering. Too much identifying makes us feel too responsible, too eager to justify ourselves by "fixing" it, thereby violating the other's integrity and our own as well. We need to let others have their selfhood, their journeys, their suffering — and interests we do not share. A wife who lacks clarity about her own separate existence may find it hard to imagine that her husband relishes enterprises in which she has no part. To a man a woman's effort to probe the private recesses of his mind can feel like an unwanted intrusion.[12]

The cross-purposes in which men and women are caught become more tangled when women clutch unambiguous hopes of finding their heart's desire through a relationship with a man and when men resent their own need for what women can provide — and therefore resent the women who remind them of that unacceptable need.[13] Women's part in the mutual pain can be summed up under the heading of "sins of intrusion" and self-abnegation.

Men have their part, too, in hurting themselves and others. When men deny women the closeness the women crave, the men may not get what they want, either. As one man put it, "Pursuit of the self is resulting in a lot of loneliness." Men whose separate stance is too unambiguous also miss out on the kinds of growth that come only through wrestling with relationships. If they ignore or discount women, they forfeit opportunities for bringing their reality alongside that of one whose experience is different and clarifying their own distinctive reality and point of view.

Men offend women by withholding themselves, belittling women, or acting aggressively. Men may protect their separateness by carefully selecting and ritualizing the connections with which they are most comfortable — sex and dinner being the stereotypes. A man who is very uncomfortable about his neediness for what women have to offer can categorize those activities as "taking," or "being served." If a man is insensitive to a woman's need for a multi-faceted and integrated relationship, a basic dimension of her being is violated. A man's refusal of intimacy has enormous power when women want it so much. At its baldest, his power to withhold can take the form of desertion.

Withholding easily edges into belittling. It may be out of his own uneasiness, his fear of connection, that a man looks down on the one who is eager to connect with him. If he is very angry about needing anything a woman can provide, a man may grab what he needs in a hurtful way. In contrast to women's sins of intrusion, men hurt women primarily by their sins of withholding or acting with violence. Perhaps it is not surprising that women are more likely to cause pain to themselves, men to others.

If we put the pain of women and the pain of men in the same frame, the mutual exacerbation becomes clear. Yearning for loving attentiveness, she wants to be "searched and known." When she offers the gift she values, he experiences being "searched and known" as a violation of his boundaries. He offers the respectful space he wants, and she feels lonely and uncherished. If she is wholly submerged in her need for connectedness, the other is pushed into grasping the freedom end of the polarity. Then she feels hurt and he feels besieged. Lynn and Al struggled with this issue in their therapy.

> The more she went out to Al, it seemed, the more he withdrew. He would complain that she was intruding in his life; she would back off again, her self-esteem dashed. . . . Lynn would encourage him to go into his studio at night and work, and then she would hang around waiting for him, "in case he wanted a late supper or something." Al, *feeling* her presence waiting for him, felt smothered by it.[14]

Women weep because they are abandoned. Men fear that they will be trapped and "unmanned" if they are caught within a woman's web of intimacy.

If the push away from the feminine characterizes masculinity, and the drive toward connectedness characterizes femininity, we find here a clue to the tragic dimension of male-female relationships. It may explain the fatal progress toward Diane's dinnertime terror on the kitchen floor, her husband's violence, and her acceptance of it. When we fall out of the creative tension between freedom and intimacy, and instead are driven to fly apart or fuse, our differences become a source of wounds rather than enchantment.

Man, the Measure of All Things

We have hinted at yet another troubling side to the encounter between connected women and separated men: men come out on top, and women come out on the bottom. Let us look now at how that happens.

Since the man's need to claim his identity requires separation from woman, that separation strikes him as a good and necessary thing. Because separating is what he needs, and he experiences it as progress, it seems, in fact, better than *not* separating. Not only does a man's primal life experience encourage him to withdraw from the feminine, but a hierarchical valuing is introduced in which he can feel *superior* by doing so. Life is seen as a struggle away from what he needs to renounce, which then seems evil, and toward what he needs to embrace, which then appears good. Because sequential steps seem essential to a man's progress, he finds hierarchies of development the natural way to make sense of his struggle. If he then applies to women the developmental hierarchy that has emerged so clearly out of his own experience, and notices that most of them appear to be at rung three on his six-rung ladder, he naturally concludes that they are inferior creatures.

A woman's life, however, is put together quite differently. She sees no need to renounce relationships in order to find herself. Being close to other people is just the natural way to live. Her identity as a woman has come to her right along with her mother's milk. Since selfhood and connectedness fit together comfortably, she feels no necessity for choosing between them. Where he sees "either/or," she sees "both-and." Holding differences together with much greater comfort, she does not summarize her experiences with hierarchical developmental schemes.

And so the saying in the Genesis story comes true: "your desire shall be for your husband, and he shall rule over you." *The woman's desire to connect has resulted in her overvaluing the man; the man's need to separate has led him to undervalue the woman.*

Once connection and separation have been translated into her desire and his rule, the dominant-subordinate arrangement reinforces itself at every subsequent turn. If his rule includes access to more of this world's resources, her wish to be connected becomes a dependent wish, because she needs what he controls. If, for her, learning from him seems quite natural, while for him, learning from her represents a step backward down the ladder, his ways more easily become human ways.[15] As group theorist and trainer Carol Pierce has pointed out, the relationships between dominants and subordinates are invisible to the former and of all-consuming importance to the latter. To his original tendency to separate is now added a power imbalance that implies he really needn't bother very much about the relationship between them. To her tendency to connect is added the power reality that for her much depends on the quality of the relationship between them. Thus we find the sad contradiction that the point of view of the woman, who has grown more observant and therefore more sophisticated about the quality of the interaction between them, is defined by her subordinance as inferior, and her ability to effect changes in the relationship is diminished by her lack of power.

There is, of course, an alternative to this evolution of separation/connection into dominance/subordinance. Instead of assuming that developmental hierarchies based on male experience are generically valid, we could take the position that we all have different needs, depending on where we are in our life's journey and which side of the separate/connected tension requires our attention at the moment. Developmental hierarchies are seductive in their promise that *I'm going to make it just as soon as I figure out how*. Though this promise may sell a lot of how-to books, it seems largely illusory. People's life journeys do not generally seem to take the form of a triumphant ascent up the ladder of life, though we wish that could be true. Maybe the shape of the movement is more like a spiral. Or a tree, that grows ring by ring not into perfection but into the wholeness of being a tree. Maybe rings are a more appropriate metaphor than rungs.

Let us examine more closely how connectedness is translated into dependence. Men equate connectedness with dependence, because that's what they find problematic about closeness. If a man's very selfhood is discovered in denying that *he* is dependent on *her*, the most unmistakable way to assert that denial is to say that *she* is dependent on *him*. Then he can look down on a woman for being dependent, he can resent the burden of dependents, he can avoid noticing that he gets what he needs from her, and he can claim that only weak people care about relationships — all the while congratulating himself that he is in no way dependent. Concern with relationships is caricatured as "fusion" — obviously a condition of immaturity or sickness we all want to avoid. If we push the tension between connection and separation out as far as it will go, to the farthest, most destructive ends of the continuum, we arrive at *fusion* and *isolation*. It should not surprise us that the first is a specter for men and the second terrifies women.

When we shine these masculine and feminine ways of illuminating reality on the broader social scene, "man as the measure of all things" emerges again as a pattern. Individualism is seen as the mark of an enlightened society. The masculine mind, defined as the human mind, disregards the intricate threads stitching individuals together in natural and social systems. These fragile systems are consequently at risk. Western culture's resistant heresy of hyperindividualism, again, is sustained by the simple equation of masculine perceptions with human perceptions. Separation not connection, autonomy not "dependence," individuation not "being-in-relationship," individualism not corporate humanity — because they are the masculine way — come to be seen as the only right and human way. The personal, social, and ecological costs of this one-sidedness threaten human existence.

The Distant Presence of God

Symbols of separation play an important place in our traditional pictures of God. In the beginning God creates by separating the light from the darkness, the land from the sea, the day from the night, and the woman from the man. And at the end, the same

God will separate the sheep from the goats. God is free ("I am who I am" and "I will be who I will be [Ex. 3:14]"), and God is the freedom giver who leads Israel out of bondage. God's people are to keep themselves separate from defiling entanglements with the surrounding tribes, which practice nature religion.

When God is seen primarily as separate, theology is dualistic and preoccupied with sin. The separation of light from darkness slips into the triumph of light over darkness. And a focus on one's sinful separation from a transcendent Deity seems to be a preoccupation of religion in which masculine perceptions predominate.

Other religious symbols point to the nearness of God. In the Hebrew scriptures, the Shekinah, divine glory personified as feminine, represents God's immanence. The writer of psalm 139 sees God as the attentive Follower: "You search out my path and my lying down, and are acquainted with all my ways [vs. 3]." The mystics paid particular attention to the mysterious connection between God and the human soul. Said Meister Eckehart, "The essence of everything is relation."[16] Hildegard of Bingen proclaimed, "God hugs you. You are encircled by the arms of the mystery of God."[17]

While themes of separation or connection can be discerned in many parts of our religious tradition, there are also places where these thoughts appear alongside one another (the literal meaning of *paradox*). The people of the covenant are bound to God in freely chosen commitment. The Exodus travelers find themselves both alone in the desert and being fed and cared for. "Why have you forsaken me?" and "Whither shall I flee from thy presence?" are questioning cries that describe each side of the tension — in Dietrich Bonhoeffer's words, "The God who is with us is the God who forsakes us."[18]

My clearest experience of this intimate spaciousness came during a month-long working trip to Australia. During the months preceding the journey I often woke with a start at three in the morning filled with anxious disbelief: "Did I really say I would go twelve thousand miles away, all by myself, to lead conferences for a denomination I never heard of before? I must be crazy!" When it was finally time to go, to my surprise I found the twenty-seven-hour flight not at all the ordeal predicted but a time of feeling *preserved* up there in the sky. The image that came to me was "borne on eagles' wings." A flying foundation! I found myself warmly welcomed to this exotic subtropical land, where I could watch red and green parrots eating their breakfast outside my bedroom window. I was deeply moved by the tenderness of the Methodist tradition that forms part of the Uniting Church in Australia, by the strong and passionate voices of the seminarians singing Wesley's hymn about the "Amazing Love" of God. My days oscillated between adventures — exploring this curious land and leading the conferences, which seemed to go well, in spite of all my anticipatory fretting — and unaccustomed solitude. I had not lived alone for a quarter of a century. Now solitary sightseeing, taking pictures (my husband always took the pictures at home), and hours to ponder alone in my tiny flat — all seemed a delightful novelty. As I wrote in my journal early one morning in Canberra, the thought came, "I believe I am ready for my heart to be melted." So my journeying juxtaposed caring and space: a most tender intimacy and a spaciousness like all the sunny skies between here and Australia.

God as caring space embraces both our need to be loved and our need to be free. God who "hugs us" invites us to go adventuring. The space between us and God is not a space we need to try to fill but a space that preserves the glory of God, which transcends every finite thing. The space is not about some inadequacy in us that needs to be fixed but about our creatureliness.

God as caring space protects us against bondage or despair. We are not left totally bereft, which would leave us without hope; nor are we encountered unambiguously, which would destroy our freedom. A God who fixed everything would rob us of our experience. Of course, like teenagers at the breakaway stage, we want all the benefits of absolute liberty and all the privileges of intensive care. We guard our autonomy and then turn around and complain, "Why did You let this happen to me?" positing God as cosmic String Puller. Yet the paradoxical distance of God is not uncaring but in the service of my liberty. The loving and respectful distance of God holds lessons in love for us all. And while I may resist intimacy with God, if I allow it, my resistance will be melted in the most gentle and respectful way.

The story of freedom and connectedness — given *and* broken — in Genesis 2–3 provides some hints for understanding and healing the troubles we experience with living in that tension. Freedom is not simply given to the man and connectedness to the woman, but both are gifts to humankind. Significantly, symbols of freedom beckon first. The human creature, as yet sexually undifferentiated, is given the work of caring for the earth, and the freedom and responsibility to name all the other creatures. To this responsibility is added the dimension of choice: "God gives it the freedom to be responsible by commanding it to obey."[19] Then God says, "It is not good for the earth creature to be alone; I will make for it a companion corresponding to it." The story proceeds with the expected and the unexpected. It is the *man* who is to leave his father and mother and cleave to his wife. It is the *woman* who takes initiative in acting autonomously and who more quickly accepts her responsibility for the joint action in which she served as leader. As the drama unfolds, the humans' created gifts of freedom and connectedness (with God, with each other, with the plant and animal worlds) are broken and set in opposition. Freedom is split from connectedness, and man is split from woman.

Not only does loneliness cry for companionship, but encounter requires separation, hints the story. As in our experience, the gift of freedom is the prerequisite for any relationship that does not put the self or the other at risk. Sexuality *means* division. Instead of the destructive extremes of fusion and isolation we are offered a life-giving tension between connection and separation, commitment and personal boundaries. Love is moving-apart-and-coming-together.

And both human creatures find their most profound connectedness with God: "Finally, woman is not derived from man, even as the earth creature is not derived from the earth. For both of them life originates with God.... Truly neither woman nor man is an autonomous creature; both owe their origin to divine mystery."[20]

Living in the Tension Between Separation and Connectedness

What might the living out of this paradoxical center mean for men and for women? For men, it might mean a word of gospel. If your identity is given, perhaps you don't have to protect it so anxiously. Confidence in a freedom-giving love might cast out this particularly masculine fear. For men who are willing to risk being not only brave but loving, there might emerge a balance in which affiliation could be valued as highly as self-enhancement. This seems to be the lesson that the latter part of a man's life often teaches him.

Balanced in this tension, a woman might receive gifts, too. She might simply rejoice in the easy relationship between identity and intimacy that is often a woman's way, rather than letting herself be made to feel that it is not the right way. She might gladly offer her discovery that responsibility for herself and responsiveness to others do not have to contradict each other but are intimately linked. As Jean Baker Miller suggests, "Perhaps there are better goals than 'independence' as that word has been defined . . . for example, feeling effective and free along with feeling intense connections with other people."[21] Again, life seems to teach women this confidence in the latter part of their lives.

Women and men may also find their relationships blessed as they venture just to be in that paradoxical caring space. Living in this tension offers useful alternatives. Defining women and men as stereotyped opposites leaves us unfree, bereft of part of our humanity. Denying all differences means ignoring our own special character and the rich gifts we could offer the other. Perhaps the closeness that lovers experience when they know they are soon to be parted takes on special poignancy because it represents the boundary line between intimacy and separation on which we all live all the time. Moving toward other people and moving apart are the basic steps in life's great dance. Whole and free, moving comfortably between autonomous and intimate activities, we may find joy in both tenderness and adventure. The dance points beyond man and woman to the giver of a spacious love that embraces your freedom and mine. The One who *is* caring space can empower me to accept that gift and offer it to you.

PART I
WOMEN AND MEN IN TENSION

3

Thinking and Feeling

W hen you make a decision, are you more likely to be guided by your head or your heart? While both thinking and feeling play a part for most of us, we tend to prefer one way of deciding to the other, just as we naturally throw a ball with our right or left hand. It's easy to find both women and men who more often choose a course of action because of its clear rationality and desired consequences, and other men and women who are more strongly led by their values and personal loyalties. But the ancient intuition that men have a *tendency* to be led by thinking and women by feeling is borne out by modern instruments such as the Myers-Briggs Type Indicator, on which the *only* adjustment for gender is found in the preference for thinking or feeling. Sixty percent of men in the United States would rather lead with their heads; 60 percent of the women prefer to be guided by their hearts.[1]

Thinking Men and Feeling Women

The preference for thinking follows logically from the differentiated posture discussed in the last chapter. I picture the thinker

31

as a man standing on a hill, focusing a flashlight on the scene below, which is illuminated by its discriminating beam. Standing apart from the other, outside the situation, provides the necessary vantage point for an objective assessment.

Those who prefer to lead with the thinking function are purposeful and product oriented. Their focus on the generalized (as opposed to the particular) other coupled with their proclivity for objective thinking makes them people who care about truth and justice. They won't let us fool ourselves, and they will treat us fairly.

The preference for feeling, by contrast, flows more easily from a posture of connection. Those who lead with feelings approach situations subjectively, from the inside, as people who are related, even passionately engaged. The question is not so much "What are the logical consequences of this proposed action?" as "What matters to *me* here?" "Who is it that I care about?" Thus the other is not generalized but particularized. The development in women of a preference for feeling makes sense when we think back to the little girl talking with her best friend on the edge of the playground while the boys practice the rules of the game. Relating to this particular other taught her sensitivity and compassion and helped her see how it looked from her friend's point of view.

Those who lead with their feeling function are concerned with the process, not just the product. They bring their passions for people and values to the human situation and leave it glowing with warmth and harmony. Maybe a fireplace is a good symbol for feeling folk.

Thinking at Odds with Feeling

Whether we tend to lead with the head or the heart, we bring the special strengths inherent in our preference, and we are likely also to bring the weaknesses that represent a simple lack of the opposite strength. Most of us, however, encounter more serious trouble with thinking and feeling. Perhaps you have been in situations where your head and heart are giving you contradictory messages, and you end up confused, upset, and immobilized. A recent American President was chronically in conflict between thinking and feeling, with the result that nobody knew what to expect from him or how to understand the rationale for his latest decision.[2]

We make trouble for ourselves and others not only when we are hung up in the middle but when we carry our tendencies toward thinking and feeling to one-sided extremes. Western society gives people permission to rely on thinking and ignore feeling. Schools put far more emphasis on reason and objectivity than on commitment and values. One of the myths of the white male system is that we can be totally logical and objective.[3]

While we all have feelings, thinking people show them less and often seem embarrassed by them. Like crows, their intellects often perch awkwardly and tentatively on the bodies from which feelings might arise. For many a man, total reliance on thinking betrays his fear of feelings. The logical attack promises control over the situation, while feelings threaten to control *him*. In the church class my colleague and I taught, Peter put it this way: "There are more risks in feeling. It's safer with intellect — you don't expose yourself." Another man, a manager, agreed: "I've been in a lot of scary situations, physically intimidating, like in the army. But that's nothing compared to the courage you need to open up your feelings in front of the people you work with."[4] The leader of a men's class told me he had to work hard to encourage the men to move past their constant tendency to intellectualize.

Mark Gerzon describes men who could bear to express their feelings only in unimpeachably masculine settings. One found a release for his feelings with his drinking buddies: "We'd say stuff and hug each other and do all sorts of things we'd never let ourselves do if we were sober."[5] For others, the battlefield provided permission for man-to-man affection.

We often find people who rely primarily on reason a bit cool, and some of us wish they were warmer and "juicier." When the feelings do burst forth, they may seem overwhelming and out of control. A study of the lives of a hundred men by George Vaillant reveals several whose alienation from their feelings proved tragic. All his life, one subject "either had been utterly unaware of his feelings or had acted upon them so impulsively as to obscure their presence."[6] Another beat up his one-year-old baby. "The cause," believed Vaillant, "was that his child threatened to render him conscious of the pain of his own childhood. Always, he had kept that pain from awareness."[7] Our existence seems to be governed by a contradictory, unrecognized law: if we deny our feelings they will run our lives.

It may not be quite as easy to grow up in America with a total reliance on feeling and an underdeveloped thinking function as the reverse, because our schools expose feeling types to the requirements of objectivity and logic. But some people, and especially some women, do manage this imbalance, to their own detriment and that of others. Women whose lives are submerged in their relationships and in duties that serve those relationships may find it hard to stand back far enough to conceptualize and articulate their experience, with the result that neither they nor others see the value in that life of wordless care.

Life feels chaotic when we are cast adrift on an ocean of feelings without direction. Emotion without intention, sentimentality, provides a way for the powerful to bracket claims that would otherwise be inescapable, to give a perfunctory nod in the direction of "little children" or "womanly purity" and then, with those pleasantries out of the way, proceed to behave in ways that injure the objects of those exercises. How many well-meaning church people prop up sweet pictures of Jesus and the children in Sunday school classrooms without ever attending to the command to welcome the "little ones" — *those who have no power*? Sentimentality is a distortion shared by the Nazis, with their strange tearfulness over children and pets, and the women who need a fix of three Gothic romances a day to escape from the triviality of the daily round to which they have reduced their lives. A life centered around girlish crushes, *Brides* magazine, and the drama of heartbreak brackets the moral imperative to *act* caringly. In such a life, personal relationships fill the sky, and the world beyond the private sphere vanishes from sight.

Human beings seem to be subject to at least one of these three death-dealing postures: being immobilized by the conflicting claims of head and heart; wallowing aimlessly on a sea of emotion without intention; and being dominated by principles abstracted from the concrete situations that cry out for care and from the feelings in which empathy is born. Because of our masculine and feminine predilections, the split between thinking and feeling also contributes to the alienation between women and men.

The thinking-feeling split leads to the misunderstanding and lack of sympathy that frequently surface in marriage counseling. "Why can't he let his feelings show?" complains Sue, while Michael retorts, "Why can't she be logical just one time?" The accusations may escalate: Michael is "cold," "heartless," "totally inaccessible." Sue is "muddle-headed," a "fuzzy thinker," "totally incapable of standing up in the face of opposition."[8] Sue assumes that Michael should have the same control over his moods that she does over hers, but this control eludes him.[9]

Stereotypes exacerbate the misunderstandings. Emotionality is seen as womanish, and feminine traits are, of course, traits for men to avoid. It is a sad picture when, on the one hand, a man pretends that he doesn't want the soft and warm experiences for which he really does hunger — like a boy trying to follow the instructions to outgrow his teddy bear. Worse yet, if he responds to a woman's entreaties and finds a way to open his heart to her, he may find that her ancient expectations about manliness inspire instant disgust for "wimps"!

On the other hand, if a man depends on his logical skills to prop up his manliness, he will object to encountering those skills in skirts. I remember my high school reluctance to look "too smart." Perhaps, with a hesitantly raised hand and a carefully affected inarticulateness, I could appear to be more feminine and attractive to boys.

These splits encourage women to overfunction in matters of the heart, while men underfunction. When women take on all the responsibility for making relationships work, they end up emotionally undernourished, while men end up emotionally incompetent. If men are called upon to play out of their weak suit in relationships, under the threat of performing less competently than the "subordinates," it's not surprising that they deal themselves out of that game, leaving it to the women, while they throw their efforts into the "really significant" public game, where, in their turn, women take the underfunctioning posture. (This will be discussed further in chapter 8, "The Public and Private Spheres.")

And so the split brings alienation to men, contempt to women. In the film *The Search for Bountiful*, an aging woman irritated her son and daughter-in-law by singing sentimental old hymns while she pushed the carpet sweeper around in the morning, and exasperated them by periodically sneaking off to try to pay a final visit to her old home in "Bountiful," a hamlet where the trains no longer ran. The men Ma encountered — her son, the railroad officials, and the police officer in the Southern town — all treated her with a mixture of politeness, contempt, embarrassment, and a wary awe of the affective qualities that determined her life so simply, which they had parked on a dusty shelf in the back of their souls while they concentrated on getting a raise or making the trains run on time. The reasons of her heart, irrelevant to them, brought them only meaningless inconvenience.

The man who leads with his head and the woman who leads with her heart often despair of finding a way to join his passion for truth and her passion for human connection. Their attempts to reach out to each other may frustrate and baffle them. After one couple described these reachings that did not touch the other to their therapist, she reflected, "He experienced her words as a barrier to intimacy. She experienced his physical advances as a barrier to intimacy."[10]

He Reaches with Arms; She Reaches with Words

That couple's reaching seemed to halt painfully in midair, his arms empty and her voice falling on deaf ears. Let us pause and ponder that voice and those outstretched arms. For our reaching out to the other matters deeply. The longing to connect with the other that comes from our depths carries with it a yearning for our own wholeness and a hunger for God.

Head and heart do not signify only differences, problems, and separation between men and women; paradoxically, they point as well to the ways we seek to participate in the reality of the other. Here is a surprising contradiction: it is with what we feel is lacking in ourselves — with our vulnerability, with what we seek in the other, that we grope toward the other — the woman with words, the man with physical passion. Is this part of the human wisdom behind the story in Genesis 2–3, where the man reaches for the woman ("This at last is bone of my bones and flesh of my flesh"), while the woman reaches for wisdom? ("So when the woman saw... that the tree was to be desired to make one wise, she took of its fruit and ate.")

For men, "a satisfying sexual relationship naturally expands from sensation to feeling to intention."[11] Many observers trace a contrapuntal movement for women: that they tend to excel in verbal skills, that these skills are developed in order to form a connection with another, and that women *then* often wish to celebrate that relationship through a sexual encounter.

These paradoxical ways of reaching toward the other are ways of reaching toward our wholeness. A woman may often discover her masculine side as she projects it onto a "man standing on a hill with a flashlight," a man whose facility with words and ideas she admires. And a man may find his way to a "fireplace" as he reaches out toward eros, toward the personal and individual.[12] His hidden feminine self may shine out of the eyes of a woman who unaccountably "captures his heart." Embracing and owning hitherto underdeveloped functions can be an exciting aspect of the mature years' journey.

Logos and Eros

In such contrapuntal ways, we approach the other sex, our own wholeness, and God. More paradoxically yet, when our hidden other self is thrown out on the screen of myth and religious symbol, Eros appears personified as the god of love, while the Word, the divine Logos in the beginning of John's Gospel, is closely connected with the feminine personification of Wisdom, or Sophia. And yet another dimension of counterpoint emerges: Eros, who takes a mythologically masculine form, is the unitive force, while Logos/Sophia[13] signals the power of discrimination.

The New Testament hints at healing for the painful conflicts between thinking and feeling, Logos and Eros, man and woman. Greek philosophers had exalted the Logos as the mind of God, the rational principle by which the universe was ordered and brought out of chaos. But it was the author of the fourth Gospel who integrated the divine Logos with Sophia. Wisdom, or Sophia, leaps beyond mere human knowledge, technical reason, or information. She is playful and a giver of delight (Prov. 8:30). She is a mother (Luke 7:35) who sets her table and invites, "Come, eat of my bread and drink of the wine I have mixed [Prov. 9:5]."

In Logos/Sophia and Eros we encounter paradoxical symbols that leap across the chasm between human and divine wisdom, across the contradictions between head and heart, and across the agonizing space between empty arms and unheard voices.

Symbols of Wholeness

The symbolic language of the New Testament also points toward the healing of these hurtful splits.

The author of the fourth Gospel not only sensed the oneness of Sophia and Logos but insisted that this Word became *flesh*. Here is no abstract truth but rather the "word of life," which "we have looked at and touched with our hands [1 John 1:1]." It is a Word that offers bread, that scrubs feet, that curls up close to a beloved friend. It is a Word we can touch and know, a place where universal Truth is revealed in the particularity of a life, lovingly enfleshed. It is a Word that tells itself in simple stories.

The word John uses for knowledge is the same word used in Genesis for sexual union.[14] Hosea spoke of Yahweh's yearning that Israel *know* the Lord — that same word that embraces physical knowing. So *knowledge* is another biblical symbol that bridges the space between spoken words and erotic delight.

The New Testament avoidance of language that separates and intellectualizes human functions finds its counterpart in a clarity that feeling needs to be guided by intention. "Then he took a little child, and put it among them; and taking it in his arms, he said to them, 'Whoever welcomes one such child in my name welcomes me' [Mark 9:36]." This story has been distorted by a sentimental halo so often that it is easy to miss the insistence that children and their needs are to be included in practical ways in the concerns of the community.[15] Paul calls the Corinthians to the same harnessing of intention to feelings when he appeals to them not to get carried away by ecstatic emotional experiences that don't build up the community (1 Cor. 14).

Hearts and Minds in Community

These symbols of wholeness point toward a way of being at one, not only within our own hearts and minds, not only between the woman's words and the man's outstretched arms, but for the Christian community of men and women in which all the difficulties from which we suffer as individuals are writ large.

Many mainline churches suffer from a one-sided emphasis on thinking and an avoidance of the affective, the ecstatic, the passionate dimension of religious life. I certainly do not want to underplay the contributions of the somewhat abstract, ordered, and at times original minds of intuitive thinkers. But my hunch is that an overemphasis on thinking has skewed the church. The Reformation intensified (though it did not invent) the message that the way to God was through correct thinking rather than passion. Few theological seminaries I know use the holistic insights found in contemporary Christian education methods that attend to the whole person, including experiences and feelings. The dominance of powerful, confident thinkers, with their preference for objectivity and distance, as the church's intellectual elite makes the transmission of ideas through lectures the preferred, and sometimes the *only*, method of communication in the seminaries that set norms for the rest of the church. As we find ways to move past hierarchies that set academic over practical disciplines toward their integration, that imbalance may be righted.

A corrective in the direction of passion and wholeness is offered by women who say, "We want to attend worship service without keeping our bodies and feelings out of the church or checking them at the door.... We do not want either to hide or to repress the emotions we feel."[16]

This discovery of a new balance may take different practical shapes in different traditions. Too much time spent sitting and talking and listening in our word-centered, mainline churches may be offset for some by receiving gifts from Quaker or Catholic mystical traditions, for others by attending more fully to the sacramental dimension that plumbs mysteries beyond human reason, for still others by strong, warm-hearted Methodist or Baptist singing. A church too full of words may profit from the ancient injunction to "greet one another with a holy kiss." While newcomers to the church I attend (particularly men) are sometimes embarrassed when hugs and kisses are passed around the church during the Peace, the awkward feelings subside with time, and it is evident that this greeting helps alleviate the hunger of many people who are starved for touching and being touched.

Churches may suffer not only from the dominance of the thinkers' power exercised from the theological top down but from a skewing in the opposite direction that arises from the overwhelming preponderance of feeling types in parish churches. Though only 40 percent of men in the general population claim a preference for feeling, 68 percent of the clergy (most of them, of course, male) are feeling types. And the fact that the majority of churchgoers are women is probably not irrelevant to their greater preference for feeling. This numerical preponderance deserves careful attention. Though we all tend to believe that others are, or should be, like us, we can be helped by greater sophistication about personality type to attend to the important contributions that thinking laity might make to the wholeness of the body. My hunch is that many local churches would do well to add some "flashlight" strengths to the "fireplace" values at which they excel. For example, while everybody may be very nice to the parish secretary, her work is often frustrating, because her contract and organizational relationships are unclear, and her pension plan is unjust.

When our churches suffer more from sentimentality than intellectualism, it may be useful to take a harder look at bromides like "Get in touch with your feelings" and notice whether that is what is really needed in *this* situation, with the strengths and weaknesses of *this* congregation. The teenagers in our church are reportedly so sick of being asked "how they feel" that that discussion starter has long since lost its usefulness. In a church heavily dominated by feeling types, it may be more important to attend to the potential contributions of the thinking minority — *not* just in order to foist off on them uncongenial and purportedly "peripheral" duties such as financial management but to welcome their contributions to a clear statement of the congregation's purposes in ministry.

Attention to our own congregation's need to pay more careful attention to the requirements of heart or head is just one part of our response to the call to live more consciously and faithfully in the tension between feeling and thinking. The most uncharitable division in Christendom today is not between denominations but between the rational approach of many mainline churches, especially those in the Reformed tradition, and the emotional bent of Pentecostal or charismatic churches. Really nasty church fights erupt across this split when it emerges in a local church.

Our biblical and theological heritages suggest a more faithful response to the challenge to live in this tension. Instead of plucking congenial verses out of the scripture, we might notice the integration between head and heart that is so frequently upheld there. Those in mainline churches can easily diagnose the verse-plucking proclivity among the Pentecostals, while ignoring Paul's account of his own ecstatic experiences, for example. On the one hand, when rational types abandon the ecstatic dimension of religion, it falls into the margins beyond the reach of more traditional institutions. On the other hand, the emotionalism of many Pentecostal groups often seems quite disconnected from their actual human feelings. The split between these two emphases can result not only in church fights but also in unethical ecstatic religion and ethical religion bereft of spiritual power and joy. Thus we are all impoverished.

Men and women and religious communities are blessed with warm hearts and discerning minds. Yet we are often unable to receive those gifts from God and each other, to live in the tension they describe, and to discern the symbols of wholeness offered by our tradition. In the midst of our blind onesidedness or our immobilizing conflicts, our irresponsible sentimentality or our heartless rationality, our yearning for and our insensitivity toward the other sex, may we find pointers toward a grace that can heal our souls, our relationships, and our churches, a grace that can keep our "hearts and minds in the knowledge and love of God."

4

Body, Mind,
and Spirit

As we shift our gaze to peer through the next facet of our
many-dimensioned male and female humanity, we come
to the complexities of human nature that people through the
centuries have called body, mind, and spirit.

I know there is only one "me," but I can't help knowing,
too, that I'm a complicated creature, and sometimes the parts
don't seem to fit together very neatly. I am an intricate system of
bone, fat, muscle, blood, organs, of pleasure and pain. I am one
who remembers, decides, is delighted by conceptual "aha's," and
fills out tax forms. I also find myself longing for meaning, wistful
for a love that will not disappoint me, brought to tears by a Bach
chorale or a Holy Week collect. Are all these "I's" equally "me"?
Is one of these superior to the others? Are my body, mind, and
spirit generally on friendly terms, or are they at war inside me?

Men and women have often given different answers to
those questions. Men have tended to show more interest in distinguishing body, mind, and spirit than in noticing how they all fit
together. The distinctions have evolved into hierarchical rankings,
so that men have often claimed some parts for themselves and as-

signed other parts to women. And because they are dominants in Western culture, men's answers have often been accepted as human answers.

The First Split: Mind and Spirit to Man, Body to Women

When the sphere of the mind and spirit is assigned to man, the body is assigned to woman. While a man tends to approach his sexuality in a more directly physical way, he also seems to feel ambivalent about his bodily life and frequently regards it as somehow the property of the woman. *He* experiences arousal; *she* is seen as "sexy." A man is likely to attribute the physical lust he experiences so compellingly to the woman who elicits it, even though *her* feelings for *him* typically emerge as less pointedly physical, more multidimensional. As James Nelson has traced in detail, men have seen mind and spirit as separate from, and better than, the body; they have also seen themselves as superior to women; and this pair of dualisms has become intertwined.[1] Let us look at how this happens and what it does to us.

How We Live with Our Bodies

To begin with, this split could not come about unless men and women had different ways of living with their bodies, different attitudes toward being the enfleshed creatures that we are.

A man's body confronts the world *outside him*. This fact finds symbolic expression in his external sexual organs. He demonstrates his masculinity as he meets challenges and hardships that arise from the outside world. He wields his body like "a fancy power tool for subduing the environment."[2]

In reaching out to connect with a woman he loves, a man may be groping toward a reality that is also spiritual and holistic, but his *starting point* is likely to be his physical arousal. The cover of the valentine my husband gave me last year pictured a man on one knee before a woman saying, "Honey, I love you with all my heart, soul, mind and body...." The sentence ended on the inside: "...but not necessarily in that order." A man is likely to approach a woman in the reverse order, loving her with "all his body." He's confident that harmony can be restored after a fight if they can just go to bed together. As a consequence of the physical focus of his own passion, he will probably feel more deeply betrayed if his beloved sleeps with another man. I had a glimpse of this when I told my husband that I had been captivated by a male colleague in a work project, and he responded, "Well, as long as nothing happened, that's perfectly all right with me." I was amused that my intense experience of having been impaled by one of Cupid's arrows could be dismissed under the heading of "Nothing Happening" — but I knew what Bob meant, and the exchange illuminated the difference in our perspectives.

Men do seem to experience more disjuncture between body and spirit than women do. I gain a feeling for the male spirit's itch to be free of fleshly bonds from reading accounts of boys' puberty rites in primitive societies, in which the body is conquered, and the boy reaches beyond it to a world of spirit.[3]

Perhaps woman's hidden, internal sexual parts signify her greater readiness to experience her body from within. She does not need to scale mountains or crawl through jungles to encounter the challenges of nature; for her they are built in. In contrast to a man's tendency to deny the out-of-control nature of bodily life and to reach for the world of spirit and infinite possibilities, a woman's experience presses her toward an acceptance of limits, finiteness, the dimension of life that eludes her control. She feels called not so much to subdue nature as to be in tune with its processes. Perhaps a woman's bodily inwardness, the nudges toward becoming attentive to her own inner processes, her heightened awareness of limits and concreteness move her away from the directional male posture, toward a greater readiness to care for herself by caring for her body — and possibly its precious contents, as well. I've listened to clergywomen under stress speak tenderly of hot soup and warm baths as remedies.

Unlike the man she meets and loves, a woman's movement toward him is less likely to begin with physical arousal. A man is sometimes surprised to learn that "for a woman a bridge of spiritual attunement must first be built before she is able ... to ... cross the bridge of sex."[4] Her experience of dawning sexual maturity is not so much the eruption of insistent desires as the appearance of signs that she might someday become a mother.[5] She approaches the young man with holistic hopes and dreams, with the knowledge of her potential inner link with the generation to come. Her path leads in the opposite direction from his; she begins with a yearning that has many dimensions, and she may take years to find her way to full physical enjoyment.

As we trace male and female ways of being enfleshed persons, what contrapuntal patterns emerge! His directional push, his itch to be free of bodily constraints, are balanced by her more integrated inwardness, which is friendlier with its limits. In some ways she may point him toward becoming more at home with physical life; in their sexual relationship he may lead her to a fuller embodiment of her love. While she is more centered in her body, he is more focused on the physical act of lovemaking, and in it he finds himself more in control — and more out of control. While he reaches for a whole connection with her through bodily love, she will, at the end, celebrate the wholeness of that connection by enfleshing it.

The Sources of Male Splitting

This paradoxical picture of female and male embodiment helps explain the emergence of a split in which a man defines his own essential nature as spiritual and intellectual, while he consigns bodily existence to women. Splitting, says Judith Viorst, "lets him tolerate profound contradictions in his thoughts and deeds, with different aspects of his self disconnected — like separate islands — from each other."[6] Let us look more closely at how this splitting develops.

First, life presses us (and particularly the infant male) into an intolerable awareness of the ambiguity of bodily existence, whose ecstasies are ours only at the price of humiliation. Ex-marine creatures recently surfaced out of female fluids, thrust out by our mothers' muscles and blood and sweat, we emerge to a life of sucking and drowsy, milky drools, gas pains and belches, rashes erupting from the burn of our own excrement, the sweet stroking of oil on those angry red sores. Mother's body, from which we have just emerged, is the wonderful other whose comings and goings bring blessing and yearning to our so very fleshly existence. The little boy, however, often learns that he can no longer claim without humiliation the cuddling that caressed his infant days. He loses permission to complain of the bodily hurts that might elicit tender female ministrations. Kissing and hugging are all right for girls. Not for him.

Second, splitting arises from a need to gain control and a fear of losing it. That infant bodily life is so unbearably dependent, so totally out of its own control. How attractive to put distance as quickly as possible between yourself and that dependence and instead to refuse the spinach, to command the dump trucks and bulldozers in the sand box, and someday even to control the female who once made you feel so out of control. Taking command over earthbound, messy bodily life and reaching toward purity, power, and freedom — here lies the promise of control.

At puberty the body's embarrassing awkwardness erupts again, stimulated by the half-glimpsed curve of a budding breast or the newly round softness of a bottom. How natural to attribute this unacceptable lack of control to her of the rounded breast and soft bottom who stimulated all this unruliness in the first place! Here again, either sternly averting one's gaze from the delectable softness or, failing that, gaining control over *her* promises the restoration of a manageable existence.

Although handing over fleshly life to women softens the pain of living with the body's ambiguity and enhances a man's confidence about being in control, it produces problems, too — such as "the ashamed eruption of a dirty interest in this rejected body."[7] What is handed over in order to achieve control now eludes a man's control. Then, when buried impulses burst forth obsessively, the fear of being out of control is deepened and reinforced.

We are continually reminded of the ultimate loss of control by "this body of death." My body marks me as a finite creature, but it is also a gift. My life depends on it. My body experiences my pleasures, miraculously brings forth new life, and blesses my existence with the beauty of Michelangelo's David or an Ingres Odalisque, along with beauty's more accessible incarnations; but it also issues periodic reminders of my limits in its fatigue and ailments. The question, in Dorothy Dinnerstein's words, is "how to handle the prospect of the final separation without despising the body's simple wishes, without robbing the body of the poignant, cherished status that rightly belongs to loved and perishable things."[8]

Men and women tend to answer this question differently. For men, women signify not only sex but mortality. Perhaps this erotic, dying body can be handed over to women, put away in the shadows of the not-me. There its fascination will be exaggerated and its fearfulness disowned. For women, distance from the body of death is a less feasible option. Pregnancy and childbirth, care of the dying and preparation of bodies for the grave, reinforce women's acceptance of finitude.

While men may seek distance from the humiliating aspects of the body that elude control and portend death, at the same time they feel some envy of the creative powers of women. In our church course, George said wistfully, "Women can have babies and nurse them, supreme human experiences forever cut off from me." Some men, less kindly souls than George, have sought revenge against female creative powers, fearfully distancing themselves from birth with forceps or taking command over the womb by needlessly excising it or legislating control over its contents. Man's myths claim the creative powers for himself: *woman* comes from *man*; Zeus births Athena from his head.

The assignment of bodily concerns to women is locked in place by dominant-subordinate arrangements. Tasks related to our bodies' needs are generally relegated to people regarded as inferior; thus dominants are confirmed in avoiding them — and in suffering the ills that arise from tucking them out of sight, as Freud pointed out.[9]

What Splitting Does to Men and Women

Having traced some of the causes of this split, let us examine its effects in the lives of men and women.

We can see many signs that modern man is out of touch with his body. "It" is composed of disconnected parts. The parts may come off in wars. He will then be given a colored ribbon, instead. A man is often unaware of the signals his body is giving him — and anyway it would be "sissy" to pay too much attention. A man may sweat to enhance his body's strength; he often does not feel permitted to notice its weaknesses. He holds himself stiffly inside his stiff clothes, which echo the discomfort of the flesh they cover.

Like the psalmist who cried out that his "moisture was dried up as in the heat of summer," men who live as though disembodied give forth a feeling of having lost their "juiciness, wetness, greening power," to use Hildegard of Bingen's words.[10] Overresponsive to demands from outside, only dimly aware of fleshly feelings within, such men seem drained of the vital springs of energy that might have surged from synergy within. The rejected bodily life cries out for attention, calling the split-off man back to it by erotic obsessions. Men who are separated from their bodies and their emotional needs have only one acceptable channel left to connect them with those hungers: sex. And through that channel rushes a mighty torrent of pent-up needs of many kinds.

Women, too, find that standing for all human flesh brings hurtful consequences. They suffer when men insist on control over female bodies. No longer are mothers in labor accompanied by midwives, who stand by to help, knowing that they do not *own* this event; now the expert obstetrician takes charge of the birth and *delivers* the baby.

Women take the fallout when they carry the freight of the bodily life men have disowned. The "temptress" deserves any violent consequences of the lust she evokes. And her lust (which may actually be rather modest, diffuse, and spiritual) is at times painted as so voracious that it can be satisfied only by the Devil himself.

Women may exacerbate the troubles inflicted upon them by the ways they respond to the assignment of the body to them. They may obediently copy down that assignment, accepting a primary role as physical creatures whose identity is primarily sexual. Many, of course, center their lives around making themselves sexually attractive to men and see salvation in the success of that enterprise.

Other women accept the assignment by absorbing all the criticism and disgust that form its dark side. Many women struggle miserably with their bodies, sweating and starving and gagging to pare down unwanted roundness. They call their body's basic cyclical process a "curse." It is hard for many a woman to own her sexual nature gladly. She feels like a second-class person because of it. Upon her is laid the conflicting lure and opprobrium of being a temptress and bearing the burden of sexual responsibility that might logically have been regarded as jointly held.

Women may also participate in their own troubles when they accept male sexual lifestyles as human lifestyles and behave accordingly. Bowing to a unisex "liberated" norm of sexual behavior, reduced to casual sex that ignores their personal integration, is a form of collusion in their oppression that women can reject.

All these flights from ambiguity, from the muddled, messy, yet humbly dear and pleasurable bundle of contradictions that forms our bodily existence, cause both men and women serious trouble. Perhaps we avoid noticing how irrational and destructive is this whole series of hierarchical divisions (mind and spirit over body, men over women, chaste white women over lustful black women) through one of the value assumptions derived from the dividing itself: that it's "only physical" and we needn't bother about it much. Those commonly heard phrases — "It's only physical" or "differences between men and women are just biological" — are a way of saying, "We don't care about our bodies, and [by extension] about this created physical world."

The problem is that the modern mentality vacillates between two mutually exclusive attitudes: if something is "only physical" it has no reality and does not need to be taken seriously; or, what is physical is *reality*, incontrovertible fact.

The Second Split: Mind and Matter to Men, Spirit to Women

The sexual splitting that has exalted men as more spiritual and devalued women as more carnal has shifted at other times to assign matter to men and spirit to women. When men are engrossed in technological pursuits, or mind-over-matter enterprises, women are commonly assigned the task of nurturing the gentler, more spiritual side of life. If he is engaged in the real and (regrettably) ruthless practical affairs of business and industry, she must cherish the tiny flame of morality and spiritual life in the home, which becomes a haven alongside the public arena where history is made. Because women have been assigned a minor theme, their works in the spiritual arena appear trivial. Society has viewed women's volunteer efforts — which kept missionary societies and Sunday schools, charity baskets and community agencies, concerts and art galleries, going — as peripheral to the mainstream of society. The basic dynamic is the same: the dominant sex assigns to the subordinates a piece of the human action that requires some attention, marginal though it may be.

Robert Hughes describes the tender rituals performed by young Lieutenant Clark, who left his pretty young wife, Betsy Alicia, and their infant son at home in England when he set sail to deliver a load of convicts to Australia in the early days of English settlement. In his diary, this young officer tells how he survived the lonely months with the aid of

> a small ritual with the "dear picture," a miniature under a hinged glass lid. Each morning, Monday to Saturday, he kisses the glass. On Sundays he raises the tiny oval pane to kiss "my dear Alicia's picture out of the case," the image symbolically laid bare, a little closer to flesh. This act is both a denuding and a prayer, as to the effigy of a female saint . . . surely an angel and not a woman.[11]

The view of woman as the Spiritual One is not without problems for her. She may find "standing for" a man's split-off spiritual life a poor substitute for being her own real person. Although the lieutenant didn't know it, Betsy Alicia was a woman and not an angel. Her husband having set sail in December 1792, Betsy Alicia died in childbirth early in 1794.

Since such an idealized picture of woman is easily revealed as inadequate to describe the entire sex, women are split into those two categories: pure and spiritual or lewd and abased. Before Lieutenant Clark learned of the nature of pure Betsy Alicia's death, we hear of his deep disgust for the "damned bitches of convict women," who were at the same time regarded as handy for casual fornication. Clark begot a child on a convict woman, insisted the little girl be christened "Alicia," and never mentioned her mother in his diary.

Not only women, but men too, suffer from such splitting. Much modern literature makes the point that when men are out of touch with their spiritual lives, they end up just as miserable as when they are out of touch with their physical lives. What is outside the focus of the dominant sex emerges as an unconscious problem. And yet, in some strange way, these "assignments" seem to attest not only to the fragmentation of men's lives but to their yearning for wholeness.

From Splits Within Us
to Splits Between Us

Both ways of carving up human reality and relegating some
pieces to the other contribute to the alienation between men and
women.

Splitting off body, spirit, or mind begins as a solution
to the discomforts inflicted upon us by our ambiguous existence but ends as a problem. Unwillingness to stay in the
tension dissipates the energy that is generated when different
realities are held together both within us and between us. As
Jung put it, "All excessive 'purity' lacks vitality."[12] And the
"solution" of dividing human nature, separating its components, ranking them hierarchically, and assigning "lower" parts
to subordinates distorts life for everybody and creates walls of
hostility.

Women share responsibility for this sorry division when
they fail to discern and clearly state the reality they experience
as the subjects of their own lives. When women refuse to receive
unwanted pieces of men's lives, however, and courageously articulate, claim, and offer their own vision of integrity, they can
cease being part of the problem and begin being part of the
solution.

Hints for Our Healing
in the Lives of Women

Because fragments of life have been assigned to them, women
have felt urgently impelled to take these pieces and work at
joining them together again. These "assignments" may, in a paradoxical way, provide the occasion for women to offer a gift to
themselves, to their sisters, and to their brothers. Let us trace
these patterns of integration within the souls of women, in
women's ways of crafting their lives, and in the ways their lives
touch others and influence the broader spheres of culture and
nature.

Women's integrated inner reality is seen in their sense of
their bodies as *themselves* enfleshed. For a woman, there is no clear
dividing line between sexual and spiritual. "For my wife, it's all
sex — even making the bed," said Bruce wonderingly.

Marjorie Bankson uses the metaphor of *Braided Streams*[13] to describe how women pull together the sexual, vocational, and spiritual strands of their lives. Sometimes women delay the full expression of one stream in favor of another; this postponement of their longed-for integration may leave them frustrated and angry. Unlike men, who often major in vocation while simultaneously minoring in sexual expression, women commonly undergo major shifts in their lives, picking up first one strand, then another. As one generation gives way to another, the *order* may shift, while the serial braiding pattern continues.

We women cannot live in integrity, craft our lives responsibly, or offer our gifts to special people or the world's concerns that loom beyond them, unless we claim and proclaim our own reality. We do not have to deny men the validity of their experience, but neither do we have to own it when it doesn't fit us. We may try to understand men's fearful, enchanted, or proprietary attitudes toward women's bodies, but we do not have to let their perceptions determine our self-image.

As women claim and proclaim their enfleshed reality, we might celebrate our appreciation of creatureliness, context, and concreteness. This gift, an extension of our sense of personal embodiment, is made manifest in simple, practical forms of service. Starting with concrete situations often suggests more relevant acts of service than starting with abstract ideals and then applying them in specific contexts. Women will do well to *respect* the specific things they do to help, uphold the validity of their approach to service alongside more typically masculine approaches, and gain confidence for extending practical service beyond the private sphere.

Hints for Our Healing in the Symbols of Our Faith

Symbols help make us whole again because they grasp all of us and point us to truth that is not accessible to any fragmented approach — one limited to the mind, for example. Symbols stir not only our minds but our imaginations, hearts, feelings, will, spirit — our whole enfleshed selves. They therefore affirm us as many-dimensional, inseparably whole people.

Body, Mind, and Spirit United in Scripture

Our uneasy relationship with our bodies is congruent with our Christian heritage as a whole. But the Bible people strongly affirm bodily life and its interconnectedness with mind and spirit. Their language is concrete and specific. Biblical writers are not in the business of conveying spiritual principles abstracted from their context. That would be to claim an unambiguous grasp of the transcendent truth that always eludes such a grasp. Instead the Bible tells stories in which transcendent meanings are enfleshed in very specific human events. The phrases "just physical" and "purely spiritual" are foreign to the symbolic language of the Bible, which always speaks about meaning but never claims to have seized it, instead pointing to it obliquely through the concrete. The insides of things and the outsides of things are congruent and inseparable.

In the Bible, people are all of a piece. We are animated bodies. When the psalmist says, "Therefore my heart is glad, and my soul rejoices; my body also rests secure [16:9]," he isn't dissecting himself and analyzing the pieces; he is looking at a whole self through different aspects of its wholeness. Paradoxically, we, who have all kinds of words to speak of that whole human being — such as "self," "individual," and "person" — seem to have lost touch with the reality, while the Bible people show a profound appreciation for the oneness of human nature, even though they have no special words for it. Any one of a number of words will do.

The word flesh, according to many scholars, means the whole person — a finite and mortal person ("He remembered that they were but flesh [Ps. 78:39]"). But "flesh" also can be "the perfect embodiment for the divine Logos"[14] in John's Gospel; if we "eat the flesh of the Son of Man" we receive his life (John 6:53). Flesh and spirit do not contradict one another: God will pour out God's "spirit upon all flesh." "Flesh" never has the purely sexual connotations we habitually read into the phrase "sins of the flesh."[15] To be "one flesh" with another includes, but isn't limited to, physical union.

The word body, too, can mean "self," "person," or "personality." When Paul says in 1 Thessalonians 5:23, "May your spirit and soul and body be kept sound and blameless at the coming of our Lord Jesus Christ," he isn't thinking of "a person as

having three parts, but as a unity which may be viewed from three
different points of view: his relation to God, his personal vitality,
and his physical body."[16] Far from being inferior, "your body is
a temple of the Holy Spirit... therefore glorify God in your body
[1 Cor. 6:19, 20b]." This admonition contradicts the Hellenis-
tic view of the soul or mind as the temple and the body as the
prison of the soul.

The Consistent Unity of Body,
Mind, and Spirit in Scripture

The unity of body, mind, and spirit in scripture is spelled
out consistently through the whole story. Not only did the He-
brews describe themselves as animated bodies, they spoke of
God's hands molding the dry land (Ps. 95:5) and of God's face
shining on them (Ps. 31:16). God makes a creature who is "very
good," "naked and not ashamed." The psalmist exults:

> For it was you who formed my inward parts;
>   you knit me together in my mother's womb.
> I praise you, for I am fearfully and wonderfully made.
>   Wonderful are your works;
> that I know very well.
>   My frame was not hidden from you,
> when I was being made in secret,
>   intricately woven [!] in the depths of the earth.
>   — Psalm 139:13–15

The goodness of this naked creature from the earth points a way
out of the twin traps of squeamishness and obsession about sex.
The story says humans are created for some very down-to-earth
activities: to serve the earth and to come together as "one flesh."

This earth creature is not only connected with the earth
and with its mate but is related to God in ways that might as-
tonish us by their earthiness if overfamiliarity had not inoculated
us against surprise. Circumcision as a sign of a special covenant
with God is odd enough; the possibility of a person being "uncir-
cumcised in heart and ears [Acts 7:51]" sounds odder yet, until
you stop and reflect how all-of-a-piece we are in the biblical view.
Another term for a special relationship with God is being "born
again." Somehow this is made possible through a gift of body
and blood, like the birth through our mothers. Even though the

celibate fathers of the church seemed to see the need for a new birth as evidence of the inadequacy of the old one, the choice of this word could just as well be an affirmation of our birth!

Through one birth, God proclaims the blessedness of all births. A fitting beginning for a story of *incarnation*, the symbol of this birth helped Christians hold their truth against the Gnostics and Arians, who preferred a more spiritual religion, just as many people do today. Though it is on the books, "incarnation" is not a working part of most people's daily lived theology.

Jesus was criticized for eating and drinking and making friends of sinners, sexual and otherwise. His passionate, dying body is echoed in our own. Much of his energy was focused on people's bodies — washing them, feeding them, touching them to make them well. Here is a Lord who healed with spit and who seemed to slide easily between the healing of bodies and the healing of souls, as the paradoxical story in Mark 2:2–11 makes plain. Some friends lower a paralyzed man through the roof. Jesus' words, "Your sins are forgiven," do not seem responsive to the implied request. To the scribes' shocked accusations of "Blasphemy!" he replies, "Which is easier to say to the paralytic, 'Your sins are forgiven,' or to say, 'Stand up and take your mat and walk'? But so that you may know that the Son of Man has authority on earth to forgive sins' — he said to the paralytic — 'I say to you, stand up, take your mat and go to your home.' And he stood up." Miracles like this are an embarrassment to our modern tendency to limit the Bible's scope to a "spiritual" sphere. Miracles are a sign that the New Being breaks into the physical world, too.

In the story of the woman taken in adultery, Jesus contradicts the assumption that sexual transgressions are somehow the property of women. Every time I read this story I am astonished again that the man in this adultery case is not there. He is not mentioned. He must have had *something* to do with the reported misbehavior! But no, all the men are ready to throw stones at her. In response to their righteous finger pointing, Jesus doodles. Then he puts male responsibility back in the picture.

To the disciples' unbelieving amazement that their executed Lord really is standing before them, and not some spirit, Jesus speaks the words: "Touch me and see; for a ghost does not have flesh and bones as you see that I have [Luke 24:39]." Then he asks them, "Have you anything here to eat?" and breakfasts off a piece of broiled fish (vs. 41–43).

The Physical and Spiritual Bound by the Sacraments

The sacraments are an ongoing reminder that we will glimpse the transcendent through things we can taste and touch and feel and see and smell. Jesus didn't say, "This is my spirit," but rather "This is my body, which is given for you [Luke 22:19]. . . . Eat my flesh [John 6:54, 56]." Things in themselves will not make much difference in our lives. Abstract truths are either elusive or arrogant. But sacraments carry on the biblical tradition by telling us that the relationship between matter and spirit is tensive and therefore alive. Through bread, wine, and water, we can reach toward the transcendent meanings we have no way to touch apart from the created unity of body, mind, and spirit.

Living the Oneness of Body, Mind, and Spirit in the Body, the Church

Instead of just giving lip service to incarnation and the resurrection of the body, how might congregations center their everyday lives around those central themes of the Christian faith? How might we live out a celebration of the gift of our bodily life and a realization that our life is one and whole? How might the church be more fully "one body in Christ"?

Being Concrete

First, we have to be concrete. You can't have a community without physical people in a physical space. And you can't love God and other people without embodying this love in action. So we can't begin and end with theology — it's only a clarifying step. Our ideas and words are not enough; they need to become flesh in the church as body. Today the body politic is pressing the church toward concreteness in the persons of the hungry, the mentally ill who roam the streets, all those whose needs, no longer substantially addressed by government programs, cry for attention from the churches. Students of congregations such as Douglas Walrath are pressing congregations toward a recognition of their embodiment in their communities. What does it mean that Christ Church sits on the corner of Fourth and Main, in the midst of *this* changing neighborhood, with *these* demographic characteristics? As this congregation's particular community makes claims, traditional women's service activities may suggest concrete and relevant ways to respond.

Recovering the Powers of Sacrament

Second, we can recover the power of sacrament. Since the Reformation, most mainline churches have been very full of words. Most church activities consist of sitting, talking, and listening. There are paint crews, but their purpose is to provide a suitable space for all the talking. This heavy reliance on words carries an assumption that human beings are primarily minds — speakers and listeners. A balance of word and sacrament, however, will allow our worship to touch dimensions of our life as whole persons that words cannot reach. There are many religious communities in which people live with liturgy in an empowering way. All churches can learn from them. Sacramental actions such as ritualized touching in the Peace may be especially helpful to men who are alienated from their bodies by making it safe, giving permission, to receive a hug. It was at a communion service at Kings College Chapel that James Nelson, enfolded by the erotic colors, shapes, paintings of his surroundings, felt powerfully at one:

> As I knelt at the altar rail to receive the sacrament, I found myself unusually moved by wonder, desire, and longing. More surprising than the intensity of the emotions themselves were the bodily sensations. I was feeling unmistakable sexual arousal. My entire body-self was longing for the divine.[17]

Attending to Bodily Life

Third, we can attend to our bodily life in the church, the body of Christ. Many of us were brought up to regard our bodies and our sexuality as not-good because of our parents' nervousness, which was reinforced by the church. When the theology we live by holds that our bodily life is created by God and is very good, the congruent behavior is enjoyment and responsibility in the knowledge that holy things do matter and that the Giver may be glimpsed through the gift. Carol Christ says,

Reverence for the human connection to natural processes would create an atmosphere in which the natural functions of women's bodies would be celebrated rather than ignored or treated as sources of shame. Menstruation, childbirth, and menopause might once again be viewed as religiously significant events.[18]

Our Christian tradition might also carry forward the attention to male puberty that is preserved in our Jewish heritage and might find ways to celebrate the experience of fatherhood. A sense of the holiness of natural processes would spill over into care of the earth, which has hitherto been almost totally ignored in churches.

An interest in positive care for women's bodies was recently revealed in an announcement in our church bulletin:

> BOSOM BUDDIES — A woman's support and referral network made up of 30 women who have undergone a variety of procedures such as breast surgery, hysterectomy, tubal ligation, abortion, fertility related and other feminine surgery, and are willing to share their experience with you when you are facing a similar situation. If you wish to join the network or are in need of this kind of support, please call Lee Cross or Wende McIlwain.

On the same Sunday that announcement appeared there was a chancel dance, a bodily and joyous celebration of a festival, reminiscent of frequent references to dances in the Hebrew scriptures.

Attention to bodily life is also surfacing in new concern about practicing the presence of God through breathing, walking meditation, and body prayer. I find prayer that includes upstretched arms movingly reminiscent of an experience I can't remember but have often observed in small children as they gesture "Pick me up — Oh, pick me up!" — a powerful, wordless cry that says more than many words.

Including Feminine Dimensions

Fourth, the church can redress the balance by including feminine dimensions of religion. At the time of the Reformation, the devotion to Mary, which had maintained a feminine presence in the church's life, was discarded. Thus the community's symbols mirror the realities in each man's heart. A reversal of this long trend can mean that the religious community's attention to wholeness and the feminine will heal men and include women.

Recapturing the Power of Sexual Energy

And finally, the church's ministry can be fueled by recapturing the power of sexual energy in church life. As long as we remain frightened of our own passion, we will stack the deck in favor of church life that is more dried up than loving and energetic. I don't think it's an accident that Jesus sent his friends out two by two. Possibly the pair whose hearts were set on fire on the Emmaus road were a man and a woman. Rosemary Rader describes the spiritual power of the early church's celibate marriages. A present-day priest holds that the celibate community including men and women of which he is a part "may be our most important contribution to the church." In a recorded conversation, he says,

> living with women ... there are a lot of things I could say. (Laughter.) It's wonderful. I think nothing can take its place. A woman evokes from a man, and a man from a woman, something that is not otherwise evoked. I think it is important that we develop within the monastic tradition this idea of celibate lovers — that we learn how to be highly sexed, and to have warm, intimate, passionate relationships, and yet to be willing to deliberately renounce the genital privileges and pleasures of spousal love.[19]

When churches can teach people alternatives to avoidance or impulsive discharge of sexual energy, it becomes one of the gifts of God for the people of God.

Putting It All Together and Taking It Apart: Living in the Tension

I see promise for moving toward a new balance both in women's search for integration and in scriptural assumptions about the goodness of our bodies and our oneness. But while our present imbalance cries out for unity of body, mind, and spirit, I do not believe that integration is the be-all and end-all of human life. Church and society have both overvalued masculine achievement over feminine being. What is needed now is not a rejection of male strengths but a rebalancing that includes female strengths as well. Too often recently women and some feminist men have reacted against male-dominated one-sidedness with a new and simple certainty: "Women's way is right." This reaction is essentially the same old either/or approach. We each need to notice where another's reality is somewhat different from our own, refrain from attributing our experience to the other, and rejoice in the wholeness our conjoined differences make possible.

Masculine reality has not suddenly become "wrong," any more than feminine reality has been "wrong" in the past. It is appropriate for men to begin with a physical experience of attraction to women, because their arousal is essential. Whoever designed a valentine saying "Honey, I love you with all my heart, soul, mind, and body, but not necessarily in that order" (and the man who bought it) was sensitive to women's reality and conscious of his own. Women can do the same for men. When I refuse to acknowledge the differentness of a man's sexuality and hold up feminine diffuse love as a human norm, I show myself unwilling to respect the difference of another's way. Men seem to have very sexual meanings for the word intimacy, for example. There is no call for women to correct them condescendingly.

There is a time to put it all together and a time to take it apart in order to make room for new possibilities. There is a time to attend to integration within, and a time to venture forth and master the reality out there — to reach, to stretch, to risk, to find out how it works so that it can be put together in a new way. The development of children provides an example: a perfectly good ten-year-old, at a stage of integration that incorporates all the best of childhood, has to come "unglued" in order for growth to continue. Rabbi Edwin Friedman points out that a troubled family will never change unless it comes unstuck, unfused.[20] Internal integration invites rest and the cessation from striving; this condition can be a problem as well as a gift. Settling for equilibrium in a world full of disequilibrium falls short of a responsible life: periods of equilibrium need to be disrupted because the kingdom has not yet come. Stasis invites the correction of prophetic challenge. Perhaps there has been too much integration in the private sphere, where women's influence has been strong, too much disintegration in the public sphere controlled by men. It might be useful to mix them up a little.

We must also value the male strengths found in direction, resolve, and the life that finds itself impelled to action. Some people have been so busy recapturing the internal unity promised by feminine visions of truth that they have not paid attention to

male resolve. Intentional doing, reaching out in response to a call
to exercise power in the world in order to master the reality *out
there*, accepting some disequilibrium for the sake of *movement* —
these are not only occasions for sin; they are occasions for grace.
Women particularly need to see the active posture, the acceptance
of power, as ambiguous, not simply negative, realities. Perhaps
birth is an exalted experience for women partly because it is a way
to touch that pole of intentional stretching and pushing that men
live out in other ways. We women may learn from our brothers
ways to stretch and push in the public sphere, to bring justice
to birth.

Masculine skill at discriminating, noticing *differences*, can
be put to crucially important use for all of us, men and women.
What is more important than noticing the difference between
what is mine and what is not mine? Perhaps more important than
discriminating body, mind, and spirit (our *inner* components)
is clarifying the difference between what goes on inside me and
what is going on outside me. Instead of speaking about "having"
a body, "having" a woman, what if we all spoke of owning what
is ours?

We must all claim our own reality and understand where
the other's reality is different, but we need also to reach toward
the other for wholeness. Women can reveal the inner integration
that is so often hidden today. Men can offer their external resolve
that is so manifest. Each of us needs the gifts that the other has
to offer, the gifts we celebrate in the poetry of our flesh and in
the prose of daily life.

5

Power and
Vulnerability

On Ash Wednesday I went to the Shalem Quiet Day at Washington Cathedral's College of Preachers. While I was eating lunch silently in the familiar refectory, I became aware for the first time that the room was lined with huge portraits of men. Six gold-framed bishops and former wardens of the college gazed augustly down in oil-painted dignity from their places high up on the white walls. When we moved to the chapel, my lifted eyes met the benign regard of five early church fathers staring down with cool, stained-glass faces.

Then, in the courtyard, I saw a twelfth figure, a little snow woman. She stood, arms lifted like a dancer, as the winter sun threatened to melt her fragile whiteness. Somehow the tentative presence of the snow woman, built of such light stuff, suggested a needed balance for the eleven costly images in gilt-framed oil and precious stained glass.

In the church, and in your life and mine, both power and vulnerability claim a presence. Most of us have learned that we need to acknowledge both the ways we are strong and the ways we are defenseless. We'd like to take control of our lives when that's appropriate and to notice when it's not. We want to own up to our needs, without either denying or exaggerating our help-lessness. But men and women do not always occupy the same position in this tension. Men tend to move toward positions of power, while women are often found in postures of vulnerability.

Claiming Masculine Power: The Promise and the Cost

Men are taught to claim their power. Their bodies, typically larger and stronger, have given them lessons in power since the days when they guarded the cave and hunted the antelope. The expectation that men will be more aggressive than women is confirmed not only in psychologists' studies[1] but in everyday language. To be called "aggressive" is often a compliment for a man, seldom for a woman. Common metaphors for being rendered power-less are "emasculated" or "unmanned" — as though power were inherent in male sexuality. Male humor often seems a socially acceptable way of taking a poke at somebody while remaining invulnerable.

Male expressions of power have both outward and inward directions. Energy, vitality, being up-and-at-'em, reaching out, thrusting forward in his life — these seem central to a man's way of living. Mountains and moons are there to be conquered. The Redskins and the Cowboys exist so we can find out who won.

A man's power must be directed inwardly as well. He learns that he must take control over his own power. Bodies are to be disciplined and kept in shape. A boy cannot become a man without knowing how to be aggressive, nor can he become a man without mastering his own aggression.[2]

This male claiming of power is a gift. It affirms life. It is positive. It radiates energy and vitality. George Vaillant's longi-tudinal study of men reveals a picture of masculine vitality as a wellspring of life, expressed through aggression and sex, two pre-cious channels of energy that require control without damming the rush of vitality.

A man's affirmation of his own power is a gift also in that it enables him to be intentional about life for himself and for others. The twin energy channels of sex and aggression can be harnessed in the service of love and work.[3] Thus a man's vitality fuels the quest. As he pours his energies into his chosen channels, he may discover an inner direction that unifies his life.

Yet another gift that comes from a man's claiming of his power is his opportunity to become increasingly sophisticated in the way he uses it. As they enjoy their permission to use power and to learn to control and modulate it, boys often learn how much power they can use, and they become comfortable and competent in its exercise.[4] They discover that coming to feel confident about their power can even enhance the way they deal with others. Speed Leas, who consults with churches suffering conflict, says he always tries to help people in church fights feel more powerful, because when people feel more powerful they will treat each other better. It is when we feel impotent that we're likely to turn nasty.

If power is a man's strong point, vulnerability is likely to be his weakness. The celebrated self-sacrificial courage of the soldier is bought at the price of pushing down out of sight that other reality of human life — our fear, weakness, and vulnerability. When life is out of control, a man tends to feel out of control, too. He wants to be a self-made man; he hates being weak or helpless. Vulnerability grates against his sense of himself as a man. As Mark Gerzon put it, "I never saw John Wayne walk up to a woman and say, 'I need a hug.' "[5]

When men deny their vulnerability, they impoverish their own lives, and they do harm to others. When a man pushes out of sight the helplessness that is part of being human, he does so at the cost of losing an important dimension of his own reality. If he refuses to give up control, he will miss out on the kinds of truth that elude human control. Mystery and paradox escape the grasp of his linear mind.

The man who can't ask for a hug learns to be a stranger to his feelings. Jean Baker Miller describes a couple who came to her for counseling. The husband

> wanted, first of all, to sail through every situation feeling "like a man" — that is, strong, self-sufficient, and fully competent... anything less he experienced as a threat to his manliness.... At the same time...he harbored the seemingly contradictory wish that his wife would somehow solve everything for him with such magic and dispatch that he would never be aware of his weakness at all.[6]

Avoiding self-disclosure is one strategy for wishing away weakness. Thus silent and guarded, such a man does not learn to trust.

If a man denies his neediness, it follows that he will probably not take very good care of himself. Though life seesaws up and down in a natural rhythm between the moments when "I can!" and the moments when "I can't," for such a man the latter become inadmissible. There is no respite from life's burdens. The man who is stuck in self-sufficiency is a good candidate for burnout. With no simple and acceptable ways to acknowledge the shaky places in his life, he is likely to express them in unacceptable ways — by drinking too much, or having affairs, or behaving abusively, or working too hard, or finally chucking it all in despair and taking off for Tahiti. His behavior will then be interpreted as failure, weakness, or sinfulness. And observers will be reinforced in their conviction that men must not give up control.

When a man projects his own rejected vulnerability onto women, ironically he becomes less able to get along without a woman. Isolated by his inadmissible needs, such a man may be seen looking for a replacement for the special woman — the one person in the world before whom he can acknowledge dependence — even before he makes the break with her.[7]

Not only does a man himself pay dearly for his avoidance of the unmanageable side of life, he frequently takes his discomfort about that side of life out on the women who stand for the vulnerability he can't admit. He sees women as responsible for all the out-of-control parts of his life: feelings, sexual desires, and the bodies from which they arise.

The assignment of all male weakness to a woman causes her inevitable problems. The rich complexity of life is thereby diminished for her as well as for him. His need to appear well defended inclines him to withhold himself from her, keeping his affect cool and his band of expressiveness narrow.[8]

There are costs to the whole human community as well. Just because little boys are taught not to cry, lest they be branded "sissies," we are all deprived of the gift of tears that flow not only when we know our weakness and vulnerability but also when we are deeply moved or are touched by compassion. The pool of tears at the depth of human life is one of the springs of our humanity. And the definition of power as masculine and vulnerability as feminine profoundly affects Western culture's attitude toward Mother Earth, as well. In contrast to Native Americans' sense of profound and interdependent bonds with the earth, European invaders planted their flags as a symbol that now they would claim the earth and make whatever use of it they wished. Heroes such as Daniel Boone are revered not because they tilled the earth but because they took it.[9] The same contrasts emerge dramatically between the dominant white Australian culture and the fragile fading culture of the Gagadju, aboriginal people in the Northern Territory. For the Gagadju, all life is a sacred unity. As one tribesman put it, "Earth our mother, eagle our cousin. Tree, he is pumping our blood. Grass is growing. And water. And we are all one." Few still remember the rituals, dances, stories, and songs by which the Gagadju have held together for thousands of years a sense of the unity of all life. And their children show little interest in learning their heritage and passing it on. One elder said, "Sometimes I think about this, and I cry before I go to sleep. Because nobody is coming after us." Before the force of a culture that exercises power over the earth, these people who live vulnerably within nature are dying.[10]

Finally, uncontrolled and unbalanced masculine approaches to power make preparations for war the normal state of affairs, a state in which human vulnerability becomes intolerable and in which the nurturing responsibilities of the nation look like luxuries we can't afford until we have achieved absolute security. As long as this "normal" state of affairs lasts, that time will never arrive. We will admire and emulate the quick-fisted, all-American hero, who "sees himself as the peace-loving champion of freedom — and will kill to prove it."[11]

The Feminine Paradox: Strength in Insecurity, Weakness in Power

As women live in the tension between vulnerability and power, we tend to lean the other way: we have trouble accepting our power, and we often show a paradoxical strength as we embrace our vulnerability. Women have trouble claiming power because of messages from others and because of voices from within ourselves. Unlike their brothers, girls have not been given permission to claim their power. As they grow up, girls are discouraged even more from using their drive for their own purposes, though they are rewarded for using it for others. Girls get the message that they are to drive with the brakes on.[12]

Not only voices from without, but also the nature of her own body makes power problematic and vulnerability inescapable for a woman. She is smaller than a man. Her anatomy is built around openness.[13] She may use tentative speech mannerisms that seem to acknowledge her deference to male power.

Deep in a woman's way is the wish to create closeness with others by sharing her secrets with them. What a vulnerable way to invite intimacy! Some of my earliest memories of friendship are of confiding to a new "best friend" something I had never told a living soul. In a girls' club, members take part in compulsory rituals of self-revelation in the hope that they will cement the common bond of risk created by sharing secrets. I think women often assume that confiding is a *human* path to closeness and are disappointed that a man's way to create a bond is less through baring his soul than through companionable activity, a bonding by exercising power alongside each other rather than by defenseless disclosure!

These voices from within teach not only risk and fear but also wisdom. A woman's body teaches her, if she will listen, to relax into the inescapable processes of life, to surrender, and to trust them. She soon discovers that any effort to take control in bearing or nursing a baby will just get in the way of what she needs to let happen through her. Motherhood teaches her to *attend* and to *tend*, words that speak of a watchful presence that allows space for the being and initiative of another. These lessons in letting happen what needs to happen may serve her well when she has to let go of an important relationship. As I watch women grieving for the death of a close bond, I often see them consenting just to *be* in that loss for a time, rather than rushing to fill the vacuum — bowing into the sadness and pain but not breaking.

While men are more likely to deny what is out of control, women more easily surrender possibilities of taking control and achieving. The prospect of wielding power evokes a variety of fears for women. The specter of being unlovable is a major one. "Why would a woman need power in the first place? If you were loved, you'd be protected and taken care of; you wouldn't need power. So, by definition, if you need power, you're unlovable." Deciding not to be powerful may look like a road to safety. Connie found herself blocked in her work. If she let herself succeed, she feared she'd be a "non-woman." " 'I'd be too powerful and then where would I be... I wouldn't need anyone else.' "[14]

Rejecting power may look like an easy way to be good: after all, if power corrupts, and I have no power, my innocence stands unchallenged. The prevalence of this conviction is confirmed by the numbers of children who can stop their mothers dead in their tracks with a single cry of "Selfish!" and by male coworkers who can easily make a woman feel destructive when she uses her power. A woman is seldom invited to cherish the springs of her own vitality.

No matter how compelling the fears and blandishments that urge her to remain appealingly defenseless, the woman who disowns her power (like the man who disowns his vulnerability) has a price to pay. She pays for her tortuous route to innocence or relatedness by distorting her own reality. The abdication of her own power magnifies her perception of others' power and then spirals downward into a confirmed conviction of her own help-lessness. "While the extremes of masculinity can harm others..., the extremes of femininity are harmful only — only! to women themselves."[15] The price of that impotent posture may well be "a bucketful of tears."[16] It may also be a bucketful of stress. As researchers have found, unmanageable stress is epitomized by a blue-collar woman, subject to others' agendas, caught between the demands of husband and boss, responsible for what she cannot control.

If a woman tiptoes around the possibilities of her own power and decides to go for indirect power derived from men, she is likely to be jealous of other women who are competing with her for that access. She's the kind of woman who "gives her sister the hip," pushing her out of the way as she jockeys for a more strategic position. There are often painful collisions between women who have informal power and women who have newer kinds of formal authority. A church secretary may see the new woman assistant as an intruder into the cozy relationship with the pastor that has long warmed the secretary's heart.

The woman who disowns her power not only distorts her relationships with other women, she is likely to treat men with insensitivity and contempt. She denies men the roundedness of their experience and doesn't see that they can be hurt, too. She may marry a man she can "look up to" and then protest that he doesn't give of himself emotionally.[17] If he then tries to become more vulnerable to please his wife, he may end up with a double helping of contempt for his trouble.

Just as men victimize women by denying their own vulnerability, when women deny their power, they can only snatch for control, and they may do so in hurtful ways. When men retain their innocence vicariously through women, and women gain secondhand power through men, neither has to bear the ambiguity of life in the tension. The cost of the cop-out for both is the relinquishment of fully human lives.

When women become aware that washing their hands of their power leads not to innocence but to punishment of self and others, they may be ready to offer a gift to us all: a more human definition of what it means to be powerful.

The Gift of Women:
Seeing Power in a New Way

The dictionaries, reflecting conventional assumptions, teach a meaning of power as "power *over*." Webster defines power as "possession of control, authority, or influence over others." Male definitions of power have become human definitions of power simply because men have more of the world's power. We assume that "dog eat dog" is just the way life is. Conflict — who's winning and who's losing — is what makes the news. Women's disinterest in that kind of power may say more about the deficiencies of the definition than about the impotence of women.[18]

When the possibility of owning their power begins to dawn on women, they often make a fresh assessment: what kind of power *do* they want to own? They often move to a perception of power as effectiveness, the capacity to produce a change.[19] The idea of power as effectiveness carries the sense of simple doing, without competitiveness or domination. The wish to be more powerful then becomes the desire to have more resources to offer others.[20] Women who are redefining power therefore tend to look for power *for*, not *over*, others. While conflict makes the headlines, working behind the scenes to try to see that everybody has a decent life emerges as a more important enterprise. Women want power exercised with care for others, because they know what it means to be vulnerable. When their sense of their own power enhances (instead of detracts from) others' power, they discover they can be powerful *alongside* others. Power, as women define it, is thus not a scarce commodity over which we must compete but in bountiful supply. When women can see power as "having the strength to care for and give to others,"[21] they can have an exciting time discovering that they can "go for it."

Women often feel exhilarated when they throw off their old assumptions about their powerlessness. I remember driving off to give my first lecture feeling that a clear choice was laid out before me. I could respond to my anxiety by wishing I hadn't got myself into this undertaking and being overwhelmed by fears about my own inadequacy. There seemed an equal amount of evidence to support a very different response: I could imagine myself feeling pretty confident, enjoying the challenge, being energized by engaging with the people I was about to meet. Since the second alternative seemed clearly more useful and more fun, why not pick that one? Making the decision that I didn't want to be crippled by my anxiety and that I could enjoy moving with the positive energy of this challenge felt like taking my foot off the brake and pressing down on the accelerator.

The Gift of Men:
Resolve with Compassion

In their effort to respond to women's newly emerging power, some men are so eager to throw off a suddenly suspect machismo that they collapse and go squishy instead. While the novelty of this new, soft posture initially captivated some men, as well as their mothers and women friends, it didn't wear well. Robert Bly worried over the new soft males: "Something's wrong. Many of these men are unhappy. There's not much energy in them."[22]* Too many of them mistake gentleness for passivity.[23] Many men who are unclear about their male identity find themselves unable to tap into the springs of their male vitality.

---

*© 1982 by Keith Thompson.

Simple solutions work no better for men than for women; men too must find their authentic place in the tension. In order to do so, they need to tack back and forth between the poles over time. First, as boys, they must claim their power. Then they must come about and make peace with the feminine, in women and within themselves. Finally men must find a way to bring those contrapuntal directions together; they must discover a way to exercise resolve with compassion.

Collapsing into the reality of the other is no more a solution for men than it is for women. Neither of us must give up our own reality and live according to somebody else's requirements or standards. Not only are "new soft men" unhappy with themselves, in my observation; they are also profoundly unsatisfactory to the women who encounter them. How do you encounter a bowlful of jelly? For all human beings, appropriate power means proceeding intentionally and resolutely while honoring and upholding others. And out of the conversation between women's strength and men's resolve, a more whole and human way of exercising power may emerge for both.

The Reversals of Power and Vulnerability in the Gospels

Both our power and our vulnerability, our strengths and weaknesses in living with them, point beyond us. I see signs of the source of the gracefulness with which we *do* live, hints for overcoming the contradictions within which we torment ourselves and others, in our Christian tradition. Most particularly, I see these signs and hints in the astonishing reversals of the Gospel stories and in Paul's paradoxes.

The Gospels keep pointing to a surprising Lord who knocks the props out from under the conventionally powerful and who empowers the helpless. The stories begin appropriately with a picture of the One who has all power consenting to come to us in an utterly vulnerable way, as a helpless infant born in a stable. The narrative moves on to describe one who goes out of his way to befriend losers and consequently antagonizes those who occupy established positions of power. The teachings proclaim a "kingdom" that is unlike any government we know, a kingdom in which the mighty have no dominion over the defenseless. Jesus' role as suffering Messiah is misunderstood and rejected, not only by the secular powers but by the men who follow him as disciples. It seems to be understood only by a few of the women disciples, those shadowy figures who blend into the background of the story — until they come forward under the cross.[24]

Jesus in his vulnerability invites us to acknowledge our own vulnerability. How we often struggle to deny our defenselessness and secure our defenses! We may then find the fist grasping our intentions pried open, our hand stretched out, empty, and we learn once again that it is only with open, empty hands that we can approach the Lord's table.

The Gospel stories reveal the holy dimension not only of vulnerability — but of power as well. Jesus' challenging surprises are not just for the powerful but also for those who need empowering. The stories present a picture of one who doesn't live with his power the way strong men usually do. He is constantly pointing to God ("Why do you call *me* good?") and offering his power freely to others ("You shall receive power"). Look at the stories of feeding the multitude, for example. When it becomes apparent that a lot of people are hungry, Jesus says to the disciples, "You give them something to eat [Mark 6:37].") He seems determined to counter the disciples' "I can't" with "You can!" Yet as these miraculous feeding stories are preserved and presented today, the disciples' role in feeding all those people goes unnoticed. The story reminds me of a recurrent dream in which my mother-in-law and about eighteen other people suddenly arrive for dinner, and all I have in the refrigerator is a bare turkey carcass. The anxious feeling, "I can't; I don't have enough" is a way many of us experience our lack of trust in our own powers. Yet in this story Jesus assures us, "You *can* feed them!" And he holds power and nurture together (in contrast to our tragic tendency to separate them.)

The feeding story in Matthew is followed immediately by the story of Jesus inviting Peter to walk on the water. Peter climbed out of the boat and was doing well until he grew scared. Reaching out his hand to grab Peter's, Jesus said to Peter, "You of little faith, why did you doubt [Matt. 14:31]?" Walking on water is a powerful metaphor for existence. We all live suspended over fathoms of water, Kierkegaard pointed out. The walking-on-water story isn't presented as a metaphysical trick (the point of these stories never is that) but rather presents Peter's vulnerability and the strength Jesus reaches out and offers Peter to *take*.

While these pictures of Jesus invite us into a *symmetrical* relationship with him in which we can be powerful, too, we have tended to respond with an assumption that the relationship must always be *complementary* — as the old Sunday school hymn has it, "We are weak but he is strong." Though Jesus's words to the sick who became well were, "Your trust has made you well," not "I have healed you," the latter are the words we seem to hear. Many of us seem to want to admire Jesus as a performer of supernatural tricks, in spite of his clear announcement at the very beginning of his ministry that he would not take that role and his constant beckoning to others to share his power. Our problematic response reminds me of a thirtieth reunion at Union Seminary. For the assembled group of clergy in their fifties, the focus of the gathering seemed to be on the theological giants who had taught them in seminary. As the alumni sat at the feet of Paul Tillich and Reinhold Niebuhr again in their memories, many of these parish clergy seemed to have a contrasting image of themselves as insignificant and inadequate. I'm sure our professors *intended* to empower their students; instead the gulf between such theological luminaries and ordinary pastors seemed enormous.

If we ignore the power Jesus invites us to share and insist that all power belongs to God and we are totally helpless, we miss out on an important side of the tension. "You shall receive power," says Jesus, and he makes it clear that this power is to be used in the service of love.

Paul's Paradoxes

Looking at this extraordinary leader who "cast down the mighty from their thrones and lifted up the lowly," Paul apparently concluded that the best way to make sense of it all was through paradox. "My power is made perfect in weakness... for when I am weak, then I am strong." As long as we feel self-sufficient, we are unlikely to long for God's power.

If, as Paul put it, "God chose what is weak in the world to shame the strong [1 Cor. 1:27]," we may find ourselves able to move back and forth between times of being weak in God and strong in God without suffering the hurtful effects of denying either our power or our vulnerability. As the passage in Ephesians has it, "Be strong in the Lord and in the strength of his power. Put on the whole armor of God [6:10–11]." How may we do that? In Paul's glowing description, the word stand keeps reappearing — "stand against the wiles of the devil," "withstand . . . and having done everything, . . . stand firm." *Standing* is a definition of power without violence. *Standing* in the tension between power and vulnerability means that we participate in a transcendent resolution of the hurtful contradictions that beset us.

Living in the Tension Between Power and Vulnerability

How can we live out the power of this reconciling paradox as men and women struggling day by day with our own strength and weakness? One way, as with all life's contradictions, is through the structures of time. As we move through the times when we find ourselves saying, "I can handle it" and the times when we cry out, *"I can't!"* we can live more deeply into the insight that utter dependence on God is the only kind that doesn't let us down. Little by little we may learn to discern when it is time to reach out with the active, initiating thrust, and when it is time to wait, trust, and discern when "the fullness of time" is upon us. "Don't push the river," goes an old Dutch saying. We pray for wisdom to know when we need to accept with serenity the things we cannot change, and when we must muster the courage to change the things we can and must change.

We encounter the oscillation between power and vulnerability not only in the moments and days of our lives but in longer swings that typically take different shape in the lives of men and women. As we reach toward maturity we may be liberated from the temptation to throw out whichever half of this paradoxical reality makes us uncomfortable. We may come to have the clarity of sight and the sturdiness of heart to reject the easy, one-sided answers that don't work. Instead of turning the other into our enemy, we might welcome the wisdom of her willingness to let life happen through her and learn from his strength. The task is for men to claim appropriate masculine vulnerability and for women to claim appropriate feminine power, and we may find, not answers, but clues for how to do this by looking at each other's behavior. As she moves farther down the road, a woman may come to claim for herself the power that a man knew he had all the time. A man may come to accept the vulnerability that a woman embraced long ago.

As all of us, men and women, find ourselves stretched to make new accommodations and meet new challenges during this shifting time in history; as women reach out to claim their power with new energy, and men come to terms with the loss of some kinds of dominance they had taken for granted, we may have new opportunities to move more deeply into the knowledge that strength and weakness are both essential dimensions of our common human experience.

Living in the tension between our power and our vulnerability requires that we refuse to split life apart, to deny part of its whole yet contradictory reality. When life presents itself as problem, it calls for an active stance; when life presents itself as gift, we are called to a receptive stance. Thus we are invited to embrace both our finitude and our courage. Instead of assigning the "I can" to men and the "I can't" to women, we may accept strength and weakness as belonging to all of us. When we can accept what is out of control and respond to the challenge to make a difference, we may learn to use our power to serve others without being subservient. We can then receive the gift that we have been given — and for which our lives cry out.

The tension between power and vulnerability emerges every day in practical dilemmas. When I volunteer to do a job in the church, I want to make a useful offering, but I also want to be fed. In group situations I am frequently torn: I want to own my authority and offer whatever I have that might be useful; but I don't want to take up all the oxygen in the room and deprive others of the opportunity to make their own contributions. How do I work to empower dependent or vulnerable people without acceding to their wishes to fall into my lap, as it were? Many times I find myself in this dilemma: I yearn to open my heart and reveal some rather tender things, but I know that I live in a world where it's risky to let down my defenses. I want to celebrate my triumphs when they come; and yet at the same time I know "all things come of Thee." I don't want to collapse when I encounter aggression; yet giving up the power struggle often has the serendipitous result that the opposition loses its hold over me.

Exploring the ways our personal struggles with this tension emerge in life's events may be an important agenda in our churches. It may also be useful for our congregations to look at this tension in the church as community and in the functioning of its ordained leaders.

Clergy are subject to a variety of seductions (sometimes subtle) to present themselves as invulnerable. The dynamics in the relationship between clergy and laity intensify the temptation from both sides. The myth of the holy man is alive and well in our churches. It goes like this: "God has set aside a special group of people who are not ordinary humans but who have godlike qualities of moral perfection, [who have] freedom from temptation and sinfulness and who are possessed with a special wisdom. These men . . . can answer all questions and solve all problems."[25] Clergy receive strong messages that they are supposed to be the helpers, not the helpees, as Barbara Gilbert points out in her study of clergy support. One of the pastors she interviewed said, "If as the helper I need help, then what kind of a helper am I?" The majority of clergy are male. They find themselves marginalized by the dominant secular male culture. It would be understandable if these clergymen were inclined to exercise control (only the benign control of the helper, of course) over their preponderantly female congregations. The church as an institution often feels powerless, poor, and fragile. How natural for such a vulnerable institution to say, "We know; we can help; we will make it all right for you." Understandable fears exacerbate the temptation. Clergy are well aware that they are hired leaders in a not totally rational system. They know they are the stand-in objects of deep yearnings and transcendent hopes. They know that as congregations carry out their religious work at the stormy subterranean levels of need and disappointment and anger, the ordained leader may become a lighting rod for conflict and end up being fired. The power of the temptations offered by the "holy man myth" is understandable in such a setting. Such seductions are reminiscent of those encountered by Jesus in the wilderness temptation to present himself as a religious strong man and performer of supernatural tricks.

Though the seductions for clergy to present themselves as helpers who themselves require no help are sometimes overwhelming, those who succumb are likely to find that they have surrendered their power as religious leaders. On the one hand, clergy who hang on to the "holy man myth" and hide all their weaknesses are unlikely to invite their parishioners to reveal the vulnerable and broken dimensions of their lives. Most of us feel distinctly disinclined to open up our guilty and sore spots to someone who appears to have everything under control.

On the other hand, clergy who claim the seemingly benign "helper" posture assign their parishioners the needy role of "helpee," thus perpetuating dominant/subordinate relationships, disempowering the laity, and cutting themselves off from the support that lay people might offer if it occurred to them that their pastors needed it. And so we end up with burned out clergy and laity who fall into the role of patients. We don't need "a pastor-centered ministry to sick and troubled laity," counters Pat Drake.[26] Laura Mol concurs: "We need clergy who can work in our churches as midwives, as distinct from obstetricians. For we're not sick, we're pregnant; we don't have a medical problem, we're simply in the process of giving birth."[27] Clergy who present themselves only as competent helpers not only disempower those they are charged to empower but also fail to serve as authentic examples of the dependence on God they preach about on Sunday mornings. And their disowned weaknesses, pushed out of awareness, will inevitably emerge in unguarded moments and in destructive ways.

Religious leaders, clergy or lay, who stand in the tension between power and vulnerability will invite others to claim both poles in their own lives. Vulnerable leaders lead us into religious power. Com-passion, "suffering with," is hard to do on a high. Most of us have to be emptied of our strength periodically in order to be compassionate people.

When churches help people feel powerful instead of teaching them that they are powerless, the ministry of the laity becomes a reality instead of a pious hope. When clergy see their role as equipping the saints instead of *being* the saint,[28] they can invite laymen and laywomen to join them as companions in ministry.

Churches can also encourage their members to embrace both their power and their vulnerability by noticing that men and women may have different religious needs. Christian theology has focused on correcting men's reliance on power and denial of vulnerability. If the church can "complexify"[29] its approach, it will also provide women with religious undergirding for their struggle to discover and claim their strength. The resources for this ministry are present in our Christian tradition; all that is required is a recognition that men's religious needs are not always identical with human needs. As women and men begin to share more equally in religious leadership, women will bring their gifts, which include a trustful relaxing into the darkness, and men will find healing from the stresses of having always to stay in control.

Churches as corporate bodies can also benefit from attending to the tension between power and vulnerability. They may find they need to reject blandness and claim the power of a unique identity and mission. Other churches, fragile and marginal, need to be supported by denominational structures as they offer themselves to their people out of uncertain resources, model a kind of success that doesn't fit the cultural mold of growth in membership and money, and perhaps consent to give up their corporate life when it is time. Too often, these struggling churches receive censure instead of the support they need.

During a recent after-supper walk I stopped in the cathedral's Chapel of the Good Shepherd and thought again of the patriarchs and the now melted snow woman. The chapel is open day and night and is therefore a simple place with everything pretty much fastened down. The relief of the Good Shepherd, tenderly holding a lamb in his hands, drew me close to the front of the tiny empty chapel. I felt the rough, cool stone and then put my hands on the crossed hands that cradled the sheep. Obviously many people had been moved to touch those hands, for they were worn and brown and smooth and felt almost like human skin. I remembered other statues in the cathedral — the father with his hands encircling the shoulders of the prodigal son, the bronze child Jesus by the entrance to the children's chapel, whose bright hands told how many children had polished the darkness away by reaching for them. All those hands of stone and metal carried traces of the many human hands that had reached out in yearning to touch them.

Although these images of power and vulnerability in the church came to me at the cathedral around the corner from my house, they suddenly seemed to point to that tension in the church wherever I meet it, as I thought of the contrast between the heavy, costly images of the church fathers and the light snow woman, between the powerful, high-up figures and the signs of the hunger for compassion (in the Hebrew scriptures, literally, "womb-love") revealed by unseen hands reaching out to touch and stroke the hands of a statue.

The cathedral is a powerful soaring structure of stone, statuary, and bright glass. But the little snow woman and the hidden hands that left their human traces pointed to the vulnerability that is also present and precious in the life of the church.

6

Pride and Hiding

P ride is the cardinal sin of man," we learned in Sunday school. Virtually unnoticed is the sin of self-abnegation, or hiding.

The Cardinal Sin of Man

"Man" meant "people" in that early Sunday school lesson. But if we think carefully about pride, we may conclude that the lesson is truer for male people. Men tend to exhibit both the positive and the negative characteristics of pride, that ambiguous human quality. The dictionary provides both meanings. Pride as "dignified self-respect" leads people (men, more often than women) to take initiative and focus their energies. Focus and initiative characterize responsible people who get things done.

But the dark side of pride underlies those strengths. If one has "too high an opinion of one's importance or superiority,"[1] focus and initiative can turn into controlling, overfunctioning, taking up all the space there is, so that there isn't any room left for others to exercise their own responsibility and initiative. People who are being themselves all over the place leave the rest of us out of the picture. The proud cry "I can!" then implies the unvoiced accusation: "You can't."

A total focus on one's responsibilities becomes problematic if those responsibilities take center stage. Those whose lives are based on a belief that "doing it right" will make them worthwhile people may begin to do some strange things. They may try to grab all the chances to do things well and push others aside in a competitive and even contemptuous spirit. They may define their own jobs as important and others' tasks as trivial. If what they do, and how well they do it, begins to fill the sky, they may begin to live as though their performance will justify their existence. They can forget that at bottom they are finite and dependent on others.

Male success depends on "becoming one's own man."[2] "Arriving" is a process of individuation, self-definition, separating oneself out from the herd. If a man believes that he will achieve selfhood through a Darwinian haul up from the primeval swamp, by achieving something special as a "self-made man," he may start to forget that his self was, after all, given — provided without any advance planning on his part. He may ignore the definition of human limits — God's first words to the human creature in the Genesis 2 creation story.[3] He may no longer notice that he's a temporary sort of creature who is sure to die. He may forget God's second words in that story, "It is not good that the man should be alone," and lose sight of that part of his well-being that is inextricably tied to the well-being of others.

While pride begins with an aggressive posture toward life, it ends with some painful inner realities. If a man's whole attention is directed toward getting things done out there in the world, he may begin to experience some impoverishment in his inner being. If he believes that taking charge and winning will make his life come off, he may feel fear creeping through the chinks of his hero's armor. If he succeeds in becoming "king of the mountain," will someone try to push him off? In classical literature, the tragic flaw that explained the hero's downfall was overweening pride. In his well-fortified position at the top of the heap, a man may find himself anxious, guarded, suspicious, and lonely. He discovers that simple self-confidence is illusory, and he will inevitably be shattered by life, which is wiser than his arrogance permits him to be. Denying the dark side of our lives always ends by alienating us from ourselves, other people, and God.

And then, what if taking charge and winning just isn't his style? Is he...somehow...unmanly? Aren't men *supposed* to be proud? As one young woman observed, "It's a lot more acceptable to say, 'After all, he's got his pride,' than 'He has low self-esteem.'"

Our Sunday school teachers were right: pride is the cardinal sin of *man*.

The Unnoticed Sin

While pride is a possible pitfall for all human beings, feminist theologians have become aware that women are much more likely to fall the other way — into self-abnegation, or hiding. Valerie Saiving said, "The temptations of woman *as woman* are not the same as the temptations of man *as man* ... and can never be encompassed by such terms as 'pride' and 'will-to-power.'"[4] Women more often miss the mark by taking themselves out of the picture or refusing to be their true selves than by being themselves all over the place. Sin for women more often means not knowing their own capabilities and skills, never taking credit for their successes, lacking the confidence that taking risks requires. Since the church's teaching about pride is well known, this chapter will say more about bringing women's sin to light; thus we may arrive at a more even-handed approach to the spiritual difficulties men and women suffer.

Hiding is a combination of masochism and powerlessness, fear and avoidance. While pride begins with invading others' space, hiding begins with giving up one's own. Like the prideful, we hiders measure the scope of our lives by the amount of power we think we have or should have. For people in hiding, life is measured by a deficit of power. We limit ourselves inappropriately. We fail to employ and enjoy our created gifts. Psychological studies indicate that while men overestimate their competence, women underestimate theirs.[5] One study of 150 gifted children found that 65 percent of the girls hid their ability, compared to 15 percent of the boys.[6] Unlike their brothers, girls aren't encouraged to cherish their own vitality as a precious commodity. When a girl notices that parents and teachers pay her less attention than her male classmates, she commonly concludes the cause is some failing of her own.

Sometimes we are reluctant to come out of hiding and live with vigor and assertiveness because we are afraid. If my worth depends on pleasing others, on being "good," I may avoid risky ventures for fear of failure, preferring to execute small tasks perfectly. If I fall into the common female pattern of "doing the dirty work behind the scenes while helping men to look good,"[7] at least I won't make any obvious mistakes. "Shitwork is infinitely safe."[8]

Women in hiding are afraid of not measuring up, of taking chances — and even of succeeding. We fear that defining ourselves may jeopardize the relationships we value so highly. A group of clergywomen identified a fundamental issue in relationships with their male colleagues: how do you exercise your own competence while maintaining the network of relationships in a system that has yet to become accustomed to competent women in formal leadership roles? "Veil the competence" was one tempting answer, admitted several of the women. Women often question the appropriateness of their competence, their success, and its public acknowledgment. As Susan Brownmiller notes, people often view exulting in personal victory as "a harshly unfeminine response. . . . More appropriate to femininity are the predictable tears of the new Miss America as she accepts her crown and scepter. Trembling lip and brimming eyes suggest a Cinderella who has stumbled upon good fortune through unbelievable, undeserved luck."[9]

Hiding results in part from overemphasizing our natural inclination to attend to the complex web of human connectedness in which all our lives are interwoven and from underemphasizing our need for self-differentiation. When our concern for the agendas of others and our relationships with them outweighs our sense of who we are, we may use our connectedness as a hiding place. We may hide our separateness. We may hide behind men. Hiding both our needs and our gifts — not to mention our lights, we may end up, ironically, in loneliness and isolation, for unless we are open about our hungers, our convictions, and our competence we can have little meaningful exchange with others.

Thus while hiding begins with giving up our own space, it ends by distorting our relationships with others. When we withhold the truth about ourselves, other people receive a partial and inaccurate picture of reality — including the truth about their own responsibilities and their own power. This is true in a special way of a woman's children, who may find themselves drowning when she pours all her energy into her relationships with them, not realizing that it is more than they can absorb or appreciate.[10]

Hiding perpetuates false perceptions in women's institutional relationships as well. When a woman will not trust in life, when she withholds her perceptions of reality, when she hides the gifts she has been given and refuses to respond to the call to use them, her relationships with other people are bent out of shape. I hear from other women, and I know in my own experience, how tempting it is to be very busy feeling guilty about my angry feelings instead of stating my concerns clearly and risking conflict. And of course, when we hide too many things in our own hearts instead of speaking a truth that might jeopardize our ties with others, we miss chances to work for change.

Why has "hiding" gone unnoticed so long? Probably because it isn't recognized as a sin. Hiding is a self-effacing spiritual malady. It doesn't *look* nasty, frequently, though it runs counter to life. People don't distinguish very clearly between masochism and saintliness. In fact, the dynamics are opposite, though at a quick glance they look alike. During a women's conference one group of women discovered that they were learning to identify as *sin* a lot of things that they had always thought were "nice." Several said sin was "colluding in denying the feminine." This idea of sin was brand new: most were accustomed to feeling ashamed of behavior that was quite the opposite, behavior that might more appropriately be categorized as prideful.

Women's struggle to clarify the distinction between hiding and goodness is made more perplexing because Western culture has given women positive reinforcement for "humility" and "service" without testing their underlying motives. And, of course, in a church whose religious understandings are derived from male experience, and in which the theologians have already decided that pride is the cardinal sin, the fact that women's primary spiritual problem is just the opposite can easily escape notice.

Charlotte was brought out of hiding through a dramatic and frightening experience. She had always assumed that God wanted her to be "good." And she had taken it for granted that being "good" meant fitting obediently into a traditionally compliant feminine role. Charlotte was almost always cheerful, helpful, and affirming of others. As she began to yearn to stretch out beyond that role, to explore her gifts more fully, to become all she could be, she felt torn apart — fearing she was violating the traditional picture of womanhood she had been given, uncertain whether she had any right to be so rebellious, yet feeling clearly drawn to new possibilities she had never before contemplated. In this agonizing period, she went on a retreat. During a guided meditation, an image came: Charlotte was enclosed inside a box. The box was comfortable and pretty and afforded enough room to stand up or sit down. It was a bit confining but not unpleasantly so. All of a sudden, in terror, she saw the box burst into flames. In a moment of clarity, she knew that God was calling her out of the constricted view of obedience to which she had struggled to conform for almost forty years.

The Invisible Woman

Many of us, like Charlotte, spend years not noticing that we are "in a box." We *expect* to live as we are expected to live. For the sin of hiding is the subjective side of the systemic reality that women are objectively invisible in Western culture. Like smog, the invisibility of women is so pervasive a reality that we don't see it.

Women's invisibility has many roots — physical, social, linguistic, and religious.

Physical Roots

The physical causes of women's invisibility are foundational but frequently ignored. I am convinced that we do not fully appreciate the connections between our bodies and our total experience of life. Of course the Freudians have analyzed the meaning of body differences from a male point of view, assumed to be an appropriate vantage point from which to define feminine reality. Surely no woman could have thought this up: "the girl's mind is so focused on the concrete aspect of being a 'have not' that it is hard for her to appreciate that she has something else which is equally significant."[11] Sadly, having been defined as "have nots" by men, many women come to accept this definition unquestioningly. Then too, many women find that the inevitability of pregnancy and childbirth and the experience of being "fed upon" while nursing dim their sense of their own individuality.[12] Still another intriguing connection between women's bodies and our invisibility may be seen in the hiddenness of birth in Western culture. Perhaps it isn't surprising that the aspect of procreation in which men take a proactive role receives an obsessive amount of attention in our society, while the event in which women have a starring role is so hidden that the paintings of birth by controversial artist Judy Chicago have an enormous capacity to shock. Birth is the only way we know of that people come into being. And yet man-made myths produce images of God as a potter, or God sticking a finger out to spark Adam into life, or Athena emerging fully armed from the head of Zeus.

Social Roots

Women's invisibility has social roots, too. Much has been written in recent years about the extent to which Western society sees men and male experience as normative, while women and women's experience have been presented as a sort of deviation. Public life, social institutions, work, art, and scholarship (including the fields of history, psychology, and political science) have been dominated by male perceptions of life, which then have been accepted as human perceptions. A more critical look at those assumptions has helped me understand why I lost confidence in myself and my ability during my nine years as an at-home wife and mother. Though I have had demanding jobs both before and after my stint at full-time motherhood, I found bringing up two children more challenging than anything else I ever tried. But I couldn't acknowledge the challenge of that task because I had somehow absorbed a message that raising children was something anybody ought to be able to do. In the isolation of the nursery and the park bench by the jungle gym, feeling very unsuccessful in this role I had longed for all my life, I concluded I must be quite incompetent if I couldn't do even this simple thing. It took me twenty years, and opportunities to listen to many other women's stories, to figure out that it was the difficulty of the task, not my own incompetence, that accounted for the struggle.

Linguistic Roots

Women are hidden in the English language, as well. Words such as wo*man*, fe*male*, or *man*kind imply that women are a subcategory of men. Women are so hidden by our language that a maternal maiden name has become a secret password for identifying one's bank account. No wonder women hide! Every word said and (mostly) unsaid encourages us in it. Women's lack of a place in our language has implications that far transcend etiquette or even fairness. The result of having no words that speak about our reality is that "women have not even experienced their own experience."[13] And so their experience of nothingness is deepened.

Religious Roots

Not only are women invisible in our language, they are often invisible in Judeo-Christian tradition. So often in the Old Testament narratives women are enumerated in the lists of the patriarchs' possessions, notable only because there would be no next generation without them. Of the woman who anointed Jesus in a dramatic prophecy, he says "Truly I tell you, wherever the good news is proclaimed in the whole world, what she has done will be told in remembrance of her [Mark 14:9]." But, as Elisabeth Schüssler Fiorenza points out, "The name of the betrayer is remembered, but the name of the faithful disciple is forgotten because she was a woman."[14] Near the end of Mark's story, it is remembered that "There were also women looking on from a distance [Mark 15:40]." In Luke's Gospel the women tell the apostles about the risen Lord, "but these words seemed to them an idle tale, and they did not believe them [Luke 24:11]."

Different Strokes

If pride is more typically the cardinal sin of *man* than of human beings, and if hiding, or self-abnegation, is more likely to be a woman's spiritual malady, it stands to reason that men and women have different religious needs. When it comes to the nourishment our souls crave, one man's meat is another woman's poison. Not long ago, I said to a male friend: "The wonderful thing is that I'm discovering I'm *all right*!" He replied: "I've discovered that I'm *not* all right — but that's all right."

My hunch is that we were both in touch with the truth we needed. I think the truth about ourselves, and the word of gospel that speaks to that truth, are always specific. For a woman it may be crucial to become aware that she's not as inadequate as she thought she was, in order that she may come out of hiding.

An appreciation for the goodness of creation — for her *own* created goodness — may be what was missing in her perception of
reality. A man's way of repenting and encountering grace might
very naturally take the form of discovering that he is not quite
as adequate as he hoped he was. A traditional Christian message
about sin and grace and a justification in which he can take no
pride may be just what is useful to him. For a woman the missing piece that completes the puzzle of our reality may be quite
different. The mighty are taken down a peg and the lowly ones
are raised up, we hear in the song of Mary (Luke 1:52).

Once when my infant daughter had a bad case of diar-
rhea, I got mixed up and gave her Milk of Magnesia instead
of Kaopectate. My bungled home nursing reminds me of the
unfortunate results when self-abnegating women are dosed with
spiritual remedies for pride. A strong emphasis on humility and
human failure may address the religious problems to which men
are more susceptible, but it has the effect of keeping women in
their place rather than liberating them. Reinforcing women's self-
despising attitudes can be an effective instrument of oppression.
Some fundamentalist prescriptions for the proper relationship between men and women seem to me to encourage men in pride
and women in hiding — and even idolatry. They tempt men to
be superhuman, women subhuman, instead of calling us all to
know ourselves as good and fallible creatures.

Linda, a young student, found it hard to get started filling
out forms to apply for next year's scholarships and loans. She told
a classmate that she kept eyeing the stack of forms, knowing they
had to be filled in, but somehow unable to get on with the job. He
replied, "It's your pride that keeps you from asking for money.
I have the same problem. I want to take care of myself and my
family without asking anyone for help." Linda realized that her
problem was different: who was *she* to be asking other people to
pay for her education? Her reluctance stemmed from diffidence,
not pride. She knew she had to claim a reality for herself that was
different from her male classmate's reality.

Our biblical heritage includes many words that point to
what people need when their condition is pride. Paul knew this
condition and spoke to it with power. He advised the Christians
at Rome: "I say to everyone among you not to think of yourself
more highly than you ought to think [Rom. 12:3]." He reminded

the Christians in Corinth that their gifts were not given them for their own sakes, but "for the common good [1 Cor. 12:7]." "What do you have that you did not receive? And if you received it, why do you boast as if it were not a gift? [1 Cor. 4:7]?"

Christian tradition also points to the biblical message that hiders need to hear:

> And God saw everything that he had made, and indeed, it was very good [Gen. 1:31].

> Look to him and be radiant, so your faces shall never be ashamed. ...The Lord is near to the brokenhearted, and saves the crushed in spirit [Ps. 34:5, 18].

> Let your light so shine before others that they may see your good works and give glory to your Father in heaven [Matt. 5:15–16].

> You were bought with a price; do not become slaves of human masters [1 Cor. 7:23].

> I came that they may have life, and have it abundantly [John 10:10].

> Almighty and everlasting God, you hate nothing you have made.[15]

In a broader way, the many stories of unnamed women in the scriptures, like the story of the woman with the alabaster jar in Mark 14:3–9, seem to point to the one whose name eludes us. In the face of reproaches about her waste of the precious ointment, that nameless woman's silence foreshadows the silence of her master in the passion story that follows. We might profit from contemplating these silent and hidden women as apophatic figures, living pointers to the mystery that transcends them.

Pride and Hiding: The Inner Connection

Pride and hiding must be seen not only as different sins, but also as inextricably linked at a very deep level. Both pride and hiding are ways of tidying up the ambiguity that is the truth about our lives. Each posture makes a statement about *part* of the truth about ourselves and our power and ignores the other part of the truth. For the reality is both that our lives are out of control and that our lives are our responsibility. There are two ways of opting out of that tension: one by denying the fragmentary nature of our selfhood and our power, the other by forfeiting the responsibility for doing what we *can* do. To split reality in this way is a futile effort to claim, "I am in control. I've got hold of the right end of the stick." We clutch at the "I can" or the "I can't" because we can't bear to acknowledge that we are hanging in the space between them. And we will not be able to stand the truth that we are hanging in space unless we can believe that space is caring in ways we can't *know* but can only *trust*.

Pride and hiding have something else in common: they are two forms of enslavement to self-image. Though man puts himself up first, and woman puts herself down first, both put themselves before God.[16] Enslavement to self-image seduces both men and women away from looking to God for validation and into using each other to reassure ourselves that we are OK.

Both inflated and deflated conditions betray a false center. I picture my self-image as a thin-skinned and extremely hungry beast. It stands around in the middle of the room taking up a lot of space, incessantly demanding protection and food. Whether the beast is starving or bloated, the point is that *it* is in the middle of the room instead of God. In words from the hymnal, "Cast out our pride and shame that hinder to enthrone thee."[17]* I am slowly getting wise to my tendency to translate everything that happens into the question of whether I am all right or not. In moments of freedom, it dawns on me that I don't have to busy myself with that question. It is already taken care of. It is hard to stand firmly in the middle of that paradox: knowing myself as a loved creature, finite and imperfect. I am always being tempted to move out of that center either into delusions of grandeur or into just giving up and saying "I'm no good," either taking total responsibility or denying I have any. Those two ways of missing the mark are linked: one is a cover for the other.

When I give someone a present, there are two responses that disappoint me. I am disappointed if the recipient doesn't use my present or denies that it *is* a present. Hiding oneself and behaving pridefully are like those responses to a gift. The only way I can please the Giver is to accept the gift gratefully. If I can lay aside the concerns about whether I'm JUST TERRIFIC (or not so hot) and simply try to do what's needed, then I know the service that is freedom. Then the task at hand can be fun, which may be a modern way of saying the same thing.

---

*© by The Church Pension Fund.

Having experienced this freedom, Julian of Norwich could write: "I could now stop my self hating, my blaming, and turn my life to simple tasks which make for peace — my own and others' — and see, for the first time, the good in all — and see God in all."[18]

Helping Christians Live in the Tension

In its daily life, the church could create a better fit between ecclesiastical remedies and human maladies. If the needs of women tend to be different from the needs of men, the church will be more helpful to people if it pays attention to the realities of both women's and men's lives.

First, the church can help people to accept that the "I can" and the "I can't" are both part of all human life. Just as an electric fan moves back and forth in a dependable rhythm of oscillation, so do human beings.[19] We can see this rhythm clearly when we observe a small child at a playground, dashing forth eagerly to join other children playing with trucks in the sandbox — then, feeling uncertain or suffering a scraped knee, running back to mother for reassurance or a Band-Aid. Soon the child is ready again to dash back to the engaging truck project. We never outgrow our need to oscillate between times when we must move back into dependence and times when we can move out with courage and confidence. We can see this oscillation not only in the daily rhythm between rest and work but in weekly alternations between our need to worship, to "become as little children" who seek those "everlasting arms" that will not let us down, and our Monday morning readiness to "go forth" back into the world, newly empowered for our ministries. All of us engage in both those movements of oscillation, back to our religious community to be "patted back into shape,"[20] and out to play our small but demanding part in transforming the world. And, like an electric fan, all of us can "get stuck" — either in refusing to acknowledge our neediness or in refusing to venture forth with courage. I think men are more likely to get stuck in refusing to regress to dependence and women are more likely to get stuck by curling up in a cozy church community and refusing to engage boldly in the hard Monday morning challenges. A church that attends to both ways of getting stuck will minister more helpfully to prideful men and women in hiding. A church whose vision of ministry includes the world it exists to serve will keep those out-of-church ministries constantly in mind while it pursues in-church activities, making it clear that helping out around the parish house is not a job description for adequate ministry for any adult.

Attention to the spiritual condition of women as well as men will encourage church leaders to balance their theology more evenly. An emphasis on the error of justification by works may need to be balanced by a clearer call to women to act, to risk, to engage courageously in the adventures of ministry to which they are called. It is no accident that the women's movement has been marked by an emphasis on political activism. The call to come forth, to engage in risky works, is just what many women need.

We will also be helped by a renewed emphasis on the doctrine of creation and on baptism, two of the church's primary resources for affirming the goodness and importance of each human person. Baptism gives us a chance to pay attention to our *names*. Many women are renaming themselves as a way of claiming a new, freely chosen, and more powerful identity. In a powerful experience at a women's conference, one woman found an idea for ministry with women back home in her congregation: "One of the most powerful things we did in our group was hearing one member's story of naming herself. Naming is a very important issue with women, and I think it would be helpful — not to mention energizing and empowering — to focus on names: Where did your name come from? Do you know who named you? How do you feel about your name? Would you want to change your name?" An important element in ministry with women can be found in emphasizing baptism as receiving a name, being "marked as Christ's own for ever"[21] by name, being incorporated into the household of God by name, and being sent forth in the power of the Spirit by name. As we emerge again from the waters, our own creation is celebrated. We can say with confidence, "It is good that I have been created, good that I am here."

This celebration and definition of each person can mark every part of our parish program. A congregation can avoid the kind of veneration for ordained leaders and religious heroes that makes people feel "I could never be like that." Sermons can celebrate the ordinary heroes and heroines in the congregation who struggle toward an authentic Christian identity and a life of courageous service. We can stop looking for speakers for our women's groups. Sitting at the feet of experts waiting for the pearls to drop is not what these women need, even when they ask for it because they haven't envisioned any alternatives. Instead, we can plan ways to reveal, elicit, and affirm the experiences and gifts of those present. We can devise strategies that encourage women to build on their strengths and celebrate one another's contributions.

Approaches like these will revive in a congregation some ringing themes that are often muted both in our words and in our ways of living together in church: the Creator who takes delight in creation and pronounces it "very good"; Jesus, who listened to nameless women even though that "wasn't done," who heard them out, took them seriously, and restored them to their created health and wholeness; and the human struggle articulated by Paul, who could finally say, "I know how to be abased, and I know how to abound.... I can do all things in Christ who strengthens me [Phil. 4:12–13 RSV]."

PART II
WORK

7

Working
and Succeeding:
Contrapuntal Themes

S napshots of "Mark" and "Sarah" at work may suggest ways
to move this discussion into the workplace, as we prepare
to sketch some contrapuntal themes in masculine and feminine
pictures of success and to listen for voices from our tradition that
speak to the dilemmas we experience as workers.

Mark at Work

"What do you do?" I asked Mark, when I met him at a church
coffee hour. I guess I really meant, "I'd like to get to know who
you are." What a person *does* signals who he or she might *be* as far
back as nursery school: "What are you going to be when you grow
up?" we ask. Just as naturally, people such as Daniel Levinson who
conduct studies of men look first at the occupations those men
choose.

Mark's choice — he was circulation manager at the *Washington Globe* — was made early. He grinned as he remembered
the excitement of his first job as a paper boy when he was eleven.
Getting up in the dark, entering into a business relationship with

the manager (a man he'd never met before), figuring out how to haul the loads of papers and gain entrance to apartment houses before daybreak, collecting the bills, and spending the profits on the kind of bike *he* wanted — in his telling of the story, these were all thrilling aspects of his initiation into the life of a worker. Leaving home while it was still dark meant a new kind of independence, a chance to explore freely the questions Who am I? and What can I do?

After finishing a business degree at the University of Maryland, Mark found a job as assistant to Dan McMillan, the *Globe*'s circulation manager. For about eight years Dan was Mark's mentor. "Even though this made me dependent on Dan to some degree, that felt okay at first," said Mark. "After all, I chose the job. I chose Dan. It wasn't like going back to being dependent on my parents — I didn't have any voice in choosing them. Being Dan's assistant was a way to learn the mysterious insides of this world of newspapers that I'd wanted to be a part of since I was a kid. And of course Dan had no say about how I lived my life after the office closed at five. When Dan moved on to a bigger paper, that was fine with me. I was ready for the promotion. And to tell you the truth, I was ready to get out of Dan's shadow."

Now, on his own, Mark has doubled the *Globe*'s circulation in just seven years. Although he was proud of his accomplishments and his steady raises, Mark's dedication to his work was a source not only of pride but of problems. His face was tense, his shoulders tight. His focus on priorities, promptness, and perfect performance didn't leave much time for fun. His wife, Sarah, complained when he worked late and begged off from outings with the children on Sundays. "I do try to help her with household chores on Saturdays, but she never seems quite satisfied with the amount of help I give her. *She's* got the choice, though. I saw an article in a women's magazine, ' "I'm sick of work": The back to Home Movement.' Can you imagine *Playboy* with a title like that on the cover?"

And then there was the worry brought on by the proposed merger between the *Globe* and the *Current*. In spite of Mark's record of achievement, the *Current* was a much bigger paper, and only one circulation manager would be needed. What if he lost his job? Who would he be then? What would he be worth? Lately

Mark had been haunted by the memory of his father's death just a month after his retirement party.

Sarah at Work

I had already come to know Sarah in a women's class at the church. "How in the world can I hold it all together?" she asked, more than once. Sarah had enjoyed her years at home when the children were small. She liked decorating the house, she liked the cooking, and she loved being with the children — that was the real challenge. Of course, sometimes she wondered what she had to show for all that work. "You spend an hour on Sunday dinner and it's gone in ten minutes. You clean up the house, and it looks as though it had been shot at and hit by the next afternoon. But the point of it all isn't so much that you can say, 'Look, I accomplished *this*' — what you are doing is more like warming up the home, so it's a good place to come home to. What was that commercial? 'Nothing says loving like something from the oven.'

"Of course it's a twenty-four hour job. But that's okay because there's a kind of rhythm in it: sometimes you have to push hard, and other times you can rest up for the next push. You scrub the bathroom; then you catch up with the mail while the baby's taking a nap. After you chop up vegetables, you can do the mending while the soup is simmering away, smelling good.

"And I liked being my own boss," she added. "*I* could decide how clean things had to be. If I wanted to take the afternoon off or stay up till 2 A.M. finishing a dress for Suzy, well, that was up to me. But after the kids were both in school I felt maybe it was time for a change. I didn't want to be like those women I saw wandering around department stores in the afternoon, looking for something to want. The week I found myself slipcovering my potholders and making a bathrobe for Suzy's *doll*, I thought, 'Is this a fit occupation for a thirty-five-year-old woman?' I had the choice about going back to work. But after we moved, the mortgage was astronomical. Mark makes good money, but how were we going to do all the work that needed doing on the house and save up for college bills?

"So now I've got two jobs and I feel as though I spend my life running from the office to the supermarket to running a few errands for mother to this class at church. But it's not just the running around that makes me feel stretched out. At the office, making it a good place to work or how you treat people is not the bottom line. You're there for eight hours. The boss wants to know, 'What did you produce today?' I might want to bring some different priorities in, but nobody's asked me what my priorities are. Heck, I'm the last one hired!

"The woman at the desk next to me is pregnant. They had a terrible time deciding whether or not to have a baby. Now that she is pregnant, she's not sure she's going to get her job back if she takes extra time off after the baby comes. I don't know what to think. I know she needs her job. But we need somebody at that desk doing her work, too.

"Commuting between my work at home and my work at the office is like moving back and forth between two countries where the customs are all different. Like yesterday, Mark brought me back to work after lunch and gave me a big kiss, right in front of the president of the company! I liked getting the kiss, but what does Mr. Johnson think when he sees me smooching in the lobby? Does he say to himself, 'There's a serious executive in the making?' And how *do* you move on to a more interesting job in this company anyhow? Mark had Dan to show him the ropes. My boss seems to treat me more like a good-looking woman than a serious worker. His assistant, Sally, seems to have settled into a permanent position as his junior partner. My women's group is the only place I can get some help in thinking about these questions. But they don't know what it's like at the company. Where do I get some help in holding all the pieces of my life together?"

Putting Mark's and Sarah's Pictures in the Same Frame

Of course, several moving pictures would convey more adequately than two snapshots the enormous range of work styles in the lives of women and men today. There are homes in which the roles are clearly divided along traditional lines, there are marriages in which the partners' roles are indistinguishable, there are househusbands and female primary breadwinners. There are people who are out of work. There are single people who support themselves. There are large numbers of families in which one parent has to hold down both homemaking and breadwinning roles. Fifty-seven percent of black homes are headed by women, descendants of that mythic matriarch who, says Gloria Naylor, for the sake of making slavery look benign, is pictured striding with ease through days filled with "bearing children and keeping house while doing a man's work at the side of the black male in the fields."[1] But despite this enormous diversity, we might find it instructive to explore the differences between the working worlds of two middle-class, mid-transition people like Mark and Sarah, many of whose satisfactions, quandaries, and pressures are also found in quite different lives.

If we put these pictures of male and female workers in the same frame and look at them side by side, the contrast between the man's *focused* approach to life and the woman's broader, more *diffuse* posture seems to stand out first. We will then proceed to note other *differences* (ways men's and women's patterns are not the same and might be considered to complement or enrich one another), *conflicts* (ways different approaches to work result in pain and anger), and *inequalities* (top-bottom relationships that oppress the "tops" obviously and the "bottoms" in more subtle ways).

Focus and Diffusion

Of course, any simple division between male and female characteristics becomes ragged around the edges when it rubs against the enormous variety of human situations and temperaments. Yet I see the tendency of men toward a more focused, and women toward a more diffuse, life posture emerging in these pictures of Mark and Sarah, as it does in the lives of other men and women.

The diffuse posture that often characterizes a woman's way of being in the world yields many benefits for her and for the other people in her life. She notices how everything is linked with everything else. The whole picture that spreads out around her suggests rich and varied connections among its many elements. Though there seems no way of getting "on top of" the multiplicity of tasks that fill their days, some women learn to relax into the sea of complexities that make up their lives and to trust that they will be borne up.

On the underside of those gifts, however, lie the troublesome aspects of having a diffuse posture toward life. Sarah complains of feeling terribly stretched. Women run from carpools to work and back again, stir the soup with a phone propped on their shoulder to get their church committee work done, and fall asleep over their neglected reading.

A man, in contrast, tends to feel he must focus his energies to prepare for the battles of life. Among the benefits of a focused posture is the thrilling sense of purpose and promise that fueled Mark's career trajectory. Only a man would have written a book called *Purity of Heart Is to Will One Thing*, as did the Danish existentialist Søren Kierkegaard. What an inspiring motto to bear on one's banner! Men seem to seek integration through *doing*, in contrast to a woman's way of embracing integration through her *being*. When men tell what life is all about for them, the theme of life as "an arduous struggle toward a glorious destiny"[2] appears again and again.

Yet such focus requires the surrender of all the valuable things life offers that are *not* chosen. If everything you own is stacked up in one lot, the surrounding vacant lots will eventually begin to look like a wasteland. "Is this all there is?" Mark has begun to wonder.

When diffuse and focused life postures bump into each other, men are likely to be left feeling exhausted and unfulfilled while women feel resentful. Women grow angry when they begin to notice that men turn over all the poorly paid or unpaid support functions to women, pour themselves totally into their work, and then parade the level of achievement resulting from that concentrated effort as a standard that women don't meet. One working mother said, "I worry about the men who are competing with me at work, who don't have the responsibilities at home that I do." In every age and culture those who could channel their energies into notable achievements (supported by those who did the other necessary chores) have been considered superior. So the encounter between focused and diffuse lifestyles tends to reinforce the subordinate status of the latter.

As we compare the stories of Mark and Sarah, we discover that the contrasts between focused and diffuse postures account for some of their difficulties. But there are further differences, conflicts, and inequalities.

Differences

The theme of separation seems to mark men's work, while the theme of integration emerges in women's work. Men tend to use work as a way to differentiate and define themselves. Women's attempts to round up all the fragments of their lives seem to spring from their appreciation for relationships and their yearning for wholeness.

Men's and women's choices are different. Men *talk* a lot about their decisions ("Which career?" "Which marriage partner?"); women have been offered fewer choices but may be required to make more! Traditionally men have had more options about what career they will embark upon and the extent to which they will participate in homemaking tasks. Fewer men than women have the psychological freedom to decide whether they are going to take a job or not.

While men have more autonomy in the public workplace, women have more autonomy in the private sphere of homemaking. Women have been reaching out from their traditional base of less-visible work in the private sphere to claim tasks in the public arena and are thus drawn into a realm that we intend shall be governed by justice. Men's work has traditionally been centered in the public sphere, where it has been more visible; men are now trying out tasks in the private sphere, where we intend that love shall rule our behavior. For both men and women, the new traffic between the public and private spheres seems full of possibilities for complementing one another's gifts and for enriching our common human experience.

Conflicts

When the themes of men's work and women's work are put side by side, a basic conflict surfaces between men's efforts to separate themselves and their work from the private sphere and women's efforts to hold it all together. This conflict is most acute in traditional families, where the sphere of love and the sphere of "work" are divided, resulting in a particular set of difficulties for both women and men. The woman is disappointed because the man often pays little attention to the home she values and to which she dedicates so many of her energies. If he is very clear that *work* is carried out in his workplace and that his home is to be "a haven of blessing and of peace," he may not define her efforts as "work" (and she may accede to his definition). The occasional Saturday morning project around the house, which feels like a pleasurable leisure-time activity, a break in routine, does not provide him with an experience of homemaking as a *job*. And if he is doing all the "work," he may assume that he is earning not just the bread but the right to rule the roost.

Husbands and wives who have rejected the traditional division of labor trade in the conflicts generated by the split between breadwinning and homemaking for conflicts springing from overload and from the confusion that is an inescapable component of major shifts in lifestyle. Gone are the clear set of boundaries to one's responsibilities, the consensus about norms and priorities in one's sphere of work. Now everybody has to do everything, and we don't yet know how all that is to be sorted out and made manageable. Both men and women struggle with the disjuncture between their accustomed assumptions about work and the novel requirements of their new workplace.

Men become angry when women invade their traditional workplaces and seek the success men have struggled for without extending themselves to the point of exhaustion and without taking the kinds of risks men respect. Dorothy Dinnerstein says women have had two motives for abstaining from history making: "socially sanctioned existential cowardice" and succumbing "to the privilege of enjoying man's achievements and triumphs vicariously... while enjoying immunity from the risks he must take."[3] Men are not offered those options. And women, for their part, grow angry when they are excluded from history making and discouraged from pursuing their own achievements and triumphs.

Inequalities

As men and women struggle with these demanding shifts, they are likely to find themselves out of sync. Most typically wives display more eagerness to move into the outside workplace and accommodate themselves to its prevailing norms than husbands are to accept full ownership of homemaking tasks. "I did your laundry while you were at work," reported Mark proudly, anticipating a hug. *"My Laundry!!?"* exploded Sarah. "Everything in that hamper was either yours or the kids'!" Old expectations bump up against new realities. He expects her to bake cookies while she expects him to share chores. Working women anxiously calculate whether they are actually bringing home any net income, after transportation, clothing, and child-care expenses are deducted from their salaries. "But rarely does either parent wonder why childcare is taken as an automatic deduction from the maternal side of the ledger," notes Ellen Goodman. "Why is the care of their children her business expense? . . . The partnership is psychologically divided in a way that puts children under her masthead. . . . She is paying someone to do 'her' work."[4] All these struggles between husbands and wives, of course, need to be set in the context of the large numbers of households headed by single parents (mostly women) and by other single adults who earn their bread and tend their home singlehandedly.

The perception that "work" is to be defined in male terms and that women will tend to the less important job of helping other human beings grow begins very early.

> In a third grade classroom of a parochial school in Brooklyn, some 25 boys and girls were asked what they would like to be when they grew up. Then they were asked what they would like to be if they were the opposite sex. In many cases when the girls imagined themselves as boys, they raised the conventional prestige of their career choice. In too many cases the boys simply could not wrap their minds around the possibility of being a girl. One boy succinctly verbalized his non-plussed reaction, "I'd kill myself!"[5]

The dominant-subordinate structure of Western society skews our perceptions of shifting work patterns. The perceived speed of the shift receives more attention than its perceived slowness. In fact, the proportion of women in professions is just now beginning to equal the proportion that existed sixty years ago, and the earnings of women are a smaller percentage of male earnings than they were a quarter century back.[6] The definition of "work" in male terms means that women are expected to be liberated by being allowed to work in male corporations, which are not expected to change. It means that women are perceived to be incapable of doing the work that men do. One surgeon patiently explained that women were not strong enough to stand up for the long hours required to perform complicated operations. "Who do you think is handing you the instruments," retorted Dr. Estelle Ramey, "the shoemaker's elves?"

Those whose tasks are subordinate and derivative are in fact less likely to measure up because they naturally have a low sense of ownership of work they in fact do not own. Those whose work offers little power and autonomy conclude, accurately, that the work really "belongs" to their boss. They often decide to seek meaning in other arenas of their lives. The boss may then feel somewhat condescending toward those who are less fully committed to the work enterprise. As Mark Gerzon concludes, "A world in which men compete and women cooperate is nothing more than a prescription for inequality."[7]

What Success Means to Women

In the light of the differences, conflicts, and inequalities between working men and women, what hopes — and what quandaries — does success hold for us? As women and men reach toward success in work, two contrapuntal sets of patterns emerge.

Success on the Home Front

Many girls still receive an early message: "The success that counts is to be found on the home front." "You came from me, you are mine, I love you, and nothing can ever change that." If a girl has heard this message from her mother, she may not feel a strong need to prove herself. Father may not place on her the same pressure to succeed that he puts on her brother. These parental messages may offer a growing girl greater comfort with "what is" and less impetus to move out into the world.

The next set of messages will be heard from a girl's circle of friends and schoolmates. In junior high school she will probably spend hours at her friends' houses talking about boys and friendships, diets and clothes, analyzing family relationships, and trying to figure out what makes the teachers tick. Girls have not traditionally been raised to imagine that they might have adventures — or even to want them. The ads in the magazines they read — even magazines designed for feminist working women — are not ads for safaris or new kinds of computers but for cosmetics and clothes that women might buy for themselves or for fur coats, perfume, and jewelry that are provided for elegant women by attentive gentlemen standing by in the shadows. The wedding day dawns as a moment of feminine triumph; consistently, divorce is experienced as such a shameful personal failure that many women hesitate to appear in church after a marriage fails.[8]

As she grows, a woman will hear another message that comes *through* rather than *from* her parents, peers, and culture — a message from the human species, as it were. The time it takes to raise human young and the amount of looking after they require press women toward developing the capacities for empathic care of the young and for maintaining the social and emotional complexities of family life. Here also is a nudge away from developing the expectation that they will pursue demanding enterprises beyond the sphere of human relationships.[9] The generally sanctioned and well-developed female characteristics that are essential to the preservation and enhancement of human life are just the characteristics that will not win women success in General Motors.[10]

Ambivalence About the Corporate World

Many women are ambivalent about succeeding in the corporate world. White American women do not regard standing out, or being assertive, as an unambiguously good thing. Feminine assertiveness is discouraged by male displeasure and by more concrete punishments such as withheld promotions and lower paychecks.[11] Jean Baker Miller paints the picture of successful sales workers receiving recognition for their accomplishments.

> The women get up and say things like, "Well, I really don't know how it happened. I guess I was just lucky this time," or, "This must have been a good month." By contrast, the men say, "Well, first I analyzed the national sales situation; I broke that down into regional components and figured out the trends in buying."

"The point is, of course," concludes Miller, "that the women were doing something like that too."[12] But that's not the way they talk about it.

This ambivalence has complex components. The first is that most women do not want to proceed in directions that will interfere with the human ties that are important to them. Because of their high value on relationships on the job, women don't seem to follow the male pattern of terminating their relationships with their mentors (if they can find them in the first place); in contrast, they may settle into a long-term relationship as competent, low-profile backup for a powerful man.[13] I can remember hearing from my boss, years ago, "You're the glue that holds this organization together." For a while, I liked hearing that. Then I began to question: was "glue" what I wanted to be?

A second component in women's ambivalence about rising to the top in the corporate structure is related to the first: having heard those early messages, most women place a high value on the task of nurturing. Most women have two workplaces. Therefore, to say that "women are afraid of succeeding" is too simple an explanation, based on an androcentric definition of "work" as what people do in factories and fields — a definition assumed not only by men but by many women. Women have their own space, but they often join others in looking down on it. If a woman wants most of all to succeed in marrying, creating a home, and raising children, or if she cherishes the friendships, books and concerts, and volunteer work that form an important dimension of her life as a single woman, she is unlikely to pour all her energies into paid work. While the order in which young women undertake enterprises centered around home and workplace has shifted in recent years, I hear them saying that the conflict between those enterprises is a live issue. Of course the source of the conflict arises not only within women; it is to be found in the world around them. One U.S. senator said, "I believe that women should be allowed to do anything they want to, as long as they are home in time to fix supper."[14] Black American women's conflict between the workplace and work at home takes the form not of either/or but of both/and. Since almost 60 percent of black households are headed by women, their experience tells them: you must expect to carry both jobs; just hang in there and try to survive.

A third component of women's ambivalence about pouring their energies into the workplace is related as well: not only are women torn between two ways of conceiving their life work, they commute between two cultures with conflicting norms. Women who move from a work setting where it is clear that "nurturing is what counts" to a workplace where it is clear that "competing is what counts" do not find their options attractive. They may choose to accept corporate norms and reject homemaking norms and then make their peace with inner incongruities; or they may choose to remain faithful to the values of the home and make their peace with failure in the competition. Many women find both alternatives unacceptable: one wounds the self; the other forfeits affirmation from the outside world. So they try to do it all and end by feeling like failures.

The Acceptance of Finitude

The frustration of failure may result in an acceptance of finitude. The challenge of holding together the pressures and rewards of home and work leaves many a woman feeling anxious, resentful, and tired. Surrendering any of her roles looks impossible; carrying them out adequately looks equally impossible. Accepting that multiplicity of roles means that whatever women do is considered secondary and derivative, women must then live with the reality that none of those roles is likely to validate them in the way that a man's work says "who he is."

But out of the pain of being forced into a recognition that she is not superwoman a gift may be born: an acceptance of limits, of finitude, of creatureliness.

The Experience of Nothingness

The satisfaction of self-giving carries with it experiences of nothingness. Many women feel fulfilled through caring for other people and participating in their development.[15] Yet permission to care for themselves as well is not always extended to, or accepted by, women. If self-giving is expected of, and by, women, then looking after their own needs may look like selfishness. Said Mary, "I'm glad I have to meet the school bus at 3:30 in the afternoon, because that gives me permission to leave my work at the church." Like Mary, I have avoided claiming for myself the statement "I don't choose to work like a driven person" by using home responsibilities as an excuse for putting limits on my office responsibilities. Self-giving thus can mean a giving away of the self, opening up the threat of "nothingness," which many women writers describe.

The Expectance of Pain

The ambiguities of a life lived between failure and finitude, self-giving and nothingness, may find resolution in "the Persephone Principle": pleasure is expected to be preceded by pain. The descent of Persephone to the underworld and her return ushering in the bloom of spring and the joy of her mother,

Demeter, were reflected in the mysteries celebrated at Eleusis; they emphasized such themes as "going down in order to come up" and "darkness followed by bright light," points out David McClelland, who sees this sequence recurring in women's experiences as well as in myths. The pain of labor precedes the wonder of new life. The task of homemaking is filled with interruptions: precious priorities constantly give way to immediate and often frustrating demands. McClelland noted that it was homemakers for whom the Persephone pattern predominated, while working women had learned "to respond like a man."[16]

What Success Means to Men

As I searched for patterns in masculine and feminine approaches to working and succeeding, I found the themes of work and success easily distinguishable from each other in women's lives but inseparable for men. For men, work is *about* success. The reasons for this may become clearer as we trace those patterns in men's experiences, the observations of those who study them, and the symbols used to interpret them.

Proving Yourself

A boy hears the message: "You're on your own. Get out there and do your best; perhaps you can prove that you are acceptable." Many men remember receiving messages of *being* from their mothers, in contrast to the messages about *doing* that they received from their fathers.[17] Even if mother communicates to her son that he is loved just because he *is*, that message may carry less weight than the words and nuances that come from father. After all, that boy is on his way to becoming a man, not a woman! Mother's message may also be muted if she tends to spend less time with her infant son than with her daughter. Or perhaps a boy may hear a maternal message born of frustration: "Doors will be opened to you that were never opened to me, and *you had better achieve!*"[18] Whether her voice is gently affirming or resentfully demanding, her care may provide a nest of safety in which his dream may be hatched.[19]

A boy hungers for the approval of the male parent with whom he must identify and from whom he is likely to hear, "You may be acceptable if you measure up and achieve excellence." The intensity of the son's yearning for acceptance and the conditional nature of fatherly love often join to elicit strenuous and anxious efforts.

Down through the centuries rumbles another ancient voice: the heritage of the hunters. A boy can still hear its echoes: "Be self-sufficient; be willing to join with other men but at the same time keep a wary distance from competitors; train yourself in courage and discipline; bear pain without whimpering."[20] Even if they no longer hunt, men must maintain control of the tribe's enterprise.

Pursuing a Dream

A man is expected to embark upon a quest, directing his energy toward the fulfillment of a significant dream. The dream is allowed to grow in that special space found only in childhood, "on the boundary between reality and illusion."[21] It is shaped by daydreams, stories, and "let's pretend," born out of childhood's normal fantasies of omnipotence. The excitement of the dream fuels the young man's energy and determination for the hard work that will be required to turn the dream into reality. The dream may soar (like Superman), or it may take humbler forms like the ambition of becoming a master craftsman.[22]

As we have noted, the single-pointed quest may so fill a man's life that other important things are left out. One study showed that middle-class fathers spend an average of thirty-seven seconds a day with their children. As John Lennon put it, to be *"proud* of taking care of children — it is still the exception to the rule."[23]

Climbing the Ladder

The image of climbing a ladder to success holds out both the promise of achievement and the pain of loneliness and pressure. A man is raised to achieve; his positive self-image is primarily dependent on his success in his chosen field. In order to succeed he must compete and win. And competition carries the message "Go it alone." In the aftermath of Eden, the man's lonely labors form the counterpart to the woman's subordination. She is no longer mentioned even as present in his work environment.[24] One of the lonely breed of male heroes is the Expert, whose expertise is predicated precisely on others' *lack* of expertise.[25]

Men	*Women*
1. Move out into life autonomously and do your very best; you may then be acceptable.	1. Being is more important than doing; perhaps the success that counts may yet be found at home.
2. Direct your energy toward the most important dream.	2. The prospect of success in the outside world is cause for ambivalence.
3. Climb the ladder, though it may lead you not only to success but to lonely competition, pressure, and uncertainty.	3. The impossibility of "doing it all" may yield a realization of finitude.
4. Your ascent will be followed by a fall.	4. Self-giving may issue in a sense of nothingness.
5. The question arises: are there more satisfying ways to be a hero?	5. Suffering will, in the end, prove to have been the prelude to fulfillment.

The ladder image of success depends on inequality, on excluding others from the top rung. Richard Nixon put the connection between ladders and loneliness baldly: "There can be only one number one: all the rest are losers."[26]

There is room for only one at the top of the ladder; therefore, while success is mandated, most will fail to achieve it. Each success must exceed the previous one: novelists don't want just to write another novel; they want to win the Pulitzer Prize. The either/or, if-you-don't-win-you-lose outlook intrinsic in the ladder image labels most workers as failures — losers.[27] Odds like that trigger feelings of meaninglessness and despair.

To the pain of loneliness, probable failure, and meaninglessness, the ladder image adds an intolerance of weakness coupled with relentless pressure. Even when a man is exhausted, he does not pay attention to his body and his feelings.[28] He is expected to stand up under the strain. He must always appear to know the answers. (What a contrast to Miller's women workers, who were at such a loss to account for their success!) If the job fails to fulfill the dream, a man is inclined to "give it all he's got" and put in longer and longer hours.[29] And if against all odds a man *does* succeed, his reward will be an increased load of responsibility and pressure.[30]

The Icarus Complex

The Icarus Complex joins the upward struggle toward the dream with the despair that hides under the ladder. Icarus' home-made wings melted when he flew too near the sun, plunging him into the sea. "This is the male image of achievement," says McClelland, a "straight line projecting upward to a peak of glory until...he falls.[31] In projective tests, twice as many women as men saw pain preceding fulfillment, while the same proportion of men saw achievement as the climax immediately preceding a final fall. Those whose eyes are firmly fixed on success sense failure as a specter lurking around a corner, ready to pounce.

Male clergy are caught in a peculiar conflict: though the culture proposes a ladder image or an Icarus theme for men, they are members of a community whose myth is dominated by the feminine Persephone motif. Clergymen may therefore be trapped in a painful dilemma between choosing the Icarus theme and settling for inauthenticity or choosing the Persephone motif and feeling like failures by prevalent masculine standards.

Being a Male Hero Today

How can one be a male hero today? If dreams are subject to rude awakenings, if flights crash, perhaps the clergyman's dilemma does not greatly differ from the quandary of Everyman. It is hard for a man to feel like a hero, even at home. Instead of treating men like heros, women today compete with them.

Men caught in this dilemma urgently seek some new images of male heroism, and some have been suggested by Mark Gerzon. In place of the Breadwinner, he proposes the Companion, who, though he does not give up his desire to achieve, no longer rests his manhood on the realization of his ambitions.[32] The Companion honors a broader spectrum of human concerns, and is proud to care for the baby and bake the bread. Instead of becoming the lonely Expert, men can adopt the image of the Colleague, for whom knowledge is used not to mystify but to enlighten — not as a jealously guarded credential but as a gift to be generously shared. The Colleague can learn from women because they are different from him, and he does not ignore his relationships in favor of his goals. One company calls this Colleague consciousness "enlarging the winner's circle."[33]

Men, Women, and Success

Putting these sets of themes of men's and women's view of work and success side by side suggests contrapuntal patterns that, when joined, hint at wholeness. The juxtaposition of these themes hints at our yearnings for wholeness (see p. 112).

Wanting It All

We all want it all. Women, especially, are stretched and exhausted as they run from baby to bank to Bible study. Many women want, as well, the excitement of investing themselves in a single-pointed quest, as they move through their individual lives and as they move through history. Men's hunger for greater wholeness becomes even more urgent, because diversifying their energies by attending to a broader range of life's dimensions promises healing for the stress and burnout of the lonely long-distance runner. An awareness of systems (corporate or ecological) also invites many men to balance single focus with a more integrated lifestyle. We all want it all, but a man's progress and a woman's progress tend to describe contrapuntal patterns as our yearnings reach toward each other and toward new wholeness.

Product and Process

When everybody shares work in public and private spheres, a product-oriented society may learn to attend also to process.

> If I complete a project — give a lecture or write an article — that's something tangible. I can hold on to it. Men are used to having these kinds of rewards. We want credit for the things we do, and we always find time to do them. But to be with my kids, I had to let go. . . . I had to get in touch with myself, with the experience of just being with them.[34]

Many men are joining Mark Gerzon in this discovery. Even house-work affords possibilities for "just being." Cutting up vegetables for a stir fry and arranging them on a tray, making a birthday cake for someone you love, shining silver or oiling wood, hang-ing clothes to dry in the sunshine, or picking strawberries for the morning cereal — these tasks afford opportunities for men, as well as women, to balance overly abstract work with tasks whose concreteness brings satisfaction, to complement product-oriented work with an attention to process that rounds out our lives. The Japanese have long savored the attentiveness to being in doing that has frequently been ignored by Westerners. Too often our grasping and self-important way of living has pushed us toward attention to product only, toward ends for which any means are justified, toward work marked by "thorns and thistles" rather than by a sense of gift, an openness to play, a listening heart.

Women's experiences press them to be aware of process; for example, a tense, product-oriented approach to nursing ends with a hungry baby. When caring for relationships, attending to the process of life, is no longer viewed as an inferior work mode, women may be invited to offer this balancing attentive-ness to us all. Many women can also return more appreciatively to the pleasures of homemaking when they have had a chance to achieve something "tangible" (in Gerzon's terms) in the outside world. Now that I have had a chance to fly out and try my wings, I can notice how really precious and produc-tive the nestbuilding enterprise is. I don't have to justify my existence with a clean house (is that the "sting" of work at home?) but can enjoy spending some time carrying out the tasks that create warm and beautiful space for me and others. All the outside work in the world isn't worth much unless we can come home to the care and beauty and love that make life worth living. For single people this home may include a shared life with friends or relatives, or it may be a welcoming space that offers healing solitude, room for creative projects, and a kitchen table to which friends may be welcomed. Whatever our life situation may be, perhaps we can all honor the tasks that enrich our private lives and enjoy them as a gift of freely chosen work.

Joining the Linear and the Circular

Joining linear and circular movements, the Icarus flight and the Persephone descent, sketches a pattern of wholeness for human lives. Success is a little like positioning yourself on a wave at the right moment to be picked up and carried by it — a simple but not easy process of yielding to the whole and knowing when to take the initiative. Masculine socialization toward total focus makes for unbalanced lives that lead to burnout. Feminine socialization toward assuming responsibility for everything may lead a woman to relinquish the opportunity to be all she can be. Resolve and compassion, the linear thrust of the quest and the encircling movement of nurture, join to describe a spiral, a fitting metaphor for the way we experience psychological movement. These patterns of wholeness offer promise and require stretching not only for men but for women. The feminine characteristics that are dysfunctional for success in the world as it is may be what the world needs most.[35]

If women are engaged in a loving revolution, we are called to stand in a special kind of tension. If it were easy, it wouldn't need doing! We can't expect the revolution to be blessed by the establishment and crumple up in a heap when others don't welcome our challenge. If we persist in looking to dominants to be our validators, we are bound to fail. A faithful posture means both refusing to opt out *and* refusing to attack and insist we have all the truth. This loving revolution may, for example, manifest itself in new ways of looking at management. Conceived functionally rather than hierarchically, the role of corporate managers may be like the traditional role of mother, who manages the household so others can move out, perform their unique duties, and then return to an orderly home base. It is not *necessary* to conceive of mother as superior just because she has this overarching role of providing an enabling structure.

The contrapuntal movements of the Icarus and Persephone patterns suggest a way we might join in bringing to birth a new set of options for human work. The dream presents both the promise and the implied tragic results of pressing beyond human limits, as all the classic myths of human hubris dramatize. The Persephone movement of descent suggests the terror of venturing into nothingness and the hope of being lifted up again. All of us live on the boundary: we are puny and finite; yet we have within us an infinite hunger. Since we don't know how to embrace that contradiction all at once, we attend to those realities sequentially. In the Icarus pattern, rising is completed by descent; in the Persephone pattern, descent is completed by rising.

A Religious Understanding of Work

The problems and promises we experience in working and succeeding are helpfully addressed by three themes from our religious tradition:

1. Work is part of the gift of creation.

2. We are called to a theonomous posture — our work is to be grounded in God.

3. Since work is not our lord, we can hold it both seriously and lightly.

Work as a Gift

Work is part of the gift of creation. But before all human work comes divine delight in the goodness of creation, just as "You are my Son, the Beloved; with you I am well pleased [Luke 3:22]," precedes any act of ministry on the part of the One through whom creation is to be restored. Jesus' work issues out of his confidence in the Father's love. Insofar as the theology by which we live is grounded in our assurance of created goodness and divine pleasure, we won't treat ourselves like unloved people or like slaves rather than children, and we won't act as though we have to become okay by "doing it right."

In both creation stories, work is "indigenous to creation," says Phyllis Trible.[36] The creation of work precedes the creation of sexuality, so work belongs to all human creatures and ought not therefore to be defined in male terms only. The work of production and the work of procreation are given to both human creatures. We are given the gift of eros ("flesh of my flesh") and the task of having and raising children; we are given a garden and the task of caring for the earth. The earth creature is to rule over the earth by serving or tilling it.[37] The close conjunction of eros and a garden, of love and work, as foundational in creation is echoed in many creation myths. As people wonder how the first

things came about, somehow it seems natural to spin tales about
gods begetting humans or God working clay into human form.

Made "in the image of God," we are creators, too. A creation story playful with rollicking puns tells us of God's delight
in fashioning all things; so we, too, make things and experience
delight because "they are very good." Like our divine Parent, we
encourage our children's creativity, taping their paintings on our
refrigerators and keeping our paper clips in their lopsided clay
pots. Thus if we accept the invitation to become fellow workers
with God, we will carry out our work in partnership with life,
in a discerning and attentive alternation between initiative and
response (as opposed to getting stuck in control or passivity).

The story says, too, that people and their work are finite.
Limits are set for the human creatures. Succumbing to the seductive promise "you shall be as gods" produces the opposite of the
promised result — disintegration ("to dust you shall return").
That is the human experience: when we refuse to acknowledge
that there are limits to what we can do, life starts to disinte-
grate. In contrast to a man's temptation to set about building a
tower that reaches to heaven, and a woman's temptation to act
as though she's got the whole world in her hands, we might all
keep an eye on our presumptuous urge to control what we can't
control (a temptation signaled by the tension in our bodies) and
just do our part, knowing that many of the results of our work
lie beyond our control.

When we won't acknowledge that we and all our works
are finite, work becomes alienated, although that was not the way
it was supposed to be. Work, which began as "an erotic activity
of creation," becomes "alienated labor" whether it is the labor
of farming or childbearing.[38] The work of production is carried
out alone, in sweaty toil, in ground now cursed with thorns and
thistles. The worker is separated from God, the earth, and the
erstwhile partner. What was offered as a gift has now become a
chore. The work of procreation is carried out in pain and struggle,
as well. The love song "flesh of my flesh" has been twisted to "he
shall rule." The woman suffers increased pain as she brings forth
children.

Since this tale is myth, not a progress report, we might
find it useful to read it not as linear sequence ("They sinned, so
now we...") but as a story that dramatizes the proffered gift of

work as part of God's creation and also the alienated labor into which work often becomes twisted — both of which make up the ambiguity and the possibilities of your work and mine this Monday morning.

Work Grounded in God

In our work, we are called to a theonomous posture: our work is to be grounded in God. Acknowledging that I have a Lord helps keep me from lording it over other people or letting them lord it over me. This means that my work can be redeemed from heteronomy ("the law of others"); my worth does not derive from my work. Because I am in charge of my work, I can offer it as a gift. I can achieve some balance between personal calling and institutional demands. As a theonomous worker, I can hold the institution in which I work with some lightness, and I can challenge it when it needs challenging. Perhaps women especially need to hear these words that are so difficult for us all: "Woe unto you when all men speak well of you." We are called to a loving revolution. This means that those who exercise power in the institutions in which we work probably do not already know, understand, and accept the truth of the prophetic word we have to speak. If they provided us with approval for proclaiming it, it would not be a prophetic message.

Our work is redeemed, as well, from simple autonomy. "Thine is the glory," not mine. Said Brother Lawrence, our calling lies in "doing that for God's sake which we commonly do for our own."[39] We are not responsible for everything; we are relieved of the impossible burden of trying to encompass infinity.

If we do not fall into heteronomy or autonomy, what would our work be like? Perhaps, to borrow a metaphor from the human task of procreation, it would be like moving more gracefully with the rhythms of pushing and waiting, moving intentionally in collaboration with forces beyond our control. It would mean living with both serenity and courage. It would mean doing whatever we have to do simply and in the power of the One who created us.

Theonomous work means, with Brother Lawrence, doing everything for the love of God, and, with Mother Ann, setting "hands to work and hearts to God." And so there need be no great barrier between work and prayer; but work might find its way into our prayer, and moments of prayer might keep work on its course, so "that in all the cares and occupations of our life we may not forget you."[40]

Holding Work Seriously and Lightly

Since work is not our lord, we can hold our work both seriously and lightly. The words and symbolic actions of the Christian tradition affirm in many ways that work is both a gift and a calling. It was said of Brother Lawrence that he was "neither hasty nor loitering."[41] An alert, relaxed gait is body language for being responsible but not driven. A fresh and painful realization of the blessing of work is experienced by those who have no work. They know what a privilege it is to expend one's energies productively, "to do the work you have given us to do."[42]

Ecclesiastes saw "that there is nothing better than that all should enjoy their work, for that is their lot [3:22]." Perhaps Abraham Maslow expressed a similar insight when he said that self-actualizing people have something in common: they "have overcome the work vs. joy dichotomy."[43] When I find myself oppressed by the multiplicity of the tasks that face me, I sometimes bring back to my dulled awareness the inherent giftedness of my work by approaching tasks, one at a time, as "something to play with now." If our joy is intended, it might flow freely across the boundaries we mark with labels like "work," "play," and "prayer." "I, God, am your playmate! I will lead the child in you in wonderful ways," says Mechthild of Magdeburg.[44]

"Living by grace, not works" is the classic Christian way of speaking about a way of life that trusts God, gives what God requires, and breaks down the division between duty and delight. I recently watched a Lutheran bishop whose energies clearly flowed together, both within himself and between him and other people. In response to a pastor's hesitant "I don't know whether I should say this or not...," he called out, "*Go* for it!" — and she did. I find it instructive to notice how grace is enfleshed in this or that person's way of working, as well as to observe how much stress and strain, anxious striving, and inner division mark the oppression of many people's work postures.

"Offering" our work in private prayer and corporate liturgical action is a most useful way of holding work seriously and lightly. Giving something away always lightens it up. Keeping the work moving by receiving it as a gift and offering it back in a loving exchange is a way of saying I am in charge of my work (instead of the reverse), and Another is in charge of me. This exchange of receiving-and-offering contrasts with the death-dealing posture of which the Deuteronomic writer warns: "Beware lest you say in your heart, 'My power and the might of my own hand have gotten me this wealth' [8:17]." The Hebrew scriptures speak of undue dependence on what is "made with hands" as idolatry — putting our trust in that which will surely let us down. When we become obsessed with work, our minds grow "cumbered" and "clogged," said George Fox. When you go about "crying, my business, my business, . . . your minds will go into the things, and not over the things."[45] James Dittes proposes a lighter way of holding work: "We work because it has *some* meaning, *some* interest, accomplishes *some*thing, and because it pays us."[46]

If we can affirm that "work is not *everything*, but it's *something*," it follows that we can choose to place limits on our work and our search for success. Those limits might take the form of simplifying our lifestyle. John Woolman was moved to speak to the women Friends in one society's Monthly Meeting of

> the disuse of all superfluities, reminding them of the difficulties their husbands and sons were frequently exposed to at sea, and that the more plain and simple their way of living was, the less need of running great hazards to support them in it, . . . [noticing] where people were truly humble . . . and . . . content with a plain way of life, that it had ever been attended with more true peace and calmness of mind than those have had who, aspiring to greatness and outward show, have grasped hard for an income to support themselves in it.[47]

Those Quakers of a simpler day might well commend the "disuse of superfluities" to us who have many more desires dinned into our ears and who feel so stretched and exhausted by our overloaded lives. The only way we can combat that overload is to give up old tasks when we want to claim new kinds of work.

The Quaker tradition urges limits, not only in the form of a simple lifestyle, which cuts down the wage-earning energy required to support it, but also by urging that we be discerning in our choice of tasks and concerns. Friends may request the community's help, in the form of a "clearness committee," to test whether a call is really "laid on them." Here is a prophetic corrective to our common modern tendency to pile everything we can into our lives and to seek to extend our capacities to superhuman proportions by delegating the routine aspects of our enterprises to subordinates. Some women are questioning the current generation's assumption that they must overachieve in career and motherhood simultaneously. Citing "sequencing" as a new remedy for overloaded lives, they are discovering that successful women such as Sandra Day O'Connor stayed home and took care of their children when they were small. Perhaps we will also be helped in limiting our work by envisioning God as Mother, too. Somehow I find it easier to imagine God the Mother saying, "Son (or daughter), you're working too hard. Why don't you take it a little easier?"

We can also acknowledge that work is not our lord through an awareness that it can be relinquished. In this era when we can expect to spend a hefty chunk of our lives as retired people, we may have an even greater need to see ourselves as more than workers. Perhaps many modern people would find "giving up work" for a limited time a more useful spiritual discipline than giving up chocolate.

The Christian tradition, of course, offers and mandates Sabbath rest, graciously calling us to hold our work not only seriously but lightly by putting some edges around work time. God took a day off. Jesus took regular vacations, moving away from the pressing crowds and the political struggle alone or with his friends. We too are to set limits on our work; by doing so we acknowledge that we are lords of our labors and that we are subject to the Lordship of the One who ordains the Sabbath. In contradiction to the blue law attitude toward the Sabbath as a time of grim prohibitions, restrictions, and boredom, the word holiday retains in its derivation an appreciation of the joyfulness of this holy time of rest.

Empowering the Church's People for Monday Morning

In a congregation, life's bridging place, we can bring the dilemmas, burdens, and oppressions of our daily work into conversation with the resources of our religious heritage so that the way we live with our work is transformed. This does not mean only that we talk about work at church (though that is useful); it means also that the church lives its life as a Sabbath community, as a place where process is more important than product, where ordained ministry is regarded as no more holy than lay ministry, and where the church, as the body of Christ, affirms many kinds of work.

A Sabbath Community

Church can be a place where we receive the message "You are more than a worker." One woman, a busy mother and wife of a clergyman, said, "Eleven o'clock on Sunday morning is the only hour in the week when nobody asks me for anything." It is a time for "putting away all earthly anxieties."[48] If a congregation conveys the message "You are my beloved sons and daughters in whom I am well pleased" before firing off messages about how many committee or Sunday school slots need filling, its articulated theology of justification by grace, not works, may be believable.

A Sabbath community will recognize that laity come to church in an "extradependent mode,"[49] wanting to be taken care of for a little while, to acknowledge the natural human need to be dependent sometimes — a need that must be pushed aside most of the time in the workplaces of home, office, and factory. Clergy, who function in a work mode as they offer an environment in which lay people can have those extradependent needs met, will have to be intentional about acknowledging their own needs for care and dependence and plan ways to have their needs met, preferably not through their spouses alone.

The congregation that is conscious of its identity as a Sabbath community will not live like a workaholic, a beehive of activity that competes with the workplace for its parishioners' productive energies. Congregations can adopt the Quaker practice of "laying down" committees whose work is done, instead of pumping a new shot of adrenalin into them when their day is past. The Sabbath community will take sensitive notice of the Monday-through-Saturday overload of its people, especially two-career and single-parent families. Attention to people's religious needs can form a constant and conscious dimension of the most mundane institutional tasks. Even a budget committee can take time to be a nourishing community that reflects on its group life and work to enhance the members' and the group's spiritual growth.

Many small signals can identify the Sabbath as a time of joy and playfulness, not grim duty. Even when I come to church with a troubled mind, I find myself ministered to by our associate rector, who usually looks as though she is enjoying the liturgy. When I see her smiling during the Gloria or tapping a toe to a lively hymn tune, I am helped to remember that the liturgy is not only the work but the *play* of the people. If our unseen companions in worship are angels and archangels and all the company of heaven, I can only picture them glorifying God with great joy!

Process over Product

The church as Sabbath community pays more attention to process than to product, thus providing a useful balance to the workaday world. The church supplements the marketplace question, "What have you produced?" with the ministry question, "*How* are we living?" and allows us to pause in our work of making a living to reflect, before God, on the process of living. Anne Wilson Schaef says,

> Theologians and people of the church are often guilty of pushing people toward levels beyond their present capacity. They have forgotten that wisdom is a process and are doing their best to advertise a product. We can only embrace that which we really know. A highly evolved "product" is useless unless it has real meaning for us.[50]

If religious truth is important to us because it makes sense out of life, it cannot be conveyed any other way than *through the process of making sense out of life*. You cannot "deliver" wisdom to me through your summary of the process by which you have arrived at your meanings. Not only congregations but seminaries will teach with more power when they provide learners with opportunities to bring their experiences into meaning-making dialogue with religious symbols.

A church that focuses on process rather than product provides room to acknowledge and deal with failure in the Christian community. Since we hold at the center of our symbol system a "failure" that places worldly success under judgment, our ministry is authentic and whole only when we offer the permission, safety, acceptance, and compassion that allows us to face up to the failed marriage or the loss of a job through fate or guilt or prophetic courage and to help one another find meaning in these events. The church may be the only place in our society where it is all right to acknowledge failure.

Clergy as leaders in a community that attends to process need to be watchful not to model a workaholic lifestyle. Driven clergy who rarely spend time with their families contradict in their behavior the gospel they preach on Sunday. Pastors are not assisted toward authenticity by judicatory executives who put undue pressure on the churches under their care to produce success measured by financial and membership growth. Clergy who, like Paul, look upon their fellow Christians as "fellow workers" reduce the chances of burnout for themselves and increase parishioners' opportunities for training in ministry.

Ordained Ministry No Holier than Lay Ministry

A congregation can live out a conviction that ordained ministry is not a holier kind of work than lay ministry. This message might be conveyed in many ways. Clergy who believe that the work of a parent is as much a calling as the work of a parson will not neglect their families in favor of "God's work." The church as a community will not limit its attention to church work but will make the daily ministries of its people visible and work "to equip the saints for the work of ministry" at home and in offices, shops, and factories. In-church equipping for out-of-church work happens most naturally through worship and education. A church that looks on liturgy as "the work of the people" will find it useful to engage lay people in worship planning, so that services will speak to the real concerns with which laity struggle in daily life. The offertory is a made-to-order opportunity for lifting up "the offering of our lives and labor." Lay people can bring forward the gifts of money that are the fruits of their work. Some churches have made this offering more dramatic on Labor Day or at other times when worship has been planned to focus on people's work. In one church, people brought forward symbols of their daily work. On the altar steps a baby sitter placed a teddy bear, an architect her drafting pen, and a carpenter his level.

A congregation can support and empower laity in their daily work by respecting lay people's creation of their worldly ministries and resisting the temptation to tell them how to make ministry incarnate in daily work. Remembering that wisdom is a process to be lived through together, not a product to be delivered, Christian educators can provide hospitable space where lay people can bring the issues that arise in the world of work into an encounter with the resources of their faith and learn to reflect on them theologically. In our church I have profited from opportunities offered in a class on leadership and a class on work issues entitled "Me and My Job." I helped design and teach a course called "How do I Live with My Responsibilities?" and another called "Me and My Authority," both of which brought to the surface functional religious issues in daily work.

Courses on prayer can invite members to discover ways to carry prayer out into daily work, "feathering it out into the day."[51] Couples' support groups can help husbands and wives sort out the complex negotiations men and women struggle with today as they carve out new patterns for sharing the work of earning money and making a home. In our church couples' group there have been many "aha's" as spouses discover that they don't have to wrestle with these questions in isolation, that others have found ways to honor one another's work, as well as practical methods for cutting corners and reducing the overload. The Education for Lay Ministry program of the New South Wales Uniting Church Synod offers courses in stress management for lay people throughout the Sydney area.

Of all society's institutions, surely the church offers the most promise for helping people become aware of the threat of burnout and the moral ambiguities in Western culture's values about success! Of course any list of suggestions like this needs to be accompanied by a reminder that discernment is necessary, especially in the small church, which must ascertain the one thing most needful; and it must not load up a small group of people with a multiplicity of programs that distract them from their ministry in the world.

A Variety of Gifts

The church as the body of Christ can affirm a variety of gifts and many kinds of work in which those gifts find expression. Congregations that are serious about living out "the church as body" experientially can provide people with opportunities to experiment with the interdependent ways of working implied by "body" imagery. As a laboratory for living, the church is freer than corporations, banks, or rescue squads to experiment with alternative ways of living out values within the congregational setting, which its people can then try out more boldly in other settings where such experiments don't feel so safe. It doesn't really matter what kind of doors we put on the church or where we put the organ pipes; what matters is that we live like an empowering community while we make decisions about the doors and the pipes. As we work together on church committees, we might pay attention to such "church-as-body" challenges as finding a balance between letting our own lights shine brightly and sitting back a bit to make room for others to contribute, experiencing work as exchange — a process of giving and receiving — as an alternative to the ways work is shaped in hierarchical structures.

Congregations can conduct their lives in ways that affirm both the work of procreation and the work of production. Actually the church often supports the procreative enterprise very helpfully. It is one of the few places where the whole family can participate together. Births are surrounded by clergy and lay visits and practical assistance to families in such forms as loving casseroles. Baptism points to the transcendent meanings in the incorporation of a new person into the community, and preparation for baptism and programs of Christian nurture for children support parents in their difficult and demanding role. People who don't have children can walk a fussy baby in church while parents get to hear a sermon all the way through. Church suppers and fund-raisers celebrate the arts of cooking and home crafts. Actually churches may need to attend more carefully to the provision of hospitable settings where the work of production can be supported, where workers in business and defense especially can explore the issues in their jobs without feeling under the ideological attack that sometimes aborts such ministry in liberal mainline Protestant churches.

And congregations can affirm women's work and men's work. The church has strong feminine themes in its heritage that help balance the highly masculinized secular culture. Churches as laboratories for living afford special opportunities for people to "play with" kinds of work they don't normally do and thus to live into a broader identity than society's labels of "accountant" or "housewife." If a church isn't stuck in stereotypical roles, a bachelor may expand his repertoire by volunteering in the crib nursery, and a woman who never manages finances could take a crack at the budget committee. Sometimes these experiments lead to the discovery of hidden gifts that open up a new vocation, as has happened several times in the church I attend. And the practice of recruiting male-female teams to teach or chair committees provides both members with a safe place to experiment with collegial ways of working that other work settings may not offer, as well as with opportunities to learn to manage well the sexual energy that can warm the tasks of ministry in the church and in the world.

When church leaders are intentional about living out their theology of work as they shape parish life, design education and worship, and carry out nuts-and-bolts church jobs, they will transform the local church into a place where people not only hear but experience that the contradiction between duty and delight is overcome, that all work is holy and whole, and that men and women are invited into new forms of partnership as God's fellow workers, as they walk out the church doors on their way to Monday.

8

The Public and Private Spheres

So God created humankind in his image,
in the image of God he created them;
male and female he created them.

God blessed them, and God said to them, "Be fruitful and multiply,
and fill the earth and subdue it; and have dominion . . . over every living
thing that moves upon the earth."

— Genesis 1:27–28

This picture of the beginning portrays a rich and stately unity between the human creature and the image of God, the man and the woman, blessing and responsibility, and the human tasks of procreation and dominion. Shared human responsibilities link not only male and female but by implication love and public leadership, authority and parenthood as well. The human couple's fruitfulness is shared with all other creatures, and the exercise of dominion links them with the One who brings the universe into being and orders it. These words from the first chapter of Genesis may recall for us the graced moments when we experience all the currents of our life flowing together harmoniously under God.

But the very stress on wholeness in this picture also hints at separation and disruption. For our experience includes not only graced harmony but also the daily ways we find this radiant picture of primal unity "put asunder." The image of God often does not shine through us, women and men frequently cause each other pain, our responsibilities usually don't feel like blessings, public dominion is commonly wielded in loveless ways, and parents are often puzzled about how to exercise an authority they sense is a necessary tool for their task.

During most of human history we have torn apart that pair of human tasks, assigning procreation to women and dominion to men. Though procreation clearly requires the cooperation of men and women, we have tended to view it as the proper labor of women, shared with the other animals, and carried out in their domain — the private sphere. And the dominion given to male and female has somehow tended to become a responsibility owned by men, shared with God, and exercised in the public sphere, which has come to be regarded as the appropriate arena for the labors of men. Human beings have not embraced their tasks as partners: men have often distanced themselves from their nurturing selves and their bodily lives; and women have tended to distance themselves from their public responsibilities. The earth creature was given what Phyllis Trible has called the paradoxical task of ruling over the earth by serving it, but somehow the ruling and serving have come apart: men have been more likely to rule and women to serve.

Even within the religious tradition of the writer who painted that picture of original harmony, we can see an impending divorce between procreation and dominion and between the private sphere of women and the public sphere of men. The spiritual dimension of procreation became dissociated, located in the fertility gods of surrounding pagans. It was regarded as a suspect power, to be conquered and suppressed by those who proclaimed a religion of history. And a covenant faith sealed by circumcision could not include women as full participants. Throughout most of the biblical period, women might have had some status as mothers, but as mothers they were homebound, removed from public life; they were like the veiled Muslim women who, like snails, carry their homes with them when they venture into the streets. And as Elisabeth Schüssler Fiorenza has noted, Paul relegated Christian love to private and interior life rather than to the arena of social transformation.

The forces making for a divorce between public and private arenas multiplied as the centuries flowed by. Mark Gerzon traces the nature of this split in more recent times. Before the Industrial Revolution, he points out, men and women worked at home, and women, like men, could be butchers and gunsmiths, mill and shipyard operators, whose work was evident in the village or town. But after industrialization, especially since the late nineteenth century, the world of work tended to become the province of men, invisible to their wives and children, while home and family were more clearly demarcated as the proper arena for women's efforts. Children thus learn to "equate the first sex with the world outside the home, the second sex with the world within."[1] After World War II, recalls Carol Tavris, women returned willingly to suburban homes and raising a boom of babies; "most of them believed in the legitimacy of the division of sexual labor, even when that meant that he got the sex and she got the labor."[2]

This carving up of life's territory between men and women, between the tasks of dominion and procreation, between the public and private spheres seems to make people miserable. I want to sketch briefly some of the forms that pain takes for women and for men, at home and outside the home.

The Distress of Women, Public and Private

Whether they attempt to claim a place in the world or decide to carry out a significant part of their work at home, women's troubles can take many forms. Women clearly experience greater difficulty in moving out into the world outside their homes. Although more and more women are finding ways to go public, to do so they still have to break through both internal and external restraints. Jean Baker Miller points out that "the things women are allowed to do are, in a significant way, removed from the life of one's time."[3] They are encouraged to avoid the risks that public engagement entails, as well as the anxiety that is an inescapable component of leadership. But if women respond to these discouraging messages by abandoning the effort to move out, they must live with the consequences of leaving decisions about public policy to men.

The invisible cords restraining women are many. In contrast to the emphasis that students of male development such as George Vaillant and Daniel Levinson place on the importance for men of cherishing their *vitality*, with its springs in sexuality and aggression, feminine vitality does not seem to be regarded as an equally precious resource in Western society. Miller describes one woman who experienced her confinement within the private sphere quite concretely. She "felt able to work and to think well so long as she worked on her ideas and plans in her own house. She could not bring them into the work setting. As she used to put it, 'If only I could bring my inside self outside.'"[4]

I know that as a young woman, I took it for granted that my *real* life was my private life. At the end of a day at school or work I would be released from secondary tasks to pursue the things I cared about most. Looking around me at the numbers of women who don't expect very much beyond a modest paycheck in the way of personal reward from the workplace, I conclude that the whispers I responded to then are still audible today.

Women who do reach out for a place in the world often seem very reluctant to give up control at home and are consequently too overextended and exhausted to give their best in either place. Some say they want home tasks shared equally, but then they treat their husbands like inept assistants — and that's what they get! Perhaps it feels frightening to give up a firm grip in one realm when one's place in the other realm seems so uncertain.

If coworkers identify a woman with the procreative task when she moves into the workplace, she is likely to be viewed as a sexual object in a context in which both "sexual" and "object" are a poor fit — workers are, by definition, subjects. This displacement can have many painful results: a woman may find that her talents are discounted, her female coworkers are jealous, and her male coworkers harass her.

Women experience the pain of the divorce between public and private spheres at home as well as at work. Though struggles in marriage and motherhood require enormous personal initiative, sophistication, and courage, such heroism in the private sphere generally remains unsung. It may go especially unnoticed by a husband who sees his wife's domestic routine as cozy, safe, and free of the pressures he trudges off to encounter every morning. Some women's energy is sapped by the triviality into which the at-home role can degenerate. For some, daytime television dulls the pain of emotional isolation. Talk-show host Phil Donahue may be "every wife's replacement for the husband who doesn't talk to her."[5] Perhaps women consult psychiatrists and pastors in greater numbers than men do because of their hunger for *someone* with whom they can share their experiences and feelings — a hunger that feels "feminine" to many men and from which they therefore distance themselves (except for those whose daily work requires them to respond to it). A woman's attentiveness to (and resultant sophistication in) reflecting on personal experience and emotional life may isolate her further, if her partner responds to her overfunctioning in that sphere of life by underfunctioning. I know of one family (now sundered) in which the husband seemed to join his adolescent sons in thumbing their noses at Mom. She had been granted, and had accepted, all of the emotional responsibility in the family — and was cordially hated for it. How unfair, she might well have complained, after she had poured her heart and soul into her nurturing role all those years! Too many women embark on the false quest offered by the culture: to earn their salvation by being domestic workaholics, pursuing the perfect home, gourmet meals, and a successful and happy family. Disappointment and depression are the inevitable results of pursuing such a false savior.

The Distress of Men, Private and Public

The gulf between the public and private arenas results in separate but perhaps equal misery for men. Being socialized to pour all their energies into their work, they suffer pain on the home front — the result of their failure to devote enough time and attention to keeping home life going. And since men have for some time been expected to confine their exercise of dominion to public life, many families suffer from a loss of masculine authority as well as fatherly care.

The cost of men's total commitment to public life is high.

> "I don't want your families breaking up just because you feel loyal
> to me," former President Carter told his Cabinet after taking of-
> fice in 1977.... But by the time the long-awaited White House
> Conference on Families convened in the final year of Carter's
> administration, the pattern had repeated itself. Families of admin-
> istration officials had come apart at the seams.... No presidential
> admonition could dislodge a pattern rooted so deeply in the
> masculine role.[6]

When those families come apart, says Gerzon, divorced men "refuse to understand that most mothers have been awarded by the
courts what they had all along — the daily responsibility for their
children's care."[7] For many men, their distance from home life
began with their children's birth, an event they avoided through
fear and feelings of inadequacy. Those feelings may be a large
reason — besides the positive lure of the marketplace — for men's
reluctance to involve themselves in their families.

One reason men tend to function less well at home than
at work[8] is that they are socialized in ways that are dysfunctional
in family life. "Winning" is not a very useful goal in the private
sphere. Parenthood, as I have experienced it, is an experience that
forces us to grow up, but some fathers opt out of that school of
hard knocks and as a result remain immature in intimate relationships. If dependence is a dirty word, you don't admit that
you are starved for opportunities to be dependent. So you stay
hungry. If attention to the complex demands of intimacy is "feminine," it is tempting to reduce intimacy to sex, an unimpeachably
"masculine" urge, and never explore the broader possibilities in
closeness with another person. And even though separation from
bodily and affective life may seem masculine, that separation can
ultimately undermine men's vitality, which they cherish so deeply
and on which their worldly success depends.

Nor are men without their publicly inflicted forms of pain.
Women whose lives are lived at home or who are preoccupied
with the inequalities they themselves suffer may be unaware of
the oppression men experience in the workplace — the experience
of impotence in the midst of a powerful system, for example —
and the risks, responsibilities, moral dilemmas, long hours, and
perhaps wearying travel and dreary motel rooms that are often
part of men's working lives. If women's strengths are not fully
present in the public sphere, it is men who have to get along

without them, thereby suffering not only from the loss of the specific contributions women might have provided but also from the stress of having to carry the whole load of public duties. If women are resentful because of inequalities in power and paycheck, they are quite capable of passive-aggressive retaliation in the workplace, of rendering "service" tinged with contempt.

Mutual Misery, in Human Hearts and Social Structures

If we put these two sketches of male and female pain alongside each other, the possibilities for tragic cross-purposes and mutually induced misery multiply. If the woman's life is confined to the private sphere, she may nag at him to function in that setting, as though that were the only place there were. (It is the only place she sees.) Men keep her out of the public arena, and she responds by largely ignoring it. His need to win may lead him to put in seventy or eighty hours a week on the job, removing him further from the world of his wife and children. Each feels trapped and regards the other's "freedom" with resentment. He hides or denies his profound dependence on his wife and thereby fuels his contempt for her. His emotional dependence on her is reciprocated by her economic dependence on him.

One of the most excruciating collisions results when a woman, dutifully following her cultural instructions, concentrates all her energies in the cramped space of her home. My mother-in-law was one such woman, and only after her death did I come to see her as a victim rather than an oppressor. She had been successfully indoctrinated with the conviction that her lifelong duty was to take care of her family. After decades of ironing seven shirts a week for her husband and each son, her life as a widow alternated between apathy and frenzied attempts to revive the vocation that had given her life meaning. On vacations she fed all of us relentlessly; the rest of the year she languished in front of the television, having no outlet for her energies. She had never heard any invitation to use her considerable nurturing skills outside the small circle of blood kinship. So her caretaking energies became a burden on her grown sons and their families rather than a point of connection with the wider world that needed her care. Women who exercise too much power in too limited a sphere —

a sphere that has a formative effect on our lives — become oppressive to those who inhabit it. I have seen several men respond with deep feeling and instant identification to James Thurber's drawing titled "Woman and House," in which a tiny man cowers apprehensively on the sidewalk before his house, which is being transformed into the menacing figure of an enormous woman. How ironic that women's confinement to the private sphere can be a major source of men's oppression!

Thus, the separation between the spheres of dominion and of procreation causes suffering within each human heart, where the work of the body and the work of the mind, the work of love and the work of power, are split. The life-giving energy that is generated when differences are held together in tension dissipates or turns to hostility when they are sundered.

Not only human hearts but social structures are the victims of the divorce between public and private life. How small a sphere is left for love within this division! The great commandment becomes a small one: "Love your neighbor, but not in public."[9] The men who have skipped the crash course for maturity offered by parenthood play boys' games in their sphere of dominion, threatening the destruction of both spheres. The domesticated strength of women is a strength that needs to be released into the world. Our future is at risk when the men who make public policy keep their emotional distance from our basic human enterprise, while the women who are engaged in that enterprise lack the initiative and authority to contribute to that public policy.[10] I look at those gathered to hold discussions on arms control and see an ocean of dark flannel suits. The women are not there. Ellen Goodman wrote of summit meeting news reports: "Women had no public role, so they were covered in their private role. Every item in each wardrobe was scrutinized."[11]

The unfortunate consequences of this divorce are evident in our churches as well. In our parish course "Women and Men," women were eager for dialogue about the relationships between the sexes. But it was only the male participants who raised economic or political issues in the course of our discussions. On those subjects the women remained silent. I don't think this vignette of church life is atypical. When I suggested including a session on male-female issues in a conference for church executives, a male colleague objected: "These guys don't want to spend time talking about their *private* life; they want to talk about the *work*." The assumption that relationships between men and women belong in a separate, private sphere contrasts with the expectations that inform my collegial experiences with women, where we move easily back and forth between personal experiences and the task at hand, noticing how one informs the other. I hear male clergy complain that their congregations are full of women, and there is much moaning about a feminized, privatized religion. And, apparently in reaction to this situation, there are issue-rattling attacks on the social problems of the day that sound like today's version of muscular Christianity.

Toward Remarriage: Glimpses of Hope

Given that the split between the spheres of procreation and of dominion impairs our ability to grow up and to respond to all creation's gifts and tasks, that it makes men and women miserable and distorts our individual, social, and congregational life, what possibilities are there for a "remarriage" of these spheres? I would suggest that we can glimpse some possibilities in the ministry of Jesus, in the life of the early church, and in congregational life and leadership.

The rhythm of Jesus' own life reflects an easy oscillation between public and private life. He moves with a sure instinct from times of solitude or intimacy with friends to compassionate involvement with crowds of people and deft movements into the gathering political storm. His carefully chosen public strategy never leaves him too busy to attend to a small domestic encounter — with a worn-out hostess, with children looking for some attention, with the problem of a shortage of refreshments at a wedding, or with a tearful uninvited guest at a dinner party. His easy movement illuminates how important a balance between public and private spheres is in our lives. If we settle for a permanent retreat to private life, or are continually stretched out by demands from without, we will not have an abundant life. Living in the tension between our own needs and passions and the demands of others is a source of energy and power.

Jesus' life also models a wedding between vitality and structure, nature and history, the world of women and the world of men. In him centuries of religious struggle come to a moment of reconciliation. Ancient religions centering around procreation were full of vitality, but they ignored history as they cycled through the submerged realm of nature. Ethical monotheism demanded responsibility within history, but it glorified men at the expense of women, and its heavy emphasis on will and structure often threatened to squeeze out life and spontaneity. Jesus refuses to make an idol of that structure and the hierarchy that maintains it. He is open to receiving the stranger, the marginal person, to having his outlook broadened by a Syro-Phoenician woman (not "our kind of people"), to spreading the good news through the enthusiastic testimony of a woman of Samaria.

The power of this reconciliation wrought by Jesus was still evident in the life of the early church. Schüssler Fiorenza describes the special integrative possibilities of the infant church gathered in the homes of women and men:

> The house church, by virtue of its location, provided equal opportunities for women, because traditionally the house was considered women's proper sphere, and women were not excluded from activities in it.... the public sphere of the Christian community was *in* the house and not outside of the household.[12]

Rosemary Rader lifts up the joyful partnership between Christian men and women who experienced liberation from the restrictions of patriarchal marriage through heterosexual friendships and early informal communities.[13] Though the old divisions soon reasserted themselves, we can look to the life of Jesus and the early church for a glimpse of some shining moments in which the Genesis picture was brought to life anew.

I see hopeful possibilities in today's churches, as well. Our congregations have a special opportunity to be a "bridge between the public and private spheres," to use Parker Palmer's wonderful metaphor.[14] If the world of women needs to be stretched toward the public arena, and if men need to be called to pay attention to the affective side of life, the church is a natural place for that stretching and calling to take place. People already have expectations that the church will be this bridge: they come to the church for the solemnization and sustenance of their marriages, to have their children baptized and taught, and to find leadership in peacemaking and feeding the hungry. On that bridge, women and men can meet in a space that provides some perspective on both the nuclear family, with its high emotional charge, and the huge, impersonal public sphere, which often leaves people feeling frightened, powerless, and confused.

As a bridging place, the church can encourage women and men to acknowledge the value of both spheres, even while they may, at a particular stage in life, need to invest most of their energies in one sphere. The church can encourage us not to make an idol of either the public or the private sphere, not to put down those who are engaged in the other for the present, and to choose some toehold in the other that will make our acknowledgment of its validity concrete and keep its possibilities alive for us. I know a church bureaucrat who finds baking bread for communion a way to touch the private realm for which his life affords little time. A woman caring for young children at home may be encouraged by her church to support one political initiative. Women who now enjoy many productive years after their children are raised need to be affirmed, supported, and challenged to engage in service. If they are treated as subjects, rather than objects of ministry, both their families and the world will benefit.

A new recognition of "what God has joined together" is badly needed in the battle of the sexes. A church that helps both men and women to give up the illusion that their own way is "right," to move beyond contempt and revenge, will point toward a kind of peace that will enrich public and private life. A church conscious of its place as a bridge can invite women and men to offer each other their gifts. It can encourage them, with mutual respect, to help each other grow up: to encourage women to risk moving out as co-leaders in the public sphere and men to acknowledge the hungers of the heart, to become wiser, more competent travelers in the country of intimate relationships.

New (or perhaps old) ways of looking at power and leadership will be needed. Serving and ruling must be held up as different aspects of the same reality. Overcoming the split between authority and love will provide healing power for both families and nations. We will require a heightened awareness that power must be used in the service of love and that people who are helped to feel more powerful will be able to behave in more loving ways. Churches too often encourage people to feel powerless — personally, theologically, and organizationally. The church can draw on its ancient knowledge that prophetic voices can be expected to come from those who are marginal to public power.

Churches' involvement in private and public issues will also need to be informed by a more sensitive understanding of how men and women can be most helpfully engaged, rather than by generalized assumptions about "human" (which often means "masculine") learning processes. Most women will not respond to approaches to social issues if they are approached on the basis of ethical principles and ideological abstractions; they will, however, respond to approaches that are communal, contextual, and concrete. Women's energies are aroused by specific situations involving real people who need food or sanctuary or help with an abusive spouse.[15] A balance between concerns for the particular other and the generalized other can enrich not only church programs but the world beyond, which those programs exist to serve.

The role of the clergy is crucial in the "bridge church." I think male clergy have a special opportunity here. If Phil Donahue is a wife's replacement for an uncommunicative husband, what is the clergyman? The pastor, like the psychiatrist, cares for a woman's emotional life as part of his daily work and provides what she may be starved for at home. (Some research indicates that clergy wives are just as starved as the parishioners.) Instead of accommodating to society's dysfunction by taking up the emotional slack for the men, pastors could encourage men and women to work out their issues about communication with each other. Rather than basking in the grateful admiration of his female parishioners, a clergyman could encourage women to ask assertively for what they need from the men in their lives, and he could coach the men in the affective skills he has developed through pastoral work. Clergy can recognize that women's emotional and spiritual strength is a gift that the world needs, not an aberration to be avoided or fixed. Rather than serving as chaplains to a feminized church, pastors could use their authority to support strong men and strong women in leadership, to hold up both masculine and feminine perceptions, experiences, styles, strengths, and passions. Taking a hint from the "missionary couples" of the early church, our congregations can make a habit of recruiting male-female teams for leadership positions.

Clergywomen have an essential contribution to make in this area. Previous generations have expressed concern about the effeminacy of the clergy, and it is not surprising that if Christian ministry requires feminine sensitivities, and women have been excluded from being leaders, then an effeminate style of leadership may have resulted that puts off both men and women. When male clergy don't have to cover all the bases and women's leadership is fully welcomed by the church, we can all lead one another to incorporate the gifts of women and men without surrendering our primary masculine or feminine identities. (This possibility will be pursued in more detail in the next chapter.) I hope that women will increasingly hold their share of the church's public roles as senior ministers and church executives, and that churches can thereby provide a new model of leadership for society, instead of dragging behind it.

Clergy also need to have a more sophisticated understanding of their role. We have lived through a period when clergy as people were collapsed into their role and a subsequent period when, in reaction, many pastors shrugged off their role and tried to be "just plain folks." Though one might be sympathetic to the motives for this response, it represents an abdication of the appropriate authority of the clergy in favor of a purely private and personal reality. We need clergy who accept their public responsibilities, not by abandoning their appropriate religious sphere but by accepting the role that is properly theirs as religious leaders. Nobody ever said it would be easy. But clergy who accept authority faithfully, moving in and out of their public role in a graceful rhythm, share in the struggle and joy of their Lord and encourage the rest of us to own the authority that is ours in our public and private lives.

Perhaps by pondering the biblical symbols that point to the unity for which we hunger, and by exploring the possibilities for the remarriage of public and private spheres that lie in the life and leadership of our churches, all of us can rediscover the union in which we were joined by God in creation.

9

Set Over, Set Apart,
or Set Alongside?
Men and Women
as Leaders

Leadership, of course, may be exercised in both private and public spheres. This chapter, however, will focus on leadership in the church, that bridging place between our public and private worlds. If you lead in other settings, translate this discussion to those situations, using your own experience as a guide.

What does it mean to be a leader? We have new uncertainties about the answer to this question. Which ways of being a leader are congruent with our religious tradition? Which are effective?

Here I want to explore three leadership postures. Leaders may see themselves primarily as (1) set over others, (2) set apart from others, (3) or set alongside others.

What benefits or problems does each leadership posture offer? And what do they have to do with being a woman or being a man in today's church?

"Set Over": Contemporary Challenges

For centuries, the view that leaders are set over their followers has been taken for granted in church systems. The word hierarchy was born in the church; its use in any other setting is derivative.

Today, however, criticisms of hierarchy are being leveled from many directions: from the secular culture, from those who question whether hierarchical church systems help congregations, from biblical scholars offering fresh interpretations of scripture, from women who test common assumptions about leadership by their own experience, and from men who are finding that the top rung of the ladder does not yield the anticipated promise.

Challenges from the Culture

A whole set of challenges to hierarchical structures is arising from the world around us. Secular managers have some new ideas about leadership. Supervisors and those they supervise are engaging in mutual evaluations. Executives are answering their own telephones, and junior employees are being called associates.[1] A more profound understanding of the dynamics of groups evokes some hope that when a group is freed from the strict control of dominant-subordinate relationships, more creativity than chaos will be unleashed.[2]

Hierarchical Church Structures

When the most creative managers in the secular culture are discovering more useful alternatives to hierarchical systems, it is not surprising that the church might want to look at those alternatives, too. Many church leaders are borrowing secular ideas about how to help organizations function more effectively, and they are putting these ideas to work in churches.

In the denominational hierarchical arrangements I see built-in barriers to the task of providing resources for local churches. I once attended a meeting called by church leaders of various denominations to "dialogue with laity." Each of these leaders was to locate a lay person and invite him or her to the meeting. During the long day I found myself wondering why these leaders didn't go directly to their congregations if they wanted to be in touch with lay people. After the meeting I was saddened to receive a letter reporting that that session had been the liveliest the group could remember. Here was a group of smart church bureaucrats whose organizational position so removed them from the day-to-day life of the churches that they had to engage in this tortuous exercise to achieve communication with the people their offices existed to serve. The pyramid structure of their denominations appeared not to facilitate their work but to create obstacles to it.

These hard-working executives are hampered because the progressively abstracted levels of hierarchy, removed farther and farther from the local church, tend to make their work less and less relevant. Congregations sometimes become rebellious because they find that the help they receive from farther up the hierarchy is delivered in a way that feels patronizing and disconnected from their real concerns, even when that is the last thing intended. It must be frustrating to have to work so hard to persuade people in local churches to look on the diocese or synod or district or conference as real — not a fantasy. It must be painful when clergy are reluctant to reveal their troubles to their designated "pastor to pastors" because that "pastor" has power over their next appointment. Many judicatory personnel seem isolated, spiritless, and drained of energy. How painfully confusing it must be to receive a "promotion" and then discover your work isn't as much fun as it used to be.

Hierarchical structures tend to maintain the status quo and keep things under control. But in a world that keeps changing faster all the time, churches need to be free of structures that prevent responsiveness. Some of those out-of-control moments are the very moments when new life may appear. When the pastor resigns, for example, many members go into a frenzy of fear that the church is about to fall apart. Actually it may be the beginning of a period when lay leaders will again discover "This is our church."

Of course church leaders need enough institutional authority to get their work done. We can't stop and vote every time we ask people to discuss John 1:1–18 in small groups. And there are times when things get so out of control in churches that a denomination needs to have a way to help people not to go on hurting one another and destroying the life of the community. But I do want to make the point that in general, hierarchical approaches to church leadership seem neither effective, life-giving, nor congruent with much of our religious tradition.

Challenges from Interpretations of the Bible

"There is no longer Jew or Greek, there is no longer slave or free, there is no longer male or female; for all of you are one in Christ Jesus [Gal. 3:28]." Paul's most soaring articulation of the new liberation in Christ makes it clear that racism, sexism, and anti-Semitism are now obsolete. National, class, and sexual differences are not to be ranked hierarchically, and nobody is to have special power and privilege because of accidents of birth.

One-up/one-down distinctions are not the way of the new creation or of creation itself. It is all *very good* — not ranked from bad through passable to pretty good. A careful look at the created world reveals enormous differences, but the multitude of different creatures are connected to one another interdependently, not hierarchically. One beast is large and roars loudly; another is tiny, complicated, and speedy. It is an abundant and even playful diversity.

Biblical scholarship points to the simultaneous creation of male and female in both creation narratives, thus weakening the argument that the male is better because he arrived here first.[3] "He shall rule over you" doesn't tell how human relationships are supposed to be but what happens when they get fouled up.

Prophetic critique of hierarchy forms a continuous thread through the biblical narrative. The psalmists are clear that "those of high estate are a delusion [62:9]" and warn "Do not put your trust in princes, in mortals, in whom there is no help [146:3]." Jesus taught his disciples an alternative to the relationships of dominance and subordinance practiced by others, and he demonstrated his way by serving and socializing with despised people such as tax collectors, women, and the ritually unclean.

"And call no one your father on earth, for you have one Father — the one in heaven. Nor are you to be called instructors, for you have one instructor, the Messiah. The greatest among you will be your servant [Matt. 23:9–11]." Jesus' new family of equal servants includes brothers and sisters and mothers — but this family has only one Father. That role does not belong to us. Words for God such as Lord and Father, which reflect the lifestyle of long-ago patriarchal societies, are not names but metaphors that need to be held alongside other metaphors like rock and eagle and Wisdom and Mother, which do not suggest that hierarchy is built into the divine structure of the universe.[4]

Challenges Rooted in Women's Lives

When women stop assuming that masculine experiences and assumptions constitute the human norm, many find themselves challenging one-up/one-down ways of looking at life. In *Patriarchy as a Conceptual Trap*, Elizabeth Dodson Gray made the crucial point that ranking differences hierarchically is not the only option.[5] If two things are different, one doesn't have to be better than the other. The ladder as a basic metaphor for life may appear to fit the experiences of men, but many women do not find it describes who they are and what they want to be about. Mary, presently an assistant in a downtown Episcopal church, wonders, "Do I want to be a rector? I don't know. I like working as part of a team with men and women on it. I don't want to be working all alone in some outer suburban church. And I don't think the chances of my getting a male assistant look good at this point." As she ponders her future in ministry, Mary finds she has goals other than making it to the top.

Many women are angry when they wake up to the illogical and oppressive characteristics of patriarchy. Others become bored and alienated by hierarchical institutions that neither meet their needs nor fit their perceptions of what life is all about. My friend Barbara Potter wrote that lately she was discovering a different response within herself:

> I feel as if I am suddenly waking up to patriarchy — it's like the air we breathe. And my waking up is paradoxically leading me to more affection for men, not less. As I see the ways men cling to being number one, and their subtle ways of dismissing women, I am no longer intimidated by their rhetoric and beguiling logic, and as I feel less a victim I therefore feel more loving.

Challenges from Men Disappointed with Dominance

Many men today are voicing their pain and disappointment as they discover that the dominant-subordinate arrangement does not seem to be working even for those who might have been expected to benefit from it. It hurts to be met with seething resentment or outright bursts of fury from the "losers," when you weren't fully aware you were playing a game that set you up to be a "winner." Perhaps it is even more painful to be alienated from the "loser" within. There is liberation in not having to fight so hard to stay out of the one-down position and to hold onto the one-up position. The effort it takes to hold on can leave you tense, burdened, and bone weary.

This new awareness often emerges for a man as he passes midlife. Perhaps the top rung of the ladder, now grasped, does not yield the satisfaction that it seemed to promise when he was younger. Noting this need of men in midlife "to modulate the powerful imagery of the ladder," Daniel Levinson quotes Yeats:

> ...Now that my ladder's gone,
> I must lie down where all ladders start,
> In the foul rag-and-bone shop of the heart.[6]

As leaders, men and women tend to lean in different directions. Male leaders frequently see themselves as "set apart"; female leaders more often prefer to see themselves as "set alongside."

We know that no distinctions between men and women are iron-clad (remember the kangaroos), and we cherish the freedom of males to be "blue" and females "red." We celebrate the unique qualities of each individual leader. Yet social scientists have been discovering that while men and women may use the same skills and strategies as leaders, they often have different goals in mind, different styles of leadership, and different attitudes toward cooperating with others.[7] Let's look next at how male leaders tend to position themselves in relationship to their followers.

Set Apart: The Masculine Tendency to Lead by Self-Differentiation

Since the growing male originally claimed his being-as-male by breaking away from his beginnings, it will not be surprising to find him taking things apart, noticing distinctions, and leading by self-differentiation.

Edwin Friedman, family systems theorist and rabbi, advocates leadership by self-differentiation as an alternative to authoritarian or consensus leadership, two approaches that have often been considered the only options. What these two styles have in common is that both bind the leader and the group together. The authoritarian leader compels the followers to go along with him. The consensus leader in effect joins the group. Says Friedman,

"The third alternative is: 'Be yourself. Keep defining yourself and saying what you believe.' "[8]

When leaders define themselves, they model self-definition for others, encouraging the followers to define themselves, too. The leader doesn't take responsibility for the group; the leader takes responsibility for *being a leader*. Instead of trying to control the behavior of others (which is impossible, anyway) the leader puts energy into the task of being a leader and acknowledges the freedom of others. As Friedman put it in one lecture, "Functioning as a leader in the image of God means to allow others to screw up." Leaders need the fortitude not only to resist the temptation to take inappropriate responsibility for the lives of others but also to withstand the seduction of those who will try to pull the leader back into a fused, or "globbed-together," position with the group.

The vision of leadership by self-differentiation has important strengths. This view of leadership may be closest to the biblical meaning of authority: *exousia*, literally emerging "out of one's own essence or being." Authority as simply *being who you are* is a gift to others. Others are free to respond as they think best. If the others are relatively differentiated themselves, they will be able to respond to the invitation to discern and articulate their own truth. *Exousia* is not the exercise of hierarchical power.

Leadership by self-differentiation is courageous. It is the willingness to say, "Here I stand." It means taking the risk of offering the gift that only you can give, the risk that perhaps nobody else will see it that way, and that you will flunk the popularity contest. By definition, leaders do not take anxious cover in the middle of the herd.

Set-apart leaders can carry out some leadership tasks especially well. It will be easier for such a leader to delegate jobs crisply, and, when appropriate, to allow people who undertake them to fail, rather than anxiously rushing to the rescue. In these ways, the set-apart leader points to the transcendence of God.

Set-apart leadership becomes problematic when differences are ranked hierarchically. Then separation easily evolves into hierarchy, with all the attendant difficulties noted at the beginning of this chapter.

Set Alongside: The Tendency of Women to Lead by Connectedness

Let us look next at the way women are likely to exercise leadership. Just as the tendency of men to define themselves in distinction from others leads them to be attracted to leadership by self-differentiation, feminine development naturally issues in a tendency to lead by connectedness.

Attending to the Web of Connectedness

Women leaders tend to be less interested in noticing distinctions between people than in emphasizing what they hold in common. They feel less set apart by their role. When the associate rector in our church, a woman, went to administer an informal ritual of laying on of hands to Michele, who was dying of cancer, she found Michele's prayer-and-support group present. She spontaneously invited all the women to join her in laying hands on Michele. A concern for holding a group together rather than dividing it often leads women to prefer making decisions by consensus instead of voting. I find groups of women eager, as well, to include not only all the people but all parts of themselves. Words are not enough: women want to add images, drama, singing, hugging, body movement, and spontaneous ritual.

Attention to wholeness produces a different way of living with time: women are less interested in what time it is, more interested in what *kind* of time it is. They pay less attention to *chronos*, the linear ticking-by of hours, than to *kairos*, "the fullness of time." My female colleagues seem more inclined to believe that a work project will be finished "when it's ready"; male colleagues tend to set deadlines, whether or not the task actually requires them. Perhaps deeper involvement in the cyclical rhythms of life, as well as experiences like anticipating the birth of a baby or setting the bread to rise, teach that the right time includes not only will but waiting.

Set Alongside, Not Over

At a clergywomen's conference, several participants nodded agreement when one said, "I see myself as a minister *among* the people, not *over* them." Women are less likely to view themselves as experts who bring the truth to those who need it, more drawn to a role as midwife — enabling others to bring into being their own truth. When I am leading a conference, I often underscore people's ownership of their wisdom by quoting their own comments as a summary of our work together.

Women's interest in connectedness and wholeness leads them to see their offerings as complementary to those of others, rather than superior. Many women church leaders contrast their preference for a complementary relationship between leaders and followers with the traditional hierarchical view. In one conference, a woman said, "I want to share my story, not to lift it up but to open it up." Dorothy McMahon, minister of the Pitt Street Uniting Church in downtown Sydney, confesses that she had to be reminded of her convictions about ministry by Frank, "the plonko." (We might call him a "wino.")

> Every day he sits on the church steps with his bottle of wine in a paper bag alongside him. Every morning I say to him "Good morning Frank!" and he says "Good morning love!" and kisses his hand to me. That morning he had a bottle of Scotch and, after kissing his hand, said "Would you like a nip love?" A bit later I opened the doors of the church and surveyed a greater than usual mess of rubbish all over the steps. I went to get a garbage bag and, muttering to myself about disgusting people who throw their rubbish on church steps, I began to pick it up. Frank joined me and as he picked up the paper he laughed and said, "It's us plonkos that are the trouble you know love." I laughed at my own self-righteousness and joined the human race again.[9]*

Nonhierarchical leaders include more people in leadership. I hear many women, clergy and lay, expressing enthusiasm about co-pastoring, or team ministry. It is harder to model shared leadership by leading alone; two or more leaders can begin to signal an open process that moves back and forth between them. With two to share the tasks, each has a chance to move in and out of role. If the designated leaders are not the only people assumed to possess wisdom and skill, leadership becomes less an achieved and permanent status, more a functional role, temporarily occu-

*From "Called to Be Human" by Dorothy McMahon in *Listen to the Spirit* © The Joint Board of Christian Education, Melbourne, Australia, 1986. Used by permission.

pied. One pastor described her experience of moving out of role through being nursed by members of the congregation while she was sick: "I didn't like it at first, but they loved me out of that. They were energized by discovering 'we can do something for the pastor.'"

I have found the line between leaders and followers less distinct in women's groups than in others. In the evaluation following one women's conference, one woman wrote, "We've experienced being filled, but it wasn't two people up there doing the filling; we filled ourselves." Members share leadership tasks; leaders engage in the participants' activities. Being a participant leader is not unlike being a mother who attends simultaneously to her children's needs and to her own.

Ministry "alongside" questions old methods and inspires new ones. Where there is a conviction that everyone must have a chance to speak, subgroups and dyads provide that opportunity in large groups, while in leaderless small groups each can tell her story in turn, "going around the circle." These inclusive methods differ from the methods of "ministry over," where podiums and pulpits elevate and separate those who are expected to impart wisdom. In crafting new forms for "ministry alongside," women find a pattern in One who knelt to wash his friends' feet, and they point to the Paraclete, whose name means literally "called to our side."

Enemies from Within

Those who see themselves as set alongside can get into difficulties, too. It may be harder for them to define their role as separate from that of other people or even opposed to other people. If their style is self-abnegating, they help hold together the dominant-subordinate system through their hiding stance, even though they are opposed to it. Some may be so busy reacting against patriarchy that they hesitate to exercise any authority. This female script is like a dance that we have learned so well that we don't have to think about it: he leads, and she follows, smiling. I was reminded of how hard it is to stop dancing backward as I watched a woman at a women's conference not long ago. She had risen at dawn on the final morning to write a beautiful prayer that gathered up the insights of the past two days. But she was unable to present her offering without constant protestations: "This may not be what you want..." "This is just a rough idea..." "I know you'll need to make a lot of changes..."

Women who would like to be leaders are often uncertain about what kind of leaders they want to be. One woman said, "I want to be a feminine clergyperson, not a copy of a male. But what is feminine? I don't know, but I do know it isn't passivity and lace." Many women say the shortage of female role models makes feminine leadership harder. And still others are reluctant to exercise authority at all because they equate it with paternalism.[10]

Women and Men as Leaders

Women and men together can be effective leaders if they redefine the concept of authority, incorporate both masculine and feminine strengths in their leadership, and move beyond the stereotypes that limit us.

The Paradox of Religious Authority

As long as we see authority as a position one holds *over* another, the question of who's on top and who's on the bottom grasps our attention. The "tops" focus on gaining and keeping their position. They are likely to expend a good deal of energy on getting their way. The "bottoms" spend their energy admiring, emulating, and resenting the "tops." If religious celebrities are discovered to have engaged in sexual or fiscal misconduct, the "bottoms" can be delightfully entertained by the revelation that the prominent are really no better than ordinary folk! This engrossing spectator sport distracts the "bottoms" from attention to their own spiritual development, which was the presumed purpose of the whole enterprise. When we turn our attention away from the sideshows that the concept of power *over* places in center stage, we might notice that religious authority means standing in the tension between simply being yourself, on one hand, and being with other people, on the other.

Leaders need to be crystal clear that religious authority is entrusted to them by the people they lead. I give my religious leader authority so that I can receive it back again with power, enhanced by the exchange. Authority belongs to everybody, and the function of leadership is the empowerment of all.

But religious authority makes leaders lonely, too. When you, as a leader, offer yourself as a symbolic person around whom others work out their own salvation, you are undertaking to walk the way of the cross. As a religious leader, you will be lifted up, and the powers of darkness will be unleashed on you.

When people are working out their spiritual development on you, you need clarity about where you end and the other person begins. You are called to be yourself simply and clearly, taking the risk of claiming your truth and proclaiming it boldly without trying to impose it on others. If authority means *exousia*, living out of one's own essence, then all of us are called to exercise our own religious authority.

Religious leaders require both the more typically feminine gift of attention to the web of connectedness and the more typically masculine gift of self-differentiation. People and groups need their leaders to stand closer beside them at some stages of growth and in some circumstances, and they need their leaders to stand farther away at other times. Religious leaders know there are times for afflicting the comfortable and other times for comforting the afflicted.

The Gospels' picture of Jesus as a leader who lives in the tension between standing alongside and standing apart will be useful to those who would follow his example. Deciding against strategies of power during the wilderness struggle, steadily rejecting "standing over" as an inappropriate way to lead, Jesus offers himself as servant and never separates himself from "losers." At the same time, he continually defines himself, speaking his truth simply and clearly without being deflected by the reactions of hostility or misunderstanding or defensive pain that truth may call forth. The simple statement of truth is never coercive: others are free to accept it or not, to follow or to go away again. Parables conclude with an open question that invites and challenges the hearer to make a personal response. The good news in this paradox for men and women is that it is based on self-differentiation but in a way that is hospitable to women, inviting them to define in their own way, "out of their own being," what it means to them to be leaders.

The Benefits of Moving Beyond a Neuter Clergy

Throughout history laywomen and male clergy, both marginal to secular society, have been allies. For the women, this bond may have been woven of many strands: their diffuse sexuality, which embraces their spiritual yearnings; the hunger for spiritual and emotional, intellectual and aesthetic closeness, which their husbands often do not satisfy; their urge to bond with a man who wields power in a sphere to which they are granted some access. A woman may find in a clergyman, with his skill in articulating matters of mind and spirit, an appropriate screen upon which to project her masculine side and then receive it back, more fully developed. This alliance of the marginal has served to uphold values scorned by the dominant male captains of armies or industry. Throughout the centuries, women and clergy have sounded a muted but prophetic note, pointing beyond the hypermasculinized culture to a reality that transcends male and female.

The cost of this challenge has been predictable. In a culture where the feminine is seen as inferior, any taint of effeminacy discredits the prophetic message of those who urge peace instead of war, caring instead of aggressive acquisition. Laymen feel alienated from such a feminized church and inclined to bracket its message. Our need for religious symbols that embrace both masculine and feminine finds an expression in soft and sentimental stained-glass saviors, which may strike men and women as alienating hybrids. Self-doubt tugs at the cassocks of male clergy. One clergyman questioned his move from business to the ministry: "Did I go to seminary because I just couldn't hack it in the cutthroat corporate world?"

The conclusion seems inescapable that the presence of women as ordained leaders will provide the simplest way to give feminine values and realities credibility in the church. Female religious leaders will relieve clergymen of the task of incorporating both masculine and feminine strengths in ways that do not fit their own personalities, and laymen of the need to distance themselves from an organization that strikes them as emasculated. Paradoxically, the growing presence of clergywomen may make for a church that is less "feminized," more truly feminine, and more truly masculine.

A Time for Breaking Stereotypes

As we move forward toward a future that promises greater freedom for men and women to be more fully who they are in the church, we presently find ourselves in a period that offers us a unique opportunity to unhook ourselves from rigid stereotypes of what men and women should be and do. These days I hear many clergymen, especially mature ones, speaking with interest and pleasure of owning their feminine side. And women who enter a profession previously closed to them are likely to be women of resolve who have a capacity to endure challenge and loneliness. The ordained ministry now seems to include many men who exercise feminine strengths and women who exercise masculine strengths.

"Why not forget about male and female differences?" some will say. "After all, we are all individuals, all human." True. But the limitation in this popular response is that it moves us backward into an emphasis on the generic. And in Western culture "generic" still means masculine and pushes the feminine back out of sight. I think it will be more useful to rejoice that the present makeup of church leadership helps the church to offer a gift for these times, a bridge toward a future in which we can all be more wholly who we are, a time when the church can welcome more fully the lives and realities of both men and women. Many people today find the promise of that future powerfully symbolized by a male priest and a female priest celebrating the eucharist together at the altar and female and male ministers sharing preaching and worship leadership. And many find that promise, too, in the energy for ministry generated in male-female colleagueship, one of the gifts of God for the people of God.

In this time of pain and discovery, energy and depression, a new kind of church is coming toward us from the future. As we travel to meet it, all of us, men and women, must define our own gifts for leadership and appreciate the gifts of our brothers and sisters, which may be quite different from ours. As we struggle to leave behind the byways of dominance and subordinance, to move toward the paradoxical and promising intersection between being who we are and being with others, we will find that we are becoming more faithful travelers. And we will discover a distant Presence as our companion on the journey.

PART III
LOVE

10

Friendship:
The Intimate Church

From nursery school to nursing home, before and after all colleagues and lovers, after our parents are dead and before our children are born, one relationship may (but never *must*) be ours for a lifetime: friendship.

There's a freedom in friendship afforded by no other human tie. Parents, siblings, children, and coworkers are visited upon us, and we are bound to lovers with cords of passion that lessen our liberty; but we can choose our friends. While we know every "other" is a mystery, parenthood and passion can tempt us to solve the riddle of the enigmatic beloved. Friends, however, can acknowledge the mystery simply, affirm the otherness gladly. Independence is a mark of friendship that other relationships are sometimes blessed to borrow: we discover that our children can become our friends when they achieve some independence, and our parents can be our friends when *we* can stand alone. Friendship, more disinterested than passion or parenthood, offers a liberating distance. We don't aim to possess our friends exclusively, as we do lovers or spouses. And because this kind of love is friendly with distance, we discover to our joy that friendships can survive separation and even flourish across many miles and years.

It is not mere freedom but the paradox of intimacy and distance that marks off friendship as a special territory in the human heart. Here as in no other human bond we stand in the tension between freedom and connectedness, in a graced space apart from cramped family quarters and the vast uncaring world.

Equality is an essential characteristic of friendship. Parents may carry their children, bosses may direct their employees, but friends stand side by side.

Sometimes friendship is a joint enterprise, undertaken side by side; at other times friends are engaged in "the mutual exchange of private worlds."[1] Often friendship blends mutual self-disclosure and shared endeavors for the common good. Either way, friendship rests upon a foundation of commitment: my friend will be there when needed and will neither abandon me in the enterprise nor fail to cherish my confidences. There's a special kind of grace in friendship. Listening to my friend or doing something for my friend is a privilege, never a chore.

Many lament the decline of this precious brand of human love, so delicately poised between intimacy and liberty, in which we stand as equals, revealing our being and collaborating in action. Some are concerned that because we have forgotten how to live in the tensive territory of friendship, we pull strangers into position as stand-ins, instantly promoting acquaintances to the vacant post of "friend," or advertising for intimacy in classified magazine ads. While many of us need and profit from psychotherapy, I think there are people who go on year after year writing large checks to therapists when perhaps what they need most is a sympathetic friend. Others assume that love is in such short supply that they desperately clutch their one intimate relationship until it cries out in pain.

Having taken a bird's-eye look at this endangered species, friendship — at the value we place on it, the equality on which it thrives, its delicate balance between independence and intimacy, confiding and comradeship — let us trace the shape these themes take for, and between, women and men.

Women's Friendships

If you listen to women, you might conclude that they place less value on their relationships with woman friends than on a romantic encounter. But if you *watch* them, you will probably come to the conclusion that women's friendships are broader and deeper than men's and fill women's needs for intimacy in ways their relationships with men cannot do. An Alban Institute study of clergywomen found that half again as many female as male clergy turned to friends for support.[2]

The importance of equality in friendship seems to support friendships among women. Both by choice and by virtue of their subordinate status, women are less intensely involved in many kinds of hierarchical rankings that separate their brothers into the top-bottom divisions that preclude friendly, equal relationships. The Alban research on clergywomen found that more than twice as many female as male clergy turned to members of their congregations for support. As I hear them, a primary reason why women dislike role relationships of inequality is that they hinder human connectedness.

While human friendship seems to be about sharing both private worlds and public enterprises, women lean toward the self-disclosure end of that continuum, perhaps because we view creating the connection as a valuable end in itself. One woman said,

> I love my women friends for their warmth and compassion. I can share anything about my life with them and they never pass judgment or condemn.... There are no limitations on disclosure that I am aware of. The special quality of these female friendships is the openness. I have never been able to talk and share my feelings and experiences in the same way with any man.

Judith Viorst concludes, "I have heard these descriptions echoed by dozens of women of every age — and not by one man."[3] When provided with a reasonably safe structure, most women will happily share quite personal and even rather tender truths about their own lives with someone they have never seen before, and they find their experience thereby enriched.

Thus women's corner on the human friendship market emphasizes close attention to "the art of making friendship into a shape,"[4] a high value for equality, and a hunger for the exchange not only of words but of their very being.

Men's Friendships

While women's friendships are more important to them than they let on, men's friendships have a higher profile in the reporting than in actual experience. If I asked you to name some great friendships, I imagine you might think first of classical companions in arms or a biblical friendship such as David's with Jonathan ("my brother Jonathan; greatly beloved were you to me; your love to me was wonderful, passing the love of women [2 Sam. 1:26]").

Though women have few words for "friend," men have many: pal, crony, buddy, mate, and sidekick. Tales and terms notwithstanding, however, a chorus of observers reports that most men don't seem to have close friends. A lot of men don't know anybody very well except their wives. Last summer I listened to some Canadian clergymen talking about their loneliness:

"I have fishing buddies, yard-work buddies, drinking buddies, colleagues on the job, and 'couples' friends. I need more than that. I need friendships where I can talk about my personal needs and struggle."

"Most men I know are not willing to go beyond those male areas."

"I know what the reaction would be if they did."

"What do you do if those normal male bonding areas like sports are not your thing?"

"I think we are seen to be wimps."

"It's especially hard since we're clergy. How much can we open up?"

"I don't have time for friendships, especially now that I'm married."

"I can't tell you what it means to me that I don't have to be careful with you guys."

One man wrote in his end-of-class reflection, "I have become aware of my own deep longing for male friendship that can be on my terms and not the socially acceptable and expected level of 'buddies.'"

Even when men do sidle up to their buddies, their behavior often seems full of conflict, marked many times by sarcasm and backslapping,[5] reminiscent of the wrestling with which boys express affection for one another. Men often require liquor or the terrors of the battlefield to provide them with permission to

show affection for their friends. Many observers attribute this behavior to anxiety about intimacy. One notes how often a tentative
hug is accompanied by vigorous back pounding, which demonstrates that nothing sensual is going on.[6] Others see a major cause
of homophobia in men's belief that their longings to be tender,
dependent, and vulnerable are unacceptable.[7] To entertain those
longings is to be "like a woman." Thus, paradoxically, a man often feels safer having those needs met *with* a woman and keeping
male friendships distant and segmented.

The equality required by friendship seems to discourage
as many male friendships as it encourages female ones. Those
ladders of success don't have room for many men to stand on
the same rung. Twice as many male as female clergy in the Alban
study turned either to their spouses or to their senior pastor for
the support that the women were more likely to find with friends
or parishioners.

One man said of his three friends:

> There are some things I wouldn't tell them. For example, I
> wouldn't tell them much about my work because we have always
> been highly competitive. I certainly wouldn't tell them about my
> feelings of any uncertainties with life or various things I do. And
> I wouldn't talk about my marriage and sex life. But after that I
> would tell them anything. [After a brief pause he laughed and said:]
> That doesn't leave a hell of a lot, does it?[8]

Male friendships tend to be centered not around exchang-
ing private worlds but about standing shoulder to shoulder in
action. Men tend to divide their friendships into separate categories — different buddies for fishing and work and a woman
for intimacy. Here that familiar male "dividing up" theme may
serve to protect men from forms of closeness that embrace all
spheres of human life. If a friend is someone to *do things with*,
this compartmentalization follows naturally. While male friendships may be lacking in personal intimacy, they are rich in the
loyalty it takes to stand side by side in a common enterprise. Sol-
diers will die for each other. A man may be willing to give up
his life for his friends. An Australian friend told me, "You can
rely on a mate. Mateship is demonstrated not in words but in
action."

Friendships Between Women and Men

If women find closeness and confidantes in their friendships, and men's fellowship is marked by distance and doing, how can women and men be friends? Friendship becomes tricky when people come to it with different expectations. I've heard some women say it is hard to be silly with men, and that an ice cream pig-out requires feminine, not masculine, companionship, just as some male antics and activities are best shared with "the guys." And when women and men don't regard each other as equals, they find it hard to be friends. When men are very unsure of themselves, and are trying to prove they have nothing in common with women, they find it impossible to be friends with women.

I can still remember my daughter running home from kindergarten with the tearful tale that Eric no longer wanted to be her friend. No more holding hands in singing class. No more whispered conversations from mats snuggled side by side on the floor at rest time. Eric had just learned that boys were not supposed to be friends with girls. I don't think girls ever learn that norm, except as a face-saving "we'll-get-back-at-them" maneuver. The pattern seems to continue into adulthood: I frequently hear a woman saying she'd like to keep on being friends with a man when a romantic relationship comes to an end, but that the man does not share that wish. That either/or masculine posture often contradicts her desire in ways that end by hurting both.

When these conflicting postures can be resolved, however, a friendship between a man and a woman, poised delicately in that role which is neither lover nor stranger, can provide one of life's most rewarding relationships. For both men and women here is a relationship that has no requirement for exclusivity and that therefore can touch many levels yet remain respectful of the larger context of both friends' lives. Perhaps it is just because friendships between men and women *are* so tensive that they have such a graced possibility of being one of those places where the holy shines through. Perhaps more than any other relationship, friendships between women and men are alive with ambiguity, contradiction, energy, and paradox. Some of the most precious and most spiritually powerful relationships in my life have been friendships with male companions on the way, which held together a clear respect for each person's life context in the world beyond our meeting and an energy that shimmered around the edges of the friendship. The power of such a friendship lies in its "not becoming either a union of lovers or a marriage or . . . retreating into the cool and safely negotiated corridors of an acquaintance," to use Wendy Wright's precise and elegant words.[9] Thus, she holds, "friendship between a man and woman can be a medium for radical personal and shared transformation."[10]

We may helpfully pursue our exploration of this mysterious spiritual power in friendship by looking at the pictures of Jesus and his friends painted by the evangelists.

Jesus and His Friends

> This is my commandment, that you love one another as I have loved you. No one has greater love than this, to lay down one's life for one's friends. You are my friends if you do what I command you. I do not call you servants any longer, because the servant does not know what the master is doing; but I have called you friends, because I have made known to you everything that I have heard from my Father.
>
> — John 15:12–15

While many today assume that a relationship with Jesus is to be sought primarily in the confines of one's own closet, a reading of the Gospels gives us a different message: the very center of the story is to be found in conversations and actions in the circle of friends around Jesus. Jesus' promise to be with us when two or three are gathered sends a message that the importance of that circle of friends is not limited to the few years of his earthly life.

The Gospels carry the message that friendship was and is a most valuable and vulnerable human reality. When we ask our friends to befriend us, as Jesus did with great openness, we take the same risk he did: we may receive a free gift of loyalty and love, or we may be misunderstood and abandoned in our loneliest and neediest hour. Perhaps you, like me, have experienced something like the abandonment Jesus knew in the darkness of that last night in the garden, and you can feel some comfort that in that pain of loneliness we are not quite alone just because he knew it, too. There is no more telling expression of incarnation, of vulnerability, of the relinquishment of power than Jesus' willingness to put himself in that place where those for whom he had given everything could turn away and let him down.

Here in the Gospels, too, is the picture of one who could stand steadily in that tension between intimacy and respect for freedom that characterizes those moments when we can be a true friend or know ourselves truly befriended. Jesus invites but never nags; he asks questions that challenge the other to define his or her own reality freely. He offers love with open hands to his friends, both men and women. (It is now clear that Jesus was not the leader of an all-male team.) One of the most telling signals of Jesus' intimacy with a woman friend emerges in the exchange between Mary Magdalene and Jesus by the opening of the empty tomb:

"Mary!"

"Teacher."

"Do not hold on to me [John 20:16–17]."

To me the conclusion seems inescapable that she was in the habit of giving her friend a hug. Here, as in the intimate picture of the feet washing with tears and hair (Mark 14:3–9), is a portrait of a warm friend who accepted emotional and physical closeness with comfort.

The intimacy of Jesus' friendships with men is evident in the pictures of him crying over the death of his friend Lazarus and lying right up against the beloved disciple at supper. These pictures of vulnerability and intimacy without seduction can speak powerfully to reluctant men and to women yearning for closeness.

With both his male and female friends, Jesus seems to move easily between mutual self-revelation and companionship in action. In John's story, Jesus tells them that he calls them *friends* because he has not kept them ignorant of what he was about but instead has told them everything (John 15:15). Time after time his behavior toward his friends shows his passionate concern to know and be known. Mary's listening is affirmed over Martha's bustling. The shy bleeding woman's surreptitious touch is met by an instant and empathic understanding of her need. Jesus knows what kind of person Nathanael is by just looking at him as he sat under a tree. Nathanael's amazed question, "Where did you get to know me?" is quickly followed by his confession of faith (John 1:48–49). The woman at the well drops her water jar and runs to tell her friends, "Come and see a man who told me everything I have ever done [John 4:29]." Jesus is clearly touched by the depth of understanding in Mary's prophetic anointing.

Being and doing are no longer at odds: the conflict we so often experience between feminine being and masculine doing is pushed toward the resolution of paradox. Not only mutual revelation but also caring and courageous actions for one another by Jesus and his friends are upheld throughout the story. "I have called you friends, for I have made known to you everything that I have heard from my Father." In John's Gospel, the very next line goes like this: "You are my friends if you do what I command you [John 15:14–15]." Alongside the active friendship of the twelve men who traveled with Jesus we hear of the women friends who held the role of breadwinners as well as companions on the road: Mary and Joanna and Susanna and "many others, who provided for them [Jesus and the disciples] out of their resources [Luke 8:1–3]."

Jesus' consistent offering of companionship to all kinds of riffraff scandalized some observers. "A friend of tax collectors and sinners [Matt. 11:19]," said some, outraged. But generally the surprised disciples kept their shocked reaction to Jesus' policy of equality and affirmative action to themselves. When they approached the well, the twelve "were astonished that he was speaking with a woman, but no one said, 'What do you want?' or 'Why are you speaking with her?' [John 4:27]." Jesus' treatment of his friends as equals is demonstrated by his willingness to care for his friends like a servant and his insistence that they *were* his friends, not his servants.

God, our Great Companion

"Jesus," says Sallie McFague, "is a parable of God's friendship with us at the most profound level."[11] In pointing to God as friend, Jesus carries on the tradition of Hebrew stories about a God who is on friendly terms with a chosen people. Pondering Jesus as "parable" opens up for us a picture of the Holy

One who travels with us and remains by our side in our adventures and troubles. The metaphor of "companion" means literally one who shares bread with us as we travel alongside each other. "Bread for the journey" — those were the words a United Church of Canada minister spoke as she administered the sacrament. Her words pointed to the great Companion on my journey, on the journey of all God's traveling people. Aside from our families, it is our *friends* with whom we break bread, who invite us to their tables or join us at ours. We all have warm pictures in our minds of friendships celebrated at table, as well as bleak memories of times when there was no friend with whom to share our meal. In a recent teaching assignment, my loneliest moments came as I carried my supper tray out of the cafeteria line and stood shuffling uncertainly while I searched in vain for a familiar face next to an empty chair. It is our *expectation* that friendly intimacy be an important part of gathering at the table that makes such moments painfully awkward.

When we put the intimacy of warm dinner-table pictures next to our experience of God as the One whose absence leaves us desolate, we see that the paradox of intimacy and distance marks our relationship with God, as it marks every friendship. This tensive quality in important human friendships may be heard in Jonathan's parting words to David, "The LORD is between you and me for ever [1 Sam. 20:23 RSV]." I too have known moments when the space between me and my absent friend seemed to be full of God.

The metaphor of God as Companion also holds in tension the concerns about friendship as being or doing. Breaking bread on the journey implies a pause just to be together in the midst of a purposeful journey. At many other points in our tradition, however, an encounter with God means a challenge to do hard things, things we don't want to do and are afraid we can't do. Friendship, which pulls together the themes of mutual self-disclosure and standing alongside each other in the midst of difficult enterprises, seems an appropriate symbol for our relationship with God. The metaphor of God as Companion, the One who shares bread with us along the road, thus emphasizes God "alongside" us rather than "above us."[12]

The Intimate Church

Father Daly reflected on the daily routine of his parish life:

> People are always dropping by to see if "you've got a minute, Father." Catholics don't usually make an appointment with their parish priest, as they would with their dentist or lawyer. At first this seemed odd to me after some years in the business world. But then I realized that it is because they don't think of the priest as a professional, but as their friend, and it's okay to just drop in on a friend.[13]

Surprises often highlight the truth that we didn't expect. Father Daly's insight that his parishioners saw their relationship with him as friendship is echoed and extended in a very different tradition — that of the Quakers. Here is a branch of the Christian family who choose "Friends" for their name, for whom friendship is found, not in the relationship between pastor and parishioner but *within the community itself*, which therefore has no need of priests. Following these Roman Catholic and Quaker leadings, let us pursue this theme of friendship into the congregation — our deep need for friendship, our yearning to have that need met within the Christian community, and some ways that yearning might be fulfilled in our participation in that group of companions on the way we call the church.

Earlier we met Peggy, who took the risk of telling her priest, and then other members of her little church in Maine, the crippling secret of her sexual victimization by her father, a secret that had made her feel alienated and worthless since childhood. Peggy and her congregation have taught me much about the dynamics of the intimate church. In many churches, Peggy's courageous self-revelation would have remained under the heading of "pastoral counseling," confided only to the priest in the confessional. Instead it became a catalyst for the ministry of the whole community. Here, ministry did not stop with the priest but moved on through him. This "counseling appointment" turned into an invitation to the community to discern, own, and carry out *its* ministry. Malcolm Burson's modeling of openness, intimacy, and expression of affection is picked up by parishioners, who make these comments:

"He talks about feelings in sermons — that gives people permission to talk about things."

"I find Malcolm open in the pulpit. He has shared his own struggles with faith."

Malcolm himself says that he supposes "there aren't many churches where the rector kisses everybody." As Peggy, encouraged by her priest, took the risk of speaking about what had seemed unspeakable and would surely reveal her as unacceptable, ministry to Peggy rippled through the congregation. People responded, "One of our own is hurting." One member said, "It's not much more than saying, 'Okay, sister, you've got a problem. You've trusted us.' It's simple. It's shocking that that simple response should turn out to be a big deal." The ripples spread out farther: other victims of family abuse were emboldened to tell their stories. Those who were strangers to this form of abuse could yet perceive the shadow of victim or abuser in their own hearts, and so this painful story emerged not as a strange problem in the lives of strangers but as a sign of the brokenness in which each of us participates in our own way. As the pain became owned by the whole community, so did healing power. Not only survivors but nonabused persons picked up initiatives for ministry with victims of family abuse. Believing itself led by God through these experiences into a new kind of ministry, the parish instituted the Center for Family Nonviolence as a way to carry the ministry out into the community, the state, and the diocese, and into the church beyond it.[14]

For me, this parish vignette illustrates how the themes we have been considering — equality, living in the tension between intimacy and freedom, and attention to people's needs to know and be known and also to work side by side — may be enfleshed in parish life. Tracing the interweaving of these themes may point to ways this kind of intimate community can avoid problems encountered in the traditional pastor-centered church and unlock energy for ministry both within the ministering community and radiating out from it.

In the pastor-centered church, ministry is seen as the function of the "professional" minister. In the pastor-centered model, Peggy's confession would probably have remained a secret confided to the pastor. The ordained minister is seen as the credentialed expert with special training in pastoral counseling; he or she is the uniquely appropriate recipient and guardian of the secrets of the confessional. These secrets point to a view of ministry located within the pastor-parishioner encounter rather than within a community of companions.

Although both clergy and laity need intimacy, they often encounter problems when they expect to find it in a relationship with such heavy role expectations. This may be especially true in the common circumstance when the pastor is male and the parishioner is female. If the pastor is isolated both by his male script and by parishioners' exalted perceptions of his religious power, and if the ordinary church member is disempowered — by her female script, by a belief that she as a layperson has no power, and by whatever troublesome event has led her to seek counsel — they meet on dangerous ground. Quoting a comment that "the pulpit has always been a libidinous zone," Jay Lowery says, "the temptation to sexual use of the star-fan relationship is great."[15] "Star-fan relationship" is a shocking term to describe what goes on between clergy and laity, but it is too often an accurate one! Both parishioner and clergyman may be lonely. He often seeks to have all his needs for intimacy met by his wife and finds that the marital bond cannot bear that weight of need, particularly when the clergy wife role isolates her and provides her no place to have her own emotional and spiritual needs met. The female parishioner-with-a-problem may be lonely because the men in her life do not provide her with emotional and spiritual nourishment. While the situation encourages both of them to look for intimacy in their encounter, the relationship is defined as a professional and priestly one in which intimacy is inappropriate. If the pastor-parishioner relationship is viewed on a professional helper-recipient model, it is the helper's duty to move the recipient crisply out of that relationship into autonomy. The encounter also sets the stage for sexual attraction, which, if acted upon, so blatantly violates professional and priestly ethics that the pastor's career is likely to be destroyed, the ordained ministry in general discredited, and the parishioner's faith and psychological well-being seriously damaged.

When intimacy is sought, not primarily in a top-bottom, one-to-one relationship between pastor and parishioner but in the ministering community, the energy for human closeness is less likely to entrap people, more likely to feed them and encourage them for ministry. When intimacy is located in the community, the pastor seeks not to be *the* minister but to encourage the growth of a community of ministering people. Thus ministry is multiplied. While Malcolm did not abandon his pastoral role, he sought to share it with the congregation by urging Peggy to count many people among her friends and pastors and by working to empower a community that could respond by ministering with Peggy, receiving her gift of ministry, and expanding ministry throughout the congregation and beyond it. Then the "official" pastor can conclude, as Malcolm put it, "There is lots of pastoral counseling going on I know nothing about." The telling of "secrets" is not attached to clerical power but becomes the natural self-revelation that a community of trusted friends invites. Self-revelation is not just a private affair, on appointment with the pastor, but is modeled for the community from the pulpit. The intimate church thus becomes a friendship of equals in which the clergy are recipients as well as enablers of care. "Malcolm ... needs others to tell him he's all right," said one parishioner. Instead of talking about "what he is doing with his people," and wondering "Will it last when he leaves?" observers speak of "what those people in Old Town are doing." If the rector kisses everybody, people sense that he does this as a way of modeling an intimate and affectionate community and because "that's just his way." Affectionate behavior is thus relieved of the loaded-up character that comes from a view of the ordained leader as the official dispenser of God's love. The troublesome results of *that* view were evident when "Father Ron," priest of a church near a women's college, held students on his lap and told them that God loved them. In contrast, the intimate church sets friendly closeness in the context of a community of equals in a way that enhances both ministry and mission.

Because the intimate church locates ministry in a community of equals rather than in the role of one professional, it lives corporately in the tension between distance and closeness, freedom and intimacy, just as individual friends do. And in the church, equality makes possible a quality of closeness that is not exclusive. At its best, the church can create a hospitable and warming climate that extends the special quality of friendship to all who come through its doors. Both clergy and laity benefit from this open intimacy. Clergy who minister within a community of friends suffer less stress and isolation. Paradoxically, their vulnerability is reduced at the same time that they are enabled to be more vulnerable. Laity suffer less from hurt feelings produced by the kind of mixed expectations that resulted when Betsy and Michael invited their pastor and his wife to dinner. When they discovered that he reported those three hours as part of his sixty-hour work week, they decided not to invite the Bradfords again. They had intended their invitation as a bid for friendship, not a request for professional services.

When the church is a society of friends who live in the tension between intimacy and freedom, this community joins women's and men's ways of being friends in a way that can meet the needs of both, rather than assigning distance to males and closeness to females. The intimate church affords many opportunities for women to find close relationships and gives men permission to express affection and discover friendships with a depth that transcends the compartmentalized encounters that leave them feeling lonely.

Congregations are uniquely equipped to support the intimacy and the decision not to act it out inappropriately that provide the foundations for transforming relationships, as many people discover. Churches can provide people with permission to come close to one another and practice in managing sexual attraction so that energy is released for spiritual growth and ministry. Many may find that committed spiritual friendships provide that permission and practice.

Among the challenges facing the intimate church is the need to work at staying open. When people find the deep and nourishing relationships for which they have been yearning, they find it easy to become so absorbed in those friendships that newcomers find no way to break into a coffee hour conversation. In our church the pastor consistently holds before members the need to be hospitable, employing a variety of strategies such as suggesting that people talk to somebody they don't know before they start talking with their friends. Intimacy probably isn't any easier than isolation, but most people find it a good deal more satisfying. And churches that take seriously their position as a bridging place between the loaded-up closeness of family life and the impersonal requirements of public life can be warmed and supported by friendship to return to their ministries in both spheres with renewed energy and courage. When people tell their stories, taking the risk of allowing themselves to be known at some depth, and express their affection for one another, they are also being energized for ministry.

The intimate church is flexible enough to provide intensive care, empowerment, or release, as needed at different stages on life's way. We all have times when we are beaten down by life's hard blows and other times when we have the strength to move out confidently in our ministries. We need religious communities that give us permission to "oscillate" from one of those postures to another, teach us how our wounds can provide occasions for us to become healers, and remind us of the fragility of our lives, our loved ones, and our enterprises — a fragility that is present even in our sturdiest hours. St. James's Church did not define Peggy as a patient and box her into a "helpee" role but participated with her in her healing and growth, as she became one who ministered with other victims of family abuse. Nor did the church hang onto her ministry, but it released her to exercise it beyond the congregation and the community. As members of that tiny church tell one another their stories, ministry is multiplied.

In such ways all our churches may venture into the graced and tensive territory of friendship, poised between intimacy and distance. In a community that bridges private yearnings and public duties, we may find ways to join a group of friends on the way, led by one who is a living parable of our great Companion. As we stop along the road to share our lives just as we share bread, we may find both relief from loneliness and courage to act.

11

Ecstasy and Ethics

I'm so miserable I've got to talk to somebody," gulped Molly between sobs, when I picked up the telephone on that September Saturday. "Pastor Sanderson is a dear man, but I couldn't tell him about this."

I knew Molly had flown to the West Coast to teach a summer school class in June, but I didn't know that she had fallen in love with the chairman of the department, who had worked with her as she designed and taught an experimental class. Planning sessions and lunches after class were filled not only with the excitement of the joint project but with the discovery that Molly and Andrew shared, in addition to their delight in their work, a passion for baroque music and a love of cross-country skiing.

"We seemed to connect on about seventeen levels at once, including being attracted to each other," said Molly. "And including being in committed marriages. Sometimes that felt like a painful squeeze. Andrew hinted in a lot of ways that he wished he could take me to bed; but at the same time it made me love him more to know he is a faithful person. Being with Andrew was like sunshine — it shone right through my life. I don't think I've ever done such good work. And we seemed to be in the same place on our spiritual path. The love shone through there, too, and seemed to hold a hint of the love of God. I thought maybe that was the place for some of this energy between us. So I asked him to be my spiritual friend, and he said 'Yes — when it clicks like this, it would be a sin not to accept.' But something seemed to bother him. When he took me to the airport, he asked me, 'What do you do with all the sexual energy?' I said, 'Well, those feelings come and go, don't they?' but then he replied, sort of sadly, 'It sounds like that's easier for you than it is for me.' And now I've written him each month, just as we agreed, but I haven't heard from him at all. The sight of that empty mailbox just makes my stomach lurch. I don't think he's going to write. How could somebody so honorable abandon an important relationship just like that?"

Molly — and I think Andrew, too — found themselves in that common human bind, wrenched between ecstasy and ethics. When the melting flame of desire is kindled inside us, we want to give ourselves wholeheartedly to the ecstasy for which our bodies reach. At the same time we know these feelings that flood our being so insistently are not the whole of life they seem to be. There is a pull in the other direction: we also want to hold these urgent yearnings in the context of our whole self, our relationships with others and with God. Those flood waters, for all their energy and crashing insistence, also have the power to drown us. If there are no banks for the river, our life becomes an unchanneled swamp, with all our energy dissipating into the ground.

Responding wholeheartedly to this contradictory pull provides no simple solution, however. A tight-lipped no to our feelings of passion doesn't work any better for us than an unqualified yes. An obsession for ethics, for control, can leave our lives an arid structure. All concrete banks and no river does not feel like a choice for life.

That pull between ecstasy and ethics would cause Molly and Andrew pain enough without further complications. But there is no shortage of additional complexities in the world around them. It's not just a personal tug of war. The whole of Western culture seems to be yanked periodically from one side of this tension to the other. Our own inner action and reaction may flow with — or against — the tides of tradition. And though we know this is a *human* problem, the way men and women experience that problem is sufficiently different that we often bewilder each other as we move toward each other, like Molly, or hesitate and step backward, like Andrew. At times we feel as though we were caught in an awkward and embarrassing dance, stumbling over our own feet and our partner's as well.

Let us take a look at the paradoxes of passion in our lives as women and men and in the Christian tradition that surrounds and guides us.

The Sexuality of Women: An Intricate Integration

A woman's erotic nature tends to be more holistic than a man's. Her body experiences as a woman, including menstruation, pregnancy, childbearing, nursing, and menopause as well as intercourse, are more varied and less sexually focused than a man's. Sex isn't something separate. It is connected with relationships, connected with the possibilities of pregnancy, connected with her whole being, connected with her spiritual life.

Pulling sex apart from relationships doesn't come naturally to women. A girl is usually interested in a relationship with a boy long before she is interested in expressing it sexually. The heroine of a gothic novel, waiting in the candlelit turret room for a dashing hero on horseback, provides a stage set for a young girl's dreams of romance. Sexual passion is only a faint glow around the edges.[1] Though the glow becomes stronger as she matures, the indissoluble unity of love and eros continues throughout her life. We have recently witnessed the strange contradiction that many women, in their desire to connect with a man, will even attempt to set aside their need to have sex embedded in relationships.

For a girl, puberty means the possibility of being a mother before it means sexual arousal, and the awareness of that possibility is part of what she brings to a sexual encounter throughout her childbearing years.[2] The connectedness of sexuality extends to spirituality as well. Women find it life-giving to weave together "the braided streams" of their lives — the spiritual, sexual and vocational strands.[3] Molly found her love for Andrew surging through her work and her spiritual life. During the past few years religious thinkers have newly appreciated this more feminine way of connecting spirituality and sexuality.

This rediscovery of the wholeness of life is a great gift; yet as with every strength, a weakness lurks behind it. The dark side of women's integration of the sexual and the spiritual is the possibility of inappropriately confusing these spheres and idolizing men. In the third chapter of the book of Daniel, the problem with the golden idol is underscored by the refrain "the idol was *set up*." Objects of our spiritual hunger that will disappoint us and leave us hungry in the end are always objects we have *set up*. Even in these liberated days, women are prone to setting up, enshrining their relationships with men in the center of their lives. When we bring an infinite hunger to a finite relationship, we go away hungry. Then we end up hurting ourselves — not only through our disappointed hopes in the other, but also by putting ourselves down, accepting a subordinate posture. "Your desire shall be for your husband, and he shall rule over you."

The Struggle to Be a Subject

While women naturally see their sexuality as intricately woven into the whole web of their existence, they find it less natural than men simply to be a sexual *subject*, to own their passion, to go for erotic ecstasy in a straightforward, focused way. A woman has a sense that her sexuality is "hers and yet not hers." It is, as well, "a manifestation of the creative life-force itself."[4] The initiative is not hers in quite the same way that it is a man's. Like her sexual parts, the springs of her ecstasy are more complex, less self-evident. She is slower to arousal, less firmly in control of the sexual encounter. At sexual initiation her fear may need to be overcome by trust.[5] Because for her, sexual passion is so inseparable from emotional intimacy, Molly describes herself as "falling in love," while Andrew says he "wants to take her to bed." "Falling" feels more like the descent of magic than "a moment to decide." Though a woman may have less control over the sexual encounter, she has more control over her own sexual impulses. Ethical issues related to personal control are likely to be less pressing for her than for him. Her ethical questions are less likely to be about control, more likely to be about response, about responsibility. She will ponder how to hold all parts of her personal system together. This different quality of her ethical question again signals her bent toward wholeness rather than toward being simply a willing subject, one whose posture can be summed up in a direct "I want." A woman's identification with mother, everyone's common first love, tends to put her in a vicarious posture in a sexual encounter. She "feels more preoccupied than he does, while they are making love...she is apt to be busier than he is imagining herself in the other person's situation, more engrossed in the other person's access to her own body and thus less engrossed in her own access to the other person's body."[6]

Problematic Possibilities in Diffusion

These characteristics making for a more diffuse sense of self as subject are part of the feminine way of being in the world. But there are other factors that *may* further dim her sense of selfhood in ways she finds problematic. Some women may not yet be sexually awakened; physical sexuality may be dissociated, as in adolescence. Some of the columnist Ann Landers's thousands of respondents who would "rather be hugged" are probably in this category. Their sexuality needs to be pulled out of hiding. Some women may see their sexual longings as bad. In that situation "the solution of 'doing it for others' can seem to offer a ready answer."[7] A woman may see herself less as obtaining what she wants than as "giving" something to a man. Or perhaps she can contrive to leave herself out of the picture in her own mind and see him as the only subject in the encounter. A woman who does not own her own power is not likely to own her own sexuality as an autonomous person. She may be dependent on his sexual response to convince her of her own worth, or she may even use the desire of men as a tool of blackmail to achieve her own, quite different purposes. A heteronomous (subject to "the law of others") woman may be so absorbed in the reality of the other that she doesn't fully inhabit her own reality. If she spends all her time worrying about *giving* pleasure, she probably won't get much. This heteronomous posture can even take a perversely reactive twist: a few women reject their sexuality precisely *because* men find it primary.

In these ways, a woman's naturally more diffuse way of living out her sexuality may become problematic, further decreasing her sense of herself as a subject, and increasing her own collusion in defining herself as a "sex object." While rightly rejecting others' tendencies to objectify her, a woman would also do well to begin from within and attend to her own development as a sexual subject.

These two characteristics of a woman's posture in the tension between men and women are connected. When inhabiting her sexuality includes the creative powers, the loved one, the possible child, her sexual-spiritual-responsible self, and the life structures that hold all of that together, it follows that a woman's sense of herself as subject would naturally be more diffuse. Her difficulty in being simply a willing subject is the counterpart of the intricate integration of her life.

The Focused Passion of Men

For a man, by contrast, an active posture is central to his sexual stance. His physical initiative is, quite simply, *required*. As a dominant in Western culture, he receives more encouragement to take his wants seriously. His male bent toward action, toward "doing things together" as a primary way to relate to others, has been with him since childhood. He finds it natural to "make love" (literally) as a way to relate to the woman, in contrast to her need to have the relationship in good order before celebrating that connectedness physically.

The energy and vitality of this clear masculine self is not without its ambiguous side. Whatever blurs the focus of his whole-hearted, energetic, thrusting pleasure may be given over to her. Whatever unwelcome ambivalence creeps into his "go for it" posture can be attributed to the woman. If his conscience is uneasy, "*she* tempted me." His assignment of responsibility to her is the counterpart of her "I'm doing it for him." Sam Keen says, "She is a threat to his autonomy, because she stirs him to desire which, when fulfilled, renders him soft and spent.... Hence he blames the woman for what he experiences as the loss of his potency."[8] Through projection, he attempts to keep his clear sense of "I-ness" — and gives part of it away!

The active stance reveals another dark side when it is bent into the triumphant posture of proving himself by using others. The easiest way to prove himself a man today is to "make it with a girl," says Mark Gerzon. "Insecure about his masculinity and obsessed with proving it...he needs to score in order to feel he has made the team."[9]

Control and Decision

Because a man is so clearly a subject in the erotic encounter, with more direct control of the sexual act and less control of himself, issues of personal control seem central to him. He has old memories of being embarrassingly out of control connected with the new adolescent awareness of himself as a sexual person. Because he is worried about his control over himself, he feels more impelled to try to be in charge. (Can it be that many men dismiss the *importance*, though not the power, of sexual arousal because they really do not like being out of control?) In contrast to her ethic of connectedness and response we find his ethic of control.

A man's focus on control in sexual relationships often seems to issue in an either/or posture. As his marriage threatened to crumble, one man's pronouncement seemed typical: "Either I have a wife or I don't."

Perhaps his body first gives him the message that sex is a clearly defined part of him, that his desire can be awakened by a part of her, and, by extension, that she may be merely a small part of his life. While the young woman enjoys the diffuse romanticism of a love story, the young man may be aroused by pornography — explicit and split off from nonsexual considerations. The focus on parts might possibly emerge as fetishism for him but not for her. The awakening of puberty brings him experiences of sexual desire that are disconnected from relationships.[10] Men can divide lust from love, sexual passion from spiritual passion, and even see them as opposites. One man says, "We are quick to talk about sex and slow to discuss intimacy."[11]

The normal socialization toward a more integrated male sexuality is often short-circuited by the *Playboy* attitude. "Instead of being (at least publicly) a transient period of 'sowing wild oats,' the immature, dissociated sexuality of adolescent males is now presented as a desirable standard for adult men."[12] And because male dominance gives male standards generic status, dissociated sexuality has been assumed to be appropriate for women as well. A man's tendency toward dissociating sexuality from relationships is probably supported not only by male dominance but also by his hunch that he is less adept at following the trails of intimacy that have been well traveled by girls since grade school.

All these rather dubious aspects of his separated stance are balanced in part by the fact that a man is less tempted to elevate a relationship with the other sex to a godlike place in the center of his existence. While Andrew had trouble hanging in, Molly had trouble letting go.

From Dissociation Toward Wholeness

If a man is not short-circuited by regarding teenage sexuality as an adequate expression of adult behavior, he will find that maturity brings a richer integration to his erotic experience. A longitudinal study of graduates of a distinguished university for men found that "Whether a man can love friends, his wife, his parents, and his children proved a far better predictor of his mental health and of his generativity than whether at 50 he found bliss in a marital or extramarital bed."[13] James Nelson reported an "aha" in his discovery of the promise in "richly diffused sensuousness and invitation to intimacy" as opposed to "a narrow, genital focus."[14] Nelson's discovery was clearly a marker event in a *man's* journey, not that of a woman. It is a discovery that enables men and women to meet on the road and greet one another in recognition.

In maturity many men move past adolescent dissociation to a new integration of their sexuality with the rest of their lives and find themselves reaching *through sex* to that wholeness. Malcolm Burson put it this way:

> My experience feels like this: that for men, "connectedness" is just as important as you propose for women. But it's experienced very differently, heard in a different voice. It means, "this woman will be *there* for me, in all kinds of different and satisfying ways, if we get connected, in both the genital and other senses." This is frequently worked out in selfish, possessive, and patriarchal ways, but for men, it's often the *only* way out of interpersonal isolation. Women are "there" for connection in a way that other men are not, and the sexual encounter "seals," indeed, even reifies, the emotional connectedness. The paradox here is that this is seldom, if ever, understood by a man or expressed to a woman, I suppose because of masculine discomfort with acknowledging feelings of dependence, even mutual interdependence.

Offerings and Sufferings

As women and men face one another in our human desire to reach for ecstasy and to hold it in the context of a whole life, we may find that our different postures lend energy and richness to our meeting. Men are more likely to own initiative with vitality and pleasure, to live out a wholehearted enjoyment of the goodness of sex. But women move into that discovery in maturity as they enjoy learning to be sexual subjects. Women find it easier to integrate their sexuality into the many dimensions of a whole life. But men in maturity discover that the total context is more important to them than they thought. And the male gift of discrimination can remind us not to turn an awareness of the connection between sexuality and spirituality into an inappropriate *identification* of the two. These realms are like and unlike, and both the connection and the distinction need to be held in tension. Our different perceptions can enhance our mutual learning and our mutual joy. It is like a dance in which we enjoy our complementary steps or like a duet in which different voices join in contrapuntal richness.

Men and women find the tension between them creative and energizing in some moments and full of painful contradictions at others. The ties that Molly lovingly wove as a network of connectedness might have felt like "strings attached" to Andrew. One episode in the television series M*A*S*H discovers Margaret and Hawkeye in a deserted Korean house suddenly under enemy fire. Their fear brings them into each other's arms, and a terrified hug slips into lovemaking. At dawn she prepares a breakfast of K-rations and begins to chatter about how their sexual encounter will affect her troubled marriage and their future work and relationship. His eyes widen in alarm as he sees the web she is weaving around him. What's the big deal? Why all this to-do about a momentary encounter? When she finally becomes aware that he is making only the lamest of attempts to play along with her, she slugs him. When they are rescued his panic turns to ecstatic relief, which further infuriates her.

A man may regard a woman as a tease, as though she lured him on with specifically sexual bait on the hook and then refused to give what she had clearly offered. They aren't meeting out of the same sets of wants and expectations. She wants him to be attracted to her, to love her. She contemplates the weaving of an intricate relationship. If he wants only sex, her need for wholeness leaves her feeling rejected.

As men and women weigh intimacy against responsibility, they discover that they have brought different weights and measurements to the task. If he beds her, he may blame her for his guilty feelings. If he succeeds in his struggle for control over his longing for her, she emerges as the temptress he righteously spurned.

Wanting a woman you can't have is not an experience a sensible fellow like Andrew would go looking for. Molly feels totally rejected and doesn't understand why he had to be so cruel. For Molly a diffuse and multidimensional attachment might have included wistful longing, but it could have promised joy as well. Why couldn't they be friends? What Andrew apparently saw as a problem had looked like an opportunity to Molly. Their inability to notice their differences has brought bewildered suffering to her — and probably to him as well.

Ecstasy and Ethics

As we try to inhabit the space between ecstasy and ethics in our own hearts and in our relationships with the other sex, our human joy and struggle are reflected and addressed in the religious traditions to which we reach to articulate our human experience and to seek guidance.

The Garden and the Song

The first pronouncement about human sexuality in the Judeo-Christian tradition is: "and it was very good." It is not by accident that the Bible story begins with God placing us in a garden where there is everything we need to delight us. The man and the woman "were both naked, and were not ashamed": that was the givenness of the garden. The story is alive with signs of the holy playfulness of the Creator. The delight of the human lovers images divine delight in the creation of new life. "The creative process itself is erotic," says Phyllis Trible.[15] If we wanted to receive the merry puns of the creation story as "words to live by," we would best do so by joyously opening ourselves to the giving and receiving of bodily pleasure. Howard Moody points to a transcendent splendor in that

> uncontrollable moment in which we are forced to abandon ourselves to a force that seizes and shakes our whole being with its ecstasy, and, there in that exalted time, our manipulation and control are shattered, our limitation and finitude are exposed. It is wondrous and fearful.... What did we ever do to deserve a feeling so good that the body's memory lives off the sweetness of it?[16]

Karl Barth called the Song of Songs an expanded commentary on Genesis 2:25: "both naked, and not ashamed."[17] With a central metaphor of eros, this book lifts up the delight men and women are created to find in each other.

The affirmation of eros in those two garden stories forms a continuing thread in the tapestry of the Judeo-Christian tradition. According to a Jewish tradition, couples are not only permitted but commanded to make love on the Sabbath, for the sexual celebration of this special day is a uniquely appropriate blessing. The Talmud enjoins on a husband the duty of obliging his wife when he sees her sitting before a mirror anointing herself with perfume.[18] Deuteronomy 24:5 offers newly married couples the wedding gift of "one year, to be happy." And the wedding feast is a frequent Gospel metaphor for the reign of God, now and in its promised glory. This eschatological note may underline the insight that human pleasure is a gift without being ultimate. When we notice the gap between what we can grasp now and ultimate fulfillment, we can refrain from laying a destructive burden on the gift that is or obscuring the glory of which we now catch only a glimpse. The theme of eros as a sacred metaphor is continued by Luther, who spoke with "scornful wonder against celibates and grateful wonder for the gift of sex." He "thought the marital embrace might be a good posture in which to be found when Jesus returns."[19]

The Theme of Ambiguity

The goodness of human sexuality is a primary theme in the Judeo-Christian tradition, which pronounces a divine Amen to our human wish to own eros joyfully. It *is* good! There is, however, a second theme, which emphasizes the ambiguity of our situation as sexual creatures. One direction in which that theme is developed presents that ambiguity not as uncertainty about whether sex is good but as a consequence of our failure to stand in the tension between ecstasy and ethics. The way we live with the gift of our sexual nature can tumble us into a large assortment of the traditional sins — adultery, covetousness, jealousy, idolatry, pride. Caught in the grip of strong passions, my vulnerability is increased. When I feel powerless, I can get mean. A fair number of homicides result from the fury of scorned women or from the lust of greedy men. We can *use* sex — perhaps just to prove to ourselves that we are alive.[20] When dominance and subordinance govern our sexual arrangements, men use sex to bully women, and women use it to manipulate men. Then our misery arises not from our *being* sexual creatures but from our failure to live ethically as sexual creatures. The man and the woman are ashamed in their nakedness not because their sexuality is shameful but because their open trust has been destroyed, their relationship broken.

Ethics Instead of Ecstasy

Still another theme in the Christian tradition presses beyond ethical ambiguity to the abandonment of ecstasy, the loss of a belief in the goodness of our erotic natures. During many centuries, Christianity was shaped by church fathers who themselves vowed to keep their distance from mothers and who were suspicious of sex even for married people. Jerome wrote, "A man who loves his wife very much is an adulterer." The church's suspicious attitudes toward sex emerged, not out of the concerns of the whole human community but solely from male splitting and projection writ large. Women could be seen as witches who fornicated with Satan or as pure virgins who allayed men's anxiety about their own lust. The abandonment of ecstasy for ethics produced some strange contradictions. "Nothing could be more absurd than to despise the body and yet yearn for its resurrection," says Wendell Berry.[21] The focus on ethics, for which eros was discarded, was, of course, the male ethic of control, rather than the female ethic of responsibility for her network of connectedness.

The theme in the tradition that rejected the goodness of human sexuality seems to have been motivated in part by a need to find a solution for that uncomfortable male dilemma of lust or shame: embrace shame as the truth about sex and attribute lust to women. One problem with that solution is that the parts of our reality we deny and assign to others take on a demonic quality; the image of witches fornicating with Satan is picture language that describes this internal male transaction. As an institution, the church led by such men had the power to absolve the guilt of all the other men who chose secular lives, not wishing to reject desire and focus on shame. And in an age when guilt seemed the primary human problem, a monopoly on absolution was a powerful commodity.

I have a hunch that this dynamic may have an additional cause in the tendency of introverted intuitive types to become religious leaders. Most Americans prefer to take in the world through their senses — what they can see and touch and feel and smell and taste. A minority of people in our country prefer to take in information through their intuition, which attends to concepts and connections, metaphors and meanings — the natural turf of those people who choose religious professions. When intuition is the preferred function, sensing is weak, undeveloped, an arena of awkwardness and stumbling (though perhaps also of numinous power). It would not be surprising if the intuitive leaders who provide the church with their gifts of spiritual perception were least appreciative of the fleshly pleasures of life, troubled by dark fantasies about the power for evil inherent in sensuality, understandably nervous about the possibility that they themselves might yield to sexual temptations, prone to projecting the source of those lures onto others and the nature of their own struggle into a cosmic battle between flesh and spirit.

Whatever the reasons (and there are undoubtedly many more), it is a sad contradiction that those who cared so much about the purity of the faith fell into one of the most ungrateful heresies the church has ever entertained — the transformation of one of the Creator's most loving gifts into an evil snare and the refusal of our human task of living in the tension between ecstasy and ethics. In contrast with the theme in the Christian tradition that accepted that ambiguous position, the life-denying, reality-splitting posture of many medieval and Reformation churchmen abandoned it. Their influence is still present in popular religion, which persists in equating sin with sex. When gratitude is forgotten, religion is reduced to ethics.

Sexuality and Spirituality

One theme of the Christian tradition upholds the tension between ecstasy and ethics; another surrenders it, judging human sexuality as inherently sinful. This fork in the road of tradition is closely related to a second fork. What is the relationship between human sexuality and spirituality? One part of the tradition separates them, while another sees them as intimately connected.

Eros Divided from Spirit

The separation of spirit from eros expresses a more masculine way of being in the world. Ethical monotheism seems to have had its historical genesis in the overthrow of ancient maternal religion. It may have had its psychological genesis in the male need to separate from mother. During formative periods it has been shaped by men who have chosen a segmented approach; a focus on the religious life as an alternative to intimacy with women. This development is congruent with the male tendency toward either/or approaches, toward looking on sexuality and spirituality as alternatives. If sex is experienced as split off from other dimensions of life, it doesn't in fact look very spiritual; dissociated sex (pornography, for example) actually seems the *opposite* of spiritual. Spirit and sex are to be divided; "pure men" are to be separate from the fleshly feminine and from "impure people" whose religion is seen as an abomination. In the separated view, spirituality is more ethical than ecstatic. Sexuality becomes primarily an arena for ethical decisions (literally "cutting-off"). Decisions are key in the ethical/historical world. Separation is naturally followed by anxiety about being in control. And ethical behavior here means control, rather than the more feminine connectedness and response. The picture of the deity that is thrown up on the cosmic screen is that of the "unmoved Mover," "never disturbed by any passions,"[22] never acted upon but always subject, in control always. A distaste for ecstatic forms of religion naturally follows. Nervousness about ecstatic religion appears in Paul's injunction against women with unbound hair and behaving in uncontrolled and unseemly ways. The perceived need for control over feelings, which threaten to burst out of control, leads inevitably to a preoccupation with rules for sexual behavior, which are elaborated in detail by the patriarchs of the Old Testament and the fathers of the church. If passion is projected onto women, male need for control over sexuality has as its natural corollary control over females as well.

To the male characteristics of separation and control should be added a *linear* approach. Especially for celibates, sex has been seen primarily as leading to procreation. The emphasis is on product rather than process.

The separation of sexuality and spirituality naturally leads, then, to a spirituality that is squarely in the ethical tradition. By contrast, the unity of eros and spirit results in an ecstatic tradition, which displays many feminine qualities.

The Joining of Eros and Spirit in Ecstatic Traditions

Non-Christian religions that allow female images of the divine tend to see sexuality and spirituality as joined. Erotic Hindu statues symbolize intercourse within the self, just as our erotic dreams and images are often a vehicle for spiritual meaning and personal integration.[23] In the ancient Sumerian religion, Inanna ordered two primary symbols of office carved from the great Huluppu tree to celebrate her ascendancy as Goddess: a throne and a bed. In marked contrast to the "masculine" image of the God of patriarchal religions, she is an explicitly sexual being.

Sexuality and spirituality are intertwined more subtly in the Bible. The verb to know as a term for sexual intercourse suggests a connection between human knowledge-through-love and God's intimate knowledge of beloved creatures. Images of Israel as God's cherished though often faithless wife are echoed in many New Testament references to the church as the bride of Christ.

The medieval mystics, many of them women, developed these hints in more explicitly sexual ways. In many places these women trace the connections between sexual desire and spiritual longing. For Julian of Norwich, "As regards our sensuality, it can rightly be called our soul because of the union it has with God."[24]

In contrast to her celibate male predecessors, Rosemary Haughton, a present-day Roman Catholic writer and mother of ten, develops a theology out of her experiences as a woman, a mother, and a sexual person. Haughton sees in romantic passion a central metaphor for the divine. Her diffuse feminine sexuality serves as an icon for the passion of God, not a diversion from it. She sees in passion "the release of spiritual power in, and between, a man and a woman through their specifically sexual, but not primarily genital, encounters."[25] In romantic love the breakthrough of passion is "self-giving towards a wholeness intensely desired, but across a gap of 'unknowing.' "[26] Intriguing hints of Haughton's experiences as mother surface in her fondness for metaphors that are kinesthetic, organic, and spatial rather than auditory or visual. Tilden Edwards comments on the numbers of women he encounters in meditation groups whose relationship with God, often seen in traditional male imagery, is filled with erotic passion, in contrast to the more distanced posture of the few men who participate in such groups.[27]

As we trace the connection between eros and spirit, a number of themes emerge. One is the interconnectedness of pain and joy. Surely our experience of sexual longing is "a painful delight," as a friend of mine put it. The Song of Songs paints a compelling picture of the yearning, longing, searching, and impatience of the lovers, for whom the distress of separation and the anticipation of union are intricately interwoven. The word passion itself means not only intense love but suffering. Jesus looked intently toward his passion, toward "being lifted up," with *epithemia*, "intense longing," which is the same word used for "lust." Some who later pondered the mystery of that event saw the cross as a "marriage bed." And many of us experience our longing for God as a painful gift.

A second theme I see is one of yielding. "Passion," or suffering, means by extension "being acted upon," or "passive." We can open ourselves to sexual passion only through relinquishing control, even to the extent of undergoing "a little death." If God is always besieging our hearts, our passion may be a response that is nourished in us and drawn from us only as we let go, only as we die to that part of ourselves that is intent on controlling. Of course life must include both the active and passive stance, both taking charge and allowing our hearts to be melted. But limiting life to the areas over which we have control truncates existence. The religious tradition that connects eros and spirit calls us to balance our need to control with a willingness to enter into mystery. The last verse of the hymn "Come down, O Love divine" begins, "And so the yearning strong, With which the soul will long, Shall far outpass the power of human telling." Yielding control means moving toward the knowing-through-love of which the Bible speaks with double significance — a knowing that eludes the grasp of our linear minds.

Attentiveness to simple being as well as focus on doing suggests a third theme, that of unity and energy. Both sexual and spiritual passion are unitive experiences, because nothing is sought except the beloved, who is an end in herself or himself. Body, mind, and spirit are integrated, healed of splits and cross-purposes. Because we are drawn through our passions, we experience service to the beloved as freedom. When an old acquaintance asks, "Where is your passion these days?" you are being questioned about where your most motivated and undivided interest and energy are focused. There love becomes work, and work turns into play.

Churches that have become one-sided in their attention to the ethical/historical pole will receive new energy from touching again the deep and linked energies of sexuality and spirituality, the ecstatic pole. It seems inevitable that the fire of charismatic renewal had to burst forth from the somewhat dry sticks of mainline Protestantism, with its head-centered, dutiful, controlled, rather unemotional style. Paradoxically, however, such enthusiasm for renewal tends to act as a substitute for eros, fails to hold up the holiness of our sexuality, and thereby forfeits the promise of a new balance. The religious enterprise, too, struggles to live in the tension between ethics and ecstasy. If we look back across great sweeps of time, perhaps it was equally inevitable that the ancient religions celebrating the Goddess had to yield to an ethical/historical faith, for unless ecstatic energy is held in tension with that pole, it can become irresponsible. The need today in mainline churches, however, seems to be for the new energy that can be tapped by reconnecting with the ecstatic and feminine dimensions of faith.

The Song of Songs is a primary biblical text that not only affirms the goodness of human sexuality but also sings of the connection between eros and spirit. The great paradox in this poetry about human passion is that though it never mentions God, it has been seen through the centuries as a song about God's love affair with us. The fact that God is not mentioned keeps the connection light and tensive, avoiding the traps of nervous separation and simple identification. Unlike the Goddess Inanna, the God of the Bible does not engage in sexual intercourse. Ponderous efforts to haul the Song of Songs into position as an allegory are undertaken only at the cost of distorting the words. The many efforts to identify God with the man (I have not heard of any to equate God with the woman) ignore the clear equality and mutuality of the lovers. There is no "ruling over" in this story. The two toss the initiative back and forth in playful counterpoint — a picture that is true to the best we know of human erotic delight. Though attempts have been made to draw morals from the story, they, too, are like putting boots on a butterfly. The story is clearly not about marriage or procreation[28] or anything at all that we ought to do but about the delights of erotic love. Other efforts at interpretation ignore the plain meaning of the story by arguing that it is not erotic at all but spiritual. There is no way to grasp the connection and nail it down, but lovers of God have always seen the Song of Songs as a pointing finger — not unlike the poetic parallel "male and female . . . in the image of God." The "holy playfulness of lovers"[29] makes a transcendent leap to the mystery of the divine Lover — in a way that defeats all human efforts to analyze, allegorize, conceptualize, moralize, spiritualize, or otherwise seize and destroy it.

Living Between Ecstasy and Ethics

How might pondering the pull between ecstasy and ethics in our experience and in religious tradition assist our struggle to live in that tension, as individual men and women and as members of our religious communities?

The Personal Challenge

As an individual, my primary task is, first, to be aware of the reality of my own experience and, second, to behave responsibly.

I need to know what is going on in me before I can make any choices. To an awareness of the shape of my own yearnings needs to be added some perception that the other's reality may take another form and a willingness to allow the other to *be* other. A man may find his erotic nature self-evident. A woman may need to be watchful lest she lose herself in her eagerness to embrace connectedness. The affirmation of the goodness of our sexuality, which is offered to us by our Hebraic tradition, can encourage us to own and celebrate our erotic reality, to be "naked, and not ashamed." It is a gift we have been given, not something to be ashamed of. Our awareness of our personal reality can be enhanced as we examine the culture and tradition that surround us and discern how our own reality is, or is not, reflected in them.

If I don't own my own feelings, I may pretend they belong to somebody else. When people dimly sense their own desires as problematic and project them onto the desired one, they may end up treating that person like the enemy. Those who do not acknowledge the human realities of their own lives may behave in joyless and punishing ways toward the rest of the human community and toward themselves.

Acknowledging the reality of my life as a sexual creature does not necessarily mean that it is a good idea for me to reveal my feelings to a person to whom I find myself attracted. Having lived through an era when many people have rediscovered the value of honesty about feelings, many assume that candid revelations about sexual desire to the object of one's affections are de rigueur. Those confessions are appropriate at the right moment in a courtship setting. But many married people find such revelations problematic in other settings. *Knowing* what is going on in me does not necessarily mean telling everybody about it. Feelings of attraction that are not helpful to discuss may, again, be enjoyed like butterflies — not to be pinned down but allowed to flutter around the edges of a relationship.[30]

First I need to know where *I* am, and second I need to behave appropriately and be faithful to my commitments. A yes to my desiring nature does not mean an indiscriminate expression of it. When people act out their emotions sexually in a mindless way, they are more likely to be running from their feelings than assertively acting on them. Though control is an appropriate concern for many people, the problem with an ethic based on control is that it threatens to cancel our yes with a no. Our ethical purposes may be more usefully served by an ethic of response, of responsibility, which can hold our private yes in the context of other yeses. My sexual energy is good, but it is also not solely mine and needs to be held within the context of a whole life and its network of relationships. This approach offers an integration to which the symbol "one flesh" can speak in many ways. We yearn to be "one flesh" — one within ourselves, living out of an awareness that physical acts are not something other than acts of our whole selves; one with the reality of our own experience, and with the whole being of another. Because becoming "one flesh" with another is such a vulnerable form of joy, it requires trust and commitment. "Making love" implies the use of sexual arousal to fuel the giving and receiving of love — in contrast to using another person to turn me on. As Jeremy Taylor pointed out, one of its purposes is to "endear each other" amid the duties, trivia, hardships, and boredom that are inescapable components of the dailiness of married life. If making love is the most powerful form of marital "team building," then it should be used to build *that* team.

An ethic of responsibility includes responsibility to *ourselves*, as well as to the other. Responsibility for ourselves means not allowing self-respect to become a casualty of our desire to connect with another. It includes a yes to our own future in an era when irresponsible sex can cost us our lives.

And it includes a response to God, sometimes just a response of simple celebration. The encounter of male and female does point to the image of God: the mystery, the energy and joy we find in knowing-another-through-love points to our meeting with the Holy Other.

When living in the space between awareness of my own reality and response to the whole of my life is not simple but involves me in the painful contradictions Molly and Andrew encountered, my refusal to duck out of that tension by ignoring one or the other pole provides me with a faithful place to stand. My willingness to bear that discomfort may, paradoxically, bring me a structure of reasonable comfort within which I can receive some gifts of spiritual growth.

How difficult it can sometimes be to stay in that narrow space between knowing my reality fully and behaving responsibly! The ways of either repressing my feelings or acting them out seem so much easier and broader. As James Hillman put it, "We tend either to repress everything because it cannot be brought into life, or, if we do allow fantasy in, then we want to live it out immediately."[31] But the willingness to embrace both desire and responsibility, energy and structure, the water and the banks, is also a willingness to engage in the religious issues. And it is from that place that a living stream may flow.

Embracing Ecstasy and Ethics in the Church

The church, also, can benefit from moving toward a more balanced posture between ecstasy and ethics. Over the centuries both culture and church seem to tack back and forth between rules and repression on one hand and the liberation of doing what feels good on the other. Including feminine as well as masculine sexual perceptions can offer us more options. What do women see when they operate as sexual *subjects*, not just as the objects of male desire and projections? If the church does not assume that only male sexual experience is normative human experience but takes women's reality seriously as well, some new dimensions will appear. And we will offer precious gifts of understanding to one another. Women seem ready to learn from male wholeheartedness about sex when it isn't expressed at women's expense. Men seem ready to learn from women's more holistic way of being sexual creatures, which links spirituality and sexuality.

Accepting the dual task of awareness about our sexual reality and seeing the ethical life as a response to our total reality has important benefits not only for individuals but also for the community of faith.

Honest acknowledgment of our sexual nature can make ministry more caring, in very specific ways. Lack of awareness is directly connected with irresponsible acting out of our feelings. In a helpful discussion of unethical sexual behavior on the part of church leaders, Mary Pellauer makes the point that "strong 'no-talk' rules about sexuality" are a systemic factor which increases the risk of sexual exploitation.[32] A United Church of Christ survey concluded that people wanted help from their church on sexual issues, though, like Molly, they didn't expect to receive it. Nine out of ten respondents thought the pastor should provide such help, and almost as many said, "Church members should help one another with concerns about sexuality-related subjects."[33] The New South Wales Board of Education of the Uniting Church in Australia recently studied the pastoral needs of widows. The report revealed that the widows' sexual needs were eclipsed at the time of their husbands' death but often reappeared strongly after some months. "Sexual suggestions on television or in books caused physical pain with no way of alleviating this distress." Many felt a need to masturbate, some having gathered from their reading that this was an appropriate way to relieve this stress; others were "carrying heavy guilt feelings even thinking that they might do this. Nowhere had the church addressed this problem. One tried to talk to her male minister, who looked embarrassed and changed the subject, so she backed off."[34] Surely an acknowledgment of the realities of our lives as sexual people can yield more caring and helpful ministry than that!

As church leaders move away from nervous avoidance of our sexual concerns, the Christian community can tap into a great God-given energy center, which will make the church more alive, more creative, more passionate, and more loving. When body, mind, and spirit are all working together, enormous energy is let loose! Some of this energy will warm ministry, when men and women collaborate on church staffs and in lay committees and teaching teams. In order to tap these reservoirs of energy, we may need to become more sophisticated about the gifts and limitations of the intuitives who form a majority of our ordained leaders. It will be useful to round out their offerings with the complementary offerings of the majority of sensing laity who may inhabit their bodies with more comfort. Those whose primary strengths are intuitive are our natural religious leaders. But we ought to be aware of the inner discomfort about life in the flesh that they may be experiencing. A low level of physical awareness and a tendency to act out sexual feelings impulsively can be the dark side of intuitive strengths. Hierarchical attitudes about leadership serve us poorly here. We don't *have* to see leaders' weak points as normative for the church in areas where the "followers" may offer more effective leadership!

Welcoming feminine perceptions about sexuality along with masculine perceptions can offer the church more ways of looking at sexual ethics. It may be possible to push beyond the moralism that results from a one-sided emphasis on ethics bereft of ecstasy. We may be able to expand our range of ethical postures beyond control, finding new ways of affirming our sexuality in the context of a whole life, governing our behavior by our responsibilities to others and to ourselves, noticing how an awareness of the connection between eros and spirit offers us inner growth, moments of gratitude, and encounters with mystery. That connection may be a rich one for us. In its gracefulness we may find ourselves able not only to control but also to yield; in its mystery we may touch the pain and joy at the depths of our lives; in its deep bond we may know the wholeness and energy that are a gift of creation.

12

Mothers, Fathers, and God

Many Christians firmly maintain that "Father" is the traditional and immutable name for God. A growing number
of church people feel an equally passionate need to speak of God
as "Mother," too. People say they care about these words because they hope for inclusiveness and justice — or because they
honor the weight of tradition. These are important concerns. But
surely there is more at issue here. There are deeper dimensions to
these discussions that account for much of the energy with which
people advocate "justice!" or "tradition!"

What else is at stake for us in using the words Father and
Mother for God? These are potent words. They evoke some of
the most profound human experiences we know. They remind us
of how we came to be, of the ways our lives are rooted in those
who brought us forth. They may also remind us of our own experiences as men or women in bringing a new generation into
being. We may care deeply that our language be inclusive. But
we also know that the power in those cords of love and guilt,
freedom and fusion, agony and hope, that bind us to our mothers and fathers and to our children is no more neuter than it is
uniform. Most of us, I suspect, are not ready to throw out the

words Mother and Father and replace them with Parent. What experiences do these powerful words evoke for us?

Our Experiences of Mothers and Fathers

What is special about our experience of mother? Our coming into the world from an invisible place within our mothers seems mysterious. Pregnancy and birth happen *through* the mother; once they are underway she does not feel in control of them. Though she encompasses and accepts mystery, her inner space is hospitable, and she and her daughter (in work and play and dreams) will make a habit of arranging hospitable spaces for people. To become a mother, a woman receives that which is not a part of her, and she is likely to be comfortable with containing disparate elements in her thoughts and feelings as well.

There certainly are no doubts about whether her child is indeed hers. The connection is unassailable and may express itself in deep bonds of unconditional love. My joy in moments of feeling my heart all happily curled about my beautiful new daughter, my friend Kathryn's cozy delight in snuggling her children's hats down over their ears — these are commonplace experiences of the simple connectedness of motherhood. This deep physical tie finds natural expression in the ongoing tasks of feeding and washing. A woman's enfleshed worldview is concrete, attentive to the way life cycles through days and weeks and months and years (as well as rhythms no calendar can measure), and reverent toward nature's creative processes.

Our mother's power is accentuated by our infant helplessness of long ago; we depended utterly on her before all thoughts or words. To our childish perception it seemed that the provider of all joys possessed also the power to withhold them and leave us cold and wet, hungry and hurting. Even when we are grown up, our perception of other people's power can be magnified by our sense of our own weakness. How much more must this be true for babies! With that shameful memory of mother's ancient and engulfing power as our genesis, it is not surprising that the power of woman inspires ambivalence at *best*. We really must not allow ourselves to be at the mercy of anything like that again. We will instead deify mothers and blame them as the source of all ills. We will put motherhood on a pedestal and trivialize it with sentimental Mother's Day cards. She must be kept under firm control, that "nursery goddess" who first inspired in us that most agonizing of dilemmas, a yearning to be taken care of and a determination to be free.[1]

Each of us is either like or unlike that goddess of the deep bonds and the awe-inspiring power — who in Western society is also, most paradoxically (and most logically), a subordinate being. For her son, who is unlike her, nostalgia for the ancient blessing bumps up against a determination that his hard-won self-hood, his membership in the one-up club, not be jeopardized by the lure of her power. The easiest solution is to keep the females handy but under a firm thumb. A daughter's likeness to her mother may be a mixed blessing as well. Unconditional love bestowed on one subordinate by another can issue in a certain passivity and dependence on the one hand or a tranquil comfort with just *being*, on the other. How can the inheritor of the goddess claim and wield such power? Only with ambivalence.

Our experience of fathers is different. First, father inhabits his role at a little distance. While male generative organs are visible and those of females invisible, paradoxically we are bound to mothers with a stout cord of blood and flesh, to fathers with an invisible thread. A long time elapses between impregnation and birth. The earliest people were unaware of the father's contribution, and any father today may doubt that a child is really his. Quite different human experiences are initiated by ejaculating (literally "throwing out") a product of one's body than are afforded by containing diverse elements in the center of one's being. That thrown-out part cannot seem so inescapably *me*.

In some form, then, separation from the birth of his child marks a father's experience. The arrival of a child may feel separating also because it intrudes on his access to his woman. While mother is the one who is blamed, father is often the forgotten one. As the child grows, distance may continue to be an important theme: work takes father away from his child's world of naps and peanut-butter sandwiches; at the end of a day of distance he may be hauled into place as punisher. ("Just wait till your father gets home...")

What meanings emerge from our connection to the father "by an invisible thread in contrast to the flesh and blood umbilical bond of pregnancy?"[2] This thread leads us to acknowledge the reality of the invisible, the birth of spirit. This note of abstraction, this hint of immortality, is reflected in a study revealing that while women's reasons for wanting a child focus on the anticipated relationship with the child, men are more likely to speak of their own immortality. Said one father, "Even after I am gone my child will be here to mark that I have existed."[3] Here is a paradoxical conjunction between a man's investment in carrying on his name and conceivable doubts about his paternity. And man's generative capacity, while more uncertain, seems endless in contrast to woman's clearly time-bound fertility. For him, here is another nudge away from acceptance of endings, a hint that one's potency and power ought to be eternal.

Perhaps fathers do not feel they have clearly established parenthood through physical fathering but must imprint their mark on the child through purposeful parenting. This sense that his child is "not me" issues in an objectivity that paradoxically yields both freedom and expectations. Love is more conditional; responsibility is not simple response but the provision of accountability and sanctions.

Father may be the beneficiary of our love-hate relationship with mother. He starts out with a clean slate. *He* was not the nursery goddess who could leave you cold and wet. So the growing child can transfer positive parental feelings to father.[4] Father, safely out from under mother's thumb, promises a kind of liberation. He swam into our view when we began to reason, and therefore *he* appears more rational. He seems like the kind of parent a sensible sort of person could deal with: more a real *person*, less like our own private version of Mother Nature. His power appears more justifiable and objective, and it is exercised in the great world outside our front door.

This reasonable, safely separate parent, who is also a member of the dominant sex, is either like me or not like me. If I am his daughter, he is less likely to invite me into that great world. His expectations of me may be moderated because of his position at the top of the family ladder and mine at the bottom. The son, as an up-and-coming dominant, will typically be the target of serious expectations: be like me; don't be like her. Be the best. Achieve solidarity with your own gender, and do not stay tied to your mother. The father's need to imprint his expectations and the son's worry about whether he measures up to them add up to the most loaded parent-child relationship, one in which hope and guilt may well combine to produce deep uncertainty.

Parents as Pointers: God the Father and God the Mother

God as Father or Mother is both like and unlike the experiences we had of the first important people in our lives. Memories of human parents form the first curriculum of images in our lifetime learning process about the divine Parent. For one dying woman this lesson also formed the last curriculum. During many visits from the hospital chaplain, she wrestled with the agonizing question "How could God punish me by giving me cancer?" "One day," recalled the chaplain,

> I asked her how she would evaluate herself as a mother. "That's one thing I'm pretty positive about. I am a really good mother!" I had surmised this myself, having seen her interactions with her offspring, the youngest of whom was in his early 20's. "How did you, as a really good mother, discipline your kids?" I asked. "Well, for one thing, I never hit them or shamed them. We talked things through. I never sent them to their rooms without a meal or any of that stuff. I grounded them sometimes. They had to learn that there were consequences to their decisions. It was never a big problem, actually." I questioned further: "What did you do when something unexpected happened, something that wasn't their fault as near as you could tell?" "I just put my arms around them and held them close and we'd cry together..." and she stopped. As tears began to fall from her eyes I took her hand. "That's what's happening to me, isn't it?" she said, not really asking a question. "I didn't do anything, and God's just holding me and crying too...like a good mother."[5]*

Our mothers and fathers point to the power and love of God; but, as with all religious symbols, the pointing finger stops short in space, for the divine Parent transcends all human parents:

> "Can a woman forget her nursing child,
>   or show no compassion for the child of her womb?

---

*Laurel A. Burton, *Pastoral Paradigms*. Reprinted by permission from The Alban Institute, Inc., 4125 Nebraska Avenue, NW, Washington, DC 20016 © 1988. All rights reserved.

Even these may forget,
yet I will not forget you."
— Isaiah 49:15

The Gospels give a clear message that family ties are not ultimate: "Whoever loves father or mother more than me is not worthy of me [Matt. 10:37]." The directives to leave one's relatives, to repent idolizing family ties, challenge some present-day efforts to subsume the family under the divine sphere.

If parent symbols for God point to a reality that both reflects and transcends our knowledge of our human parents, we cannot comprehend the transcendence, but we can notice where the symbol participates in our experience and know that it points beyond all that we can fathom.

With these cautions against identifying the symbol with the Reality, let us look at what we might expect of religion that finds "God the Father" and "God the Mother" important ways to speak of the Deity.

To begin with, we would expect to find God the Father separate from creation, "high and lifted up." It does not surprise us that "an immanent mother-god is replaced by a transcendent Yahweh, standing above human experience, not to be identified with any human attribute, a distant patriarch overseeing all."[6] Here is a God of initiative, who promulgates the word, the law, from on high. God the Father does not contain disparate realities but creates by separating the light from the darkness. Symbols of chaos like the sea and its monsters are firmly under the control of the Deity, and divine will interrupts the rhythms of life at its pleasure. Distance from the earth includes distance from the fleshly creative powers of the female. The sons of this patriarchal faith redeem us from our ancient dependence — in early days by destroying the adherents and the symbols of feminine religion and in modern times by dismissing it in two words: "fertility cult." This transcendent Father is free and he gives *us* freedom.

Paradoxically, paternal religion is both personal and abstract. God the Father remains Other; mortals may hope for communion, not union, with God. Sky imagery hints at limitless possibilities. A focus on immortality, victory over death, and the eternal Name do not surprise us as we lift our eyes from human fathers to a heavenly Father. A high value for right thinking and following the rules leads inevitably to ethical monotheism, that crown of paternal religion, with its strong call to justice and right-eousness, its demand for responsible action in the affairs of the world. Though this is a religion of the dominants, concern is expressed for fair treatment of the lowly.

"Be perfect, therefore, as your heavenly Father is perfect [Matt. 5:48]." This lofty expectation inevitably arouses in us a fearful concern: can we ever measure up? Will this judgment find us utterly inadequate? "You are my Son the Beloved; with you I am well pleased [Luke 3:22]." Here is the divine answer to an anxiety so profound that it can be addressed only by a voice from heaven blessing the firstborn of all sons. Are we able to receive this divine yes? Popular father religion rarely hears it. Some of the more sophisticated sons of the patriarchy pay lip service to the yes but hold sin and guilt in the center of their theology.

We know the religion of God the Father well. It has been the dominant theme in the faith of our fathers for centuries, and we are the grateful inheritors of its transcendent themes of jus-tice, liberation, and personhood. But this simple linear sketch is not all we know of our faith. Jesus called his Father by the in-timate name Abba. The presence of a comma between "Father" and "Almighty" in the Nicene Creed points to the paradoxical picture of God as both Almighty and Abba.[7]

The aspects of God that are missing from the linear sketch above emerge most clearly in the theme of God the Mother. This theme is muted but inescapably present through the rich tapestry of the Judeo-Christian tradition. There are motherly images of compassion ("womb-love," from its Hebrew root) like those in Hosea:

> "Yet it was I who taught Ephraim to walk,
>   I took them up in my arms;...
> I led them with cords of human kindness,
>   with bands of love.
> I was to them like those
>   who lift infants to their cheeks.
> I bent down to them and fed them."
> — Hosea 11:3–4

There is the feminine figure of Divine Wisdom, who "has built her house,... has also set her table," and extends

the invitation, "Come, eat of my bread [Prov. 9:1, 2, 5]."
The medieval mystics, many of them women, revived feminine
themes such as Jesus as mother. "God hugs you," said Hildegard of Bingen. "You are encircled by the arms of the mystery
of God."[8]

If we want to see what this minor maternal theme might
look like pulled out from under paternal dominance, we can take
a look at the two thousand years of Mother-Daughter rites that
preceded the two thousand years of Father-Son rites just past.[9]
Some Mother images will emerge from hiding if we look back
to the time "When God Was a Woman," to use Merlin Stone's
words, which point to a full-fledged feminine religion with dimensions that far transcend the tag "fertility cult." One of the
hymns to the Sumerian Goddess Inanna, known as Ishtar to
the Semites, praises her feminine attributes, singing of "night,
animals, gardens, reeds, food, rest, lovemaking." Another hymn
sings of the masculine attributes of the Goddess: "dawn, judgment, thought, action, abstraction."[10]

The picture of God the Mother that emerges from these
diverse sources displays many common themes that are familiar
to us from our experience of human motherhood.

Unconditional Love

Phyllis Trible has pointed out literary structures of womb-
like encircling in the Hebrew scriptures. Jesus yearned to gather
the children of Jerusalem "as a hen gathers her brood under her
wings [Luke 13:34]." Just as distance provides a vantage point
for judgment, maternal closeness naturally expresses itself in love
without reservations. We need to live in the tension between
those two realities. We need unconditional love before conditional love, in our human and religious beginnings. In church
this means that we have to be lovingly drawn in, accepted without reservation, and nourished, before we are ready to receive
judgment or be sent out with power. The lack of balance from
which we suffer can be revealed by questioning half a dozen average pew sitters: the persistence of the idea that you must earn
your salvation will be quickly demonstrated, to the despair of
preachers who have been trying to straighten them out on this
matter for years.

The Goodness of Creation

"And it was very good," but somehow it didn't seem to stay that way for more than about an hour. The stories about creation in the Hebrew scriptures were turned into stories about the fall in Christian theology. Either/or, linear thinking leads to this cancellation of "original blessing" (to use Matthew Fox's words). It might be more useful to see the creation and fall myths as having a paradoxical rather than a sequential relationship.

Religion that emphasizes our sinfulness seems to be based on an assumption that we think we're fine and the main thing we need is to be let in on the truth that we're not. That isn't the central reality of my experience or the experience of many others as I hear it. If I have received enough "mother love" to know I'm loved, even delighted in, then I can more fruitfully examine the ways I'm not all right. Problems are not the only place of openness to the divine: our lives point beyond themselves at least as much in what we are given as in what we cry out for.

What's in it for us to put sin in the center? A focus on sin, paradoxically, offers a way to look at the world as potentially under our control. It may also be a way for the institutional church to encourage people to regard themselves as under *its* control. It doesn't surprise me to hear many women looking to creation theology for the recovery of a lost balance.

Embracing the Physical and Sexual Realities of Life

We worship a God to whom the psalmist said, "you kept me safe on my mother's breast [Ps. 22:9]." Jesus' motherly activities of feeding and washing flow on in the care of mother church, and in the Middle Ages suckling imagery was commonly used to speak about sacramental feeding — not surprisingly, since nursing and the eucharist are the only experiences we know in which we are fed by the body of another. It should not surprise us that the self-emptying One may be truly imaged in the self-emptying mother.

In the non-Christian maternal religions, where the Goddess was patroness of sexual pleasure, sculptors of religious art exulted in breasts and fertile bellies, and the lingam (a combined phallus and vulva) could be venerated as a holy symbol. The patriarchs put down "fertility cults." They identified feminine religion with sexuality and rejected it, sometimes violently. The tendency toward male, split-off sexuality was projected on a cosmic screen. And so we bewail the loss of the sacredness of sexuality, but we will not allow the foundation for it. We have instead celibate males propounding rules that are regarded as irrelevant by noncelibates. But Roman Catholics certainly have no copyright on the church's inability to deal with human sexuality in more helpful ways than the giving of rules and the nervously averted gaze.

A Love for Mother Earth

Feminine religion attends to the cyclical processes of life — not only those on the calendar, but birth and death, death and rebirth, winter and spring in the soul. To the transcendence and infinite possibilities of sky imagery might be added the concreteness of earth imagery with its implied acceptance of our creatureliness. We came from the earth and we will finally return to it. Nature, with its amoral creative and destructive powers, gives the message that we are not ultimately in charge, a message that balances the control promised by a view of life as history, the arena of the works of men. The patriarchal reaction against "nature religion" puts its earthly realities out of consciousness and devalues them, with the result that Mother Nature is ignored and exploited. Christianity has lost the ground for wise caring for our fragile earth with its intricate, hidden, nonlinear systems.

Including the Darkness

God as Mother is mystery that embraces life and death, as Goddess religions dramatized in their liturgies. Medieval mystics had their own way of including the awe-inspiring darkness. Acknowledging the darkness affirms that God is mystery and also that we are surrounded by divine care even in our not-knowing and in the dyings that punctuate our lives. Thus God as Mother holds accessibility and mystery together in the paradox sensed by Dylan Thomas' Welsh child, who "said some words to the close and holy darkness," and so nestled down to end his day.

I believe that women were spiritual leaders in ancient times because they had a vision of life's wholeness. The vision of wholeness means accepting death, rather than denying it. It means a willingness to venture beyond rationality toward an appreciation of mystery, of the numinous. Like Job's friends, many of us are unable to come out from behind our formulas and open ourselves to what looks like the meaningless chaos of existence.

It is probably easier for us to accept an angry and incomprehensible Father than such a Mother: if Father is angry and punishes us, he probably has a good reason. We can handle the image of a powerful Father with a fair degree of comfort. But an angry and punishing Mother flips us back to a prerational era of total dependence. We despair of domesticating the nursery goddess. God the Mother is too powerful. We turn instead to Father, who is, paradoxically, safer.

Perhaps we may be inspired to a less fainthearted faith by the mystics, who were willing to walk into that darkness.

God as Mother and Father: Pain and Promise

What, then, is the cost and what are the promises in a more balanced picture of our holy Parent? Surely the cost lies in the pain of exploring our resistance to maternal themes with courage and candor, renouncing the violence that has led to Canaanite-bashing and witch-burning in past years, to clawing and biting women priests' hands in more recent ones.[11] In less hostile guise I have seen the resistance in a liturgy task force in my own parish, a group charged with planning a sermon on God as Mother. "My mother wasn't unconditional love; she rejected me," said one man, with feeling. It was a deep and painful discussion, but beyond the hunger and the disappointment may lie religious power we are often too timid to approach. I have experienced the resistance in myself. I read an article that suggested using feminine names and pronouns for God for a month. "Good exercise," I thought, until I found myself in tears and thought the experiment might wait till sometime when I felt stronger.

The cost is the requirement that we venture out of safe territory. (I am reminded of the children in *The Lion, the Witch, and the Wardrobe* asking Mr. and Mrs. Beaver whether Aslan, the Christ figure, was quite safe. "Of course he's not safe," they replied indignantly. "But he's good.")

Some "costs" are imaginary, as I see it. There is no requirement that we enshrine Mother images and reject Father images. That kind of either/or thinking is not native to the feminine mindset. Mothers know how to contain elements whose fit defies logic.

We have touched on some of the promises: images that encourage acceptance for people who are too hard on themselves; a functional way to counter that chronic heresy that brings most people to the Bible asking "Tell me what to do"; a theological foundation that supports more helpful attitudes toward human sexuality and loving preservation of the earth.

But I see still more promises, for women and for men. A faith that balances masculine and feminine realities will be a blessing. Women will be much more helpfully ministered to by a church that does not distrust and exclude women's reality but celebrates their life-giving powers. There is also promise of healing for men who are tired of carrying the white man's burden, whose overfunctioning causes them to suffer from workaholism, stress-related symptoms, and a certain dried-up quality. With the rich perspectives that are illuminated when our realities as women and men are revealed and allowed to encounter one another, we can all begin to see the truth about our lives emerging from the shadows. When the image of God in its male and female glory is allowed to shine more brightly, we may discover to our relief and joy that monotheism doesn't have to leave us with a single-parent human family.

CONCLUSIONS

13

Different Voices in a Listening Church

Ｗe have circled around the many-faceted reality of our male and female lives, probing the ambiguous shadows, appreciating the sparkles of energy, and catching glimpses of paradox in which hurtful contradictions are somehow overcome.

During our explorations of the often painful tensions within and between women and men, we have discovered hints of resolution shining through the picture of Jesus in the Gospels, a picture of what "male and female in the image of God" looks like in a particular lived experience. Here the contradictions that plague our daily lives as men and women have been resolved. Here is a picture that reaches beyond stereotypes to embrace all the richness of male and female. The opposition between love and work is overcome. The feminine themes of self-giving and nurturing and the masculine themes of resolve and quest no longer stand opposed. Here we find a picture of one who can choose freely either to stand apart or to move close to others. We always come upon Jesus in free encounters with others, never in forced accommodation to them. He often "made no answer [Luke 23:9]" when an answer was clearly expected. Yet he pointed to his Father by telling a story about a Middle Eastern gentleman who would throw aside all his dignity, hike up the skirts of his robes, and *run* down the street to hug and kiss a rebellious and disrespectful son.

Following a sorting-out period in the wilderness, this paradoxical leader came home to tell his people what his ministry was to be about. For his first sermon in Nazareth, Jesus chose a text that announced two purposes: "to proclaim ... recovery of sight to the blind, [and] to let the oppressed go free [Luke 4:18]." "Then he began to say to them, 'Today this scripture has been fulfilled in your hearing' [Luke 4:21]."

We too are invited to participate in the resolution of contradictions, in the promised recovery of sight and release from oppression. What does it mean to live as women and men whose eyes have been opened and whose lives have been liberated? How might these promises shape the lives of our religious communities? What challenges might we encounter as we run to meet those promises? And what gifts can we offer each other along the way? To those final questions we now turn.

Challenges for Women

We are now ready to write the first chapter of a new story about women and men in our communities of faith. In recent decades we have been working our way through the preface: the struggles to include women in church leadership and to find words that acknowledge the presence of both women and men in our churches. Now that we have significant numbers of female leaders and some language that includes all of us, we can begin! The recent past is prologue. We now discover that we can explore the *experience* of women and men in the light of a tradition whose treasures appear ever more abundant as we bring them into conversation with our lives as men and women. This new story holds both challenge and promise.

We now find women in a bewildering variety of places. Some women find nothing amiss in the sexual arrangements with which Western culture presents them. Some are content with the informal kinds of power women have always had. Some are awakening. Some are enraged. Some, grateful for a newly granted place in previously all-male institutions, are fearful of jeopardizing it.

Some are honing their skills as agents of change. And of course others find themselves in in-between places or moving back and forth from one posture to another. There is no generalizing about "where women are today." But many observers discern a typical sequence of stages, each carrying its own challenge.[1]

Awakening

Change always begins at the moment when those who find themselves out of joint with things-as-they-are begin to notice and name the disjuncture between what is and what they yearn for. Until women raise their voices to claim their perceptions and proclaim their hopes, no change can take place. When a woman opens her eyes and discovers that she is oppressed, her first response is often embarrassment. Carol Tavris observes, "It can be intolerable, this embarrassment; so a common resolution at this stage is to conclude that the new information is wrong and your old ways are right."[2] In its militant form this posture is represented by the women who go on the road to give speeches about why women should stay home.

But many a woman who is waking up finds she must begin to experiment with some uncomfortable behaviors, says Carol Pierce, such as saying no sometimes and not *always* being helpful.[3] She may contemplate the possibility of claiming some new kinds of power and deciding what she wants that power to be like. And she may begin to look beyond her familiar private world to the challenges of the public arena.

Anger

In order to move out of the posture of passive servitude into the posture of freely chosen servanthood pictured in the Gospels, a woman usually needs to journey through a transitional stage in which she claims a new autonomy. When she begins to question her chronic assumption that "it's my fault" and to contemplate the possibility that the fault lies elsewhere, anger wells up within her. When she encounters others who reassure her that she's not crazy, she feels stronger, more hopeful, and often angrier.[4] Her anger sparks sources of energy she didn't know she had. This energizing anger is an important part of the awakening woman's experience. She needs to move fully into her anger so that she can receive its gifts and move *through* it.

If she builds a permanent shrine for her rage, she will become stuck in it. But she will probably have to cycle back through it periodically. For me, the return to rage has often been triggered by the very thought of my denomination's all-male (until very recently) House of Bishops. "After all," I think, "they're just a bunch of guys my age." While I don't believe the episcopal job description would fit my particular talents, I have been infuriated by the idea of belonging to a denomination that denies me that job on the basis of my sex, and I have found myself muttering, "Let them have their church." In the midst of my fuming, I know I have to acknowledge my anger so that I can move through and beyond it again. "But it *isn't* their church! They *say* it's everybody's church!"

Empowerment

Then I may find that the energy generated by my anger moves me past impotent muttering to purposeful planned action. I'll need to look for encouragement to claim my piece of the agenda for change and persevere when progress pokes along at a snail's pace. I need to remind myself that if it were easy, it wouldn't need doing. In all of this, I need help and support from others, women and men too. And I need to discern what kind of support will be most useful. As one woman worked her way through the agonizing discovery that her growth led her to challenge the beloved Southern Baptist church that had nurtured her since childhood, she said, "My needs are for affirmation and clarity, and the strength and courage to continue growing 'where I would rather not go.'"

Becoming a skillful agent for change means living in the tension between my passionate convictions and my desire to communicate effectively with the other. It means making my case in loving ways. It means resisting the lure of revenge. It means acknowledging that a man's way may appropriately differ from mine. If I don't want a man to treat me as though I had no distinctive experience, then I have to respect his otherness, resisting my impulses to say "Catch up with me" or "Do it my way." Otherwise I merely perpetuate the dominant/subordinate arrangement I claim I'm attempting to change. If I am engaged in a loving revolution, I must work for change in caring ways, responding empathetically to men who are anxious about loosening their grip on ancient power. As one who claims to want to embrace the whole web of relationships, I must not set myself over against the other but stay in the tension of loving *in spite of*. I need to pray for the recovering sexists who still make my life miserable. At the same time, I need to know that loving does not mean being only soft. The gift of "recovery of sight" lays upon me the responsibility of keeping my eyes open. The promise of release from oppression requires my active partnership in its overthrow. And to engage effectively in a loving revolution, I need skills. I need to learn that "change, over the long haul, requires organization, patience, good humor, and the ability to negotiate and compromise."[5] What a demanding task: to claim and proclaim my own reality, to meet the other in loving respect, and to develop the skills for exercising flexible strength.

Challenges for Men

Because the challenges facing men often arise in *response* to changes initiated by women, the transitions display less inner logic. (Here, as so often, the expected patterns are turned upside down.) Men, themselves in a variety of places, are required to respond simultaneously to the initiatives of women who are spread across the whole spectrum of awakening, rage, empowerment, and all the in-between places. Often, however, a man first hears the challenge from a woman who is important to him. He cares about her, her awakening stirs him, and he begins to understand and respond to her differently. Once he has accepted the need for change she has presented, his gift for generalizing may lead him to conclude that the personal *is* the political and thus to move this challenge out into the public sphere.

As he negotiates this shift in his own attitudes, challenges from all around him will continue. He may feel that these women are no longer giving him a boost; instead they compete with him and press him with new and conflicting expectations. The new energy in women is matched by a new depression among many men. The man who said, "I've had to let go of a world I assumed was my oyster" was experiencing grief, tinged with nostalgia and depression. Such a man must find a way to respond to the difficulty of these challenges with respect but not despair.

The challenge born out of his response to a woman's awakening leads a man not only outward to the public and political but inward toward the private and personal. He finds that the struggle to understand a woman is really a struggle to understand himself.[6] He is no longer content to relinquish to her the sole custody of his emotional life. He wants to own again the tasks of moving outward to forge bonds with other people and moving inward toward his own spiritual depths.[7] A support group of like-minded men may help him meet his newly perceived need to reflect and relate, which contrasts with her need for autonomy and action.

As he becomes friendlier with many dimensions of his own being that were heretofore delegated to women, he will find himself much better able to encounter women openly and honestly. He will discover within himself what Robert Bly calls "an energy that can face this energy in women, and *meet* it." As he reacquaints himself with the feminine hitherto hidden in his inner shadows, he is less often assailed by "bad moods and undermining seductions"[8] and readier to engage with real women out there in the world around him. Instead of dismissing women out of hand, avoiding them, withholding eye contact, or going limp, he will engage them in vigorous discussions, give them straight feedback, tell them when he is angry, and resolve problems with them collaboratively. Inching his way out of isolation, he will dare to be intimate.

Promises Not Only for Women But for Men, as Well

Wide-awake women have been clear about the promise at the end of the challenges of change. They are alive with the energy and excitement of new opportunities to offer what they have to give and to take on responsibilities previously denied them. They see the promise in claiming their full selfhood. Like Sarah in chapter 7, they are eager to "put it all together," to forge some congruity between their hearts and their worlds, the values of home and workplace, the private and public spheres.

Men have been less certain whether any promises await them at the end of this long hard road of change, with its uncertain signposts, and the losses, conflict, and grief they encounter on the way. But many are catching glimpses of at least five possible promises.

Relief from Loneliness

Still today "It is not good that the man should be alone." His loneliness cannot be relieved by inferior creatures but only by an equal companion. Many men are saying that loneliness hurts, that they are hungry for intimacy with one another, with women, and with God. Such men may be wooed toward a deeper intimacy with a God whom they can glimpse through feminine as well as masculine metaphors.

Relief from the Burden of Strength

I hear men saying that they are tired of the constant struggle of having always to be strong, to hold on to the "one up" position. They are tired of living in the wearying and humiliating split between public overfunctioning and private infantilization. Many long for an alternative to the ceaseless struggle to meet unrealistic expectations. As fathers and mothers begin to have more equal dreams for their sons and daughters, the heavy hopes heaped on sons may be lightened, to everybody's advantage. And when women and men share the world's burdensome tasks as interdependent partners, both may find some relief from personal isolation and inequitable demands.

Relief from Resentment and Guilt

When women are no longer assigned the posture of purity (a handy position for retaliatory hand slapping), while men are made out to be the bad guys, men can experience release from an understandable resentment. And men will find their consciences lightened when they no longer have to feel guilty just for being men, when they no longer squirm under the uneasy awareness of oppression perpetrated on women by a male-dominated society.

A Resurgence of Lost Masculine Vitality

Men's energy ebbs when they are discouraged from claiming their whole humanity. They are tempted to ignore their physical, emotional, and spiritual life in favor of a focus on intellect, power, and productivity. Their feminine side gathers dust on a shelf. Their narrowly defined sexuality does not vitalize their whole lives. As men rediscover, reclaim, and reintegrate these lost parts of themselves, they feel energized. Instead of *losing* a clear sense of maleness, they find they are able to be more distinctly masculine as they relinquish the requirement of being "generic" people.

A Religion That Brings Life More Wholeness

A man's re-ligion (that which binds back together the broken fragments of life) must by definition include all the dimensions of his life, not only a truncated "masculine" selection. His openness to *otherness* points to the Holy Other, to mystery, which is the primary characteristic of religious life. "All hiding places reveal God," said Meister Eckehart,[9] and a man's spiritual journey must wind through his own hiding places. There he may find that his ancient longings and loneliness can be met by a more whole God, including aspects we think of as "feminine," who may "mother" him in a way he can now accept and welcome.

Of course much of the promise of receiving this more whole image is not specific to women or men but is offered to the whole human community. There is promise for the *relationships* between men and women. The diffused sexuality that adds sparkle to collaborative tasks not only blesses men but delights the hearts of women. We can arrive at a place where our fascination with the other is based a little less on projection and a little more on the gifts this particular other brings to our love and work. Our interactions will be transformed when we are able to move past disdain and retaliation. And in the long run everybody will profit when our institutions make room for more winners.

The promise extends beyond the relationships of women and men to the most serious issues facing humankind. Pressing beyond the winner-loser dichotomies that end by making losers of us all may give us new hope for not only personal but global relationships in this nuclear age. We also blow on that little flame of hope when we balance the individualism that has been pushed off the high end of the scale in Western hypermasculinized society with a rediscovery of our membership in one another. A revived appreciation for the physical world not only in us but around us, for the intricate interweaving of all the world's living systems, will kindle new hope for the healing of our environment whose wounds are daily discovered. The relationships between women and men that have been dismissed as a "women's issue" are not only a "people's issue" but a "planet issue."

Employing Our Gifts for One Another

When we see the image of God as both male and female, we acknowledge both richness and finitude, an appreciation for the fullness of God's gift of creation along with the recognition that none of us can take our own partial truth and make it ultimate. Knowing I have a Creator can free me to accept my creaturely condition; acknowledging my creatureliness includes accepting the limits, the incompleteness, of being male or female. Membership in one body with many members gives me permission not to claim to have, not even to strive to have, every gift. My modest quota is an acceptable contribution to the total enterprise. We can all offer one another both our gifts and their incompleteness. Then I become a little freer to accept the differences among people as contributions toward my wholeness and toward the wholeness of our community. Appreciation for the offerings of those who are different from me is the other side of my recognition that my own offerings are limited.

For example, we need a new balance that includes feminine attention to integration within us and between us. Yet we must also value the more masculine gift of discrimination, without which integration would be devoid of meaning, content, and life-giving tension. When men assume their way is *the* way, they make themselves all-sufficient (and lonely), they deprive themselves of women's strengths, and they diminish the wholeness of reality. Women who look to men as their models withhold their own unique contributions, to the detriment of all. The counterclaim that "the feminine is the way" misses the mark, too, for women have been deprived, and deprive themselves, of power, intentionality, and the willingness to take risks and undertake quests. So women need what men do well, too. Thus through our diversity in unity not only are we offered the gift of richly fulfilling relationships; the paradoxical and purposeful picture of Jesus invites us to high callings that, in their turn, become the medium of our transformation.

Gifts for the Church from Women

"Like good stewards of the manifold grace of God, serve one another with whatever gift each of you has received [1 Pet. 4:10]."

What gifts might women employ for their male colleagues and for the whole church? I see some important offerings: serving as caring agents of change, proclaiming a vision of wholeness and connectedness, supporting men in owning their vulnerability, and avoiding kinds of "helpfulness" that really don't help.

Caring Agents of Change

Women today cannot avoid the prophetic task. Unless women steadily take initiative, there will be no change. While many kinds of witness against sexism are needed, I believe more of us need to recognize that an effort to communicate *effectively* is not a symptom of wobbly convictions. Preaching to the converted and scolding the unconverted do not add up to an effective strategy of change. I have not found that slapping men's hands improves their hearing. A posture of revenge is neither effective nor faithful. When we encounter oppression, we need to learn how to "love our enemies," help them "know what they do," and be ready to forgive them. As one woman put it, "I hope I can discover compassionate ways of helping the church broaden its focus."

Offering a Vision of Wholeness and Connectedness

For too long men have delegated to women the tending of the "connective tissue" in individual and group relationships. Male-dominated Western culture has devalued and even feared the human ties without which none of us could survive. The women's group to which I belong has been struck by how hard a similar men's group has to work at the tasks of connection. "They don't seem to notice which members of their group are in church and which are missing," said Charlotte. Said Peter of the men's class he taught, "The basic issue was, 'Are we going to dare to be intimate with one another in this class?'" I believe the church will be transformed by women's full presence in our time. It will partake of women's concern for wholeness and integration, their appreciation for the many-splendored variety in creation. And it will be more fully a body, with all the parts related functionally rather than hierarchically.

Acknowledging Vulnerability and the Need for Support

Women have something to offer men who feel they always have to "tough it out" and deny the need for help and support. One director of Christian education was pleased that she could share some of her male clergy colleague's burdens. As she saw it, "His marriage was strengthened because he didn't have to take all that parish stuff home. He could deal with it at work." Another pastor, the only woman in a group of thirty local clergy, asked for advice on premarital counseling. The men, who also wanted help in this area of their ministry, were thereby given permission to admit that need, and the clergy group decided to sponsor a two-day workshop on preparing couples for marriage. In one church, where clergy and laity gathered for the procession on the morning of the bishop's visit, one woman said, "I'm nervous." The men then acknowledged they were nervous, too. Women can encourage men to acknowledge their vulnerability and need for support.

Avoiding Giving Unhelpful "Help"

Women sometimes have far too many ideas about how to help men. As Carol Pierce has emphasized, maternalism only perpetuates the old symbiotic relationship, which prevents both women and men from fully exercising their strengths. Pierce also cautions women against assuming that a man's journey toward wholeness is like a woman's. While women may need to try out some of the plans they ponder in their hearts, men may need to become more inward and reflective about their lives.[10] Healthy energy for initiating change has sometimes been derailed into female chauvinism or moral one-upwomanship. I listened to one woman talking at length about men's need to "catch up" to where women are today, and inwardly approved her male colleague's response: "Not catch up, but respond, rather." A bid for authority based on sole proprietorship of truth others lack is not congruent with the most helpful feminine gifts in ministry.

Gifts for the Church from Men

Men also have gifts to offer the church and women, gifts such as room for self-definition, room to grow, and courage to take risks.

Room to Become

Perhaps the most needed gift men can give women is respectful and attentive space that encourages women to define themselves. Having been defined by men for so long, women badly need opportunities to differentiate themselves, to name their own realities and be heard, to develop their own styles of leadership, without being ignored or simply told they are mistaken. This space will include "the freedom to screw up," in Edwin H. Friedman's terms. When their autonomy is thus acknowledged, women may ask for advice on taking risks and appropriate confrontation. I notice that our women's group, which is so quick to notice our brothers' difficulty in keeping track of one another, is slow to admit our own reluctance to speak the truth to one another when we sense candor may cause conflict. If we asked the men's group, I imagine they could offer some coaching in "standing apart." If we were convinced of their respect, we might well be willing to ask for such help.

Self-Differentiation

Men may be enabled to offer women space to grow because men have had more practice in differentiating themselves. Men can offer lessons in speaking in one's own voice. They may model for women a more thoughtful discrimination between tasks for which they themselves must take responsibility and tasks that belong to others, providing a consequent clarity about delegating parts of the work to other people. Women can learn from men to avoid becoming inappropriately enmeshed in areas of responsibility that belong to others.

Agency and Risk

Men's skills in self-differentiation can also help them assist female colleagues who are working to increase their own sense of agency, their courage to take risks, and their ability to initiate strategies for change in the public sphere.

Are there yet other ways men might be helpful to women? Here are some suggestions from a wise woman and a wise man:

Carol Pierce says: "New behaviors are called for, but what are they? Some effective ones are:...letting a woman make her own mistakes, responding to her ideas, controlling one's desire to always have the last word, separating oneself from men telling stories at women's expense, and supporting a woman in taking initiative for herself."[11]

The mentor role is one in which men may offer women room to become and model self-differentiation and risk taking. Daniel Levinson describes how men might helpfully act as mentors to women:

> Fuller integration of the Masculine/Feminine polarity enables a man to mentor younger women with less hurtful intrusion of his masculine values and sexual needs. He can appreciate a woman's feminine qualities without having to deny or exploit them. As he seeks to develop his own feminine side, he can learn from her and have a more equal relationship. He is freer to enjoy the erotic aspects of their relationship without having to be directly sexual.[12]

The Challenge and Promise for the Church

The Celtic cross with its juxtaposition of embracing and thrusting movements might be a particularly appropriate symbol for the church today, as it strives for new faithfulness to the whole picture of human life that we glimpse in the Gospels and holds before our religious communities the vision we seek to enflesh in our lives — a vision in which those who have been divided become one again, in which we find a new inner wholeness, and in which we know ourselves sustained by the Holy now more wholly envisioned.

The listening church hears the voices of both women and men. Rather than assuming that male reality is generic human reality, and leaving female reality hidden, the listening church hears, welcomes, and is shaped by the daily lives of all its people.

A church that can help the world's men and women move through difficult challenges toward a new time of promise will be marked by an open stance that has many dimensions. Such a church will be open to the world around it — not encapsulated within its own walls, its agenda circumscribed by parochial preoccupations. This listening church will be intentional about gathering women and men from their homely and holy daily tasks in households, workplaces, and communities, and from all the struggles and anxieties those tasks evoke, to a gathered community where they may renew their dependence on the dependable, reflect on the meaning of daily life, and receive courage to move back into their daily ministries with renewed confidence and clarity about their callings. In order to engage in this complex task, a congregation must have a posture of attentive and respectful listening to the world it exists to serve.

Such a church will listen to the experience of its people. If the congregation is to perform its religious task of noticing the connections between experience and religious symbols, it will have to welcome everyday experience into full partnership in the dialogue. When religious tradition always initiates the conversation, the "application" too easily becomes a "therefore" handed down by the expert — often moralistic, sometimes even scolding — that contradicts grace, freedom, and the laity's ownership of their own ministries. Instead, take for example Steve Brown's description of how he went about raising consciousness of ecological issues in his congregation. He did not fall into the temptation of "laying it on" from the pulpit, telling people what issues they should be concerned about; he began by listening for the ecological issue that was on the minds of *these* people. Rather than trying to fire up a Kansas congregation about the problem of medical waste on East Coast beaches or preaching about aquifers in New Jersey, Brown listened to parishioners' stories to find out what local environmental issues were already on their minds. By starting with local awareness of specific problems, he found he could nourish a concern that took root in the congregation.[13]

The listening church therefore opens out ministry to the whole congregation, encouraging the growth of a community of ministering people alive with the energy that builds from equality to intimacy to empowerment. My consciousness of shared ministry in our congregation was heightened recently by a nineteenth-century-style service that marked our centennial celebration. Instead of following St. Mark's usual worship-in-the-round style, the chairs were lined up in rows facing the high altar, so that we all looked past the backs of other people's necks toward the clergy. Only male clergy appeared in the chancel, and lay participation was limited to hymn singing. If our usual lay worship task force had planned the service, I could detect no sign of their work. The rector stood at the top of steps, which made him look very tall, while our kneeling posture made us very small. The anachronism was enlightening: I found it difficult to believe that only twenty years ago I would have accepted without question all those signals that ministry is performed *by* clergymen *for* laity.

Not only is the ministry of the listening church owned by the whole congregation, it hears voices of truth from many traditions, moving beyond the denominational divisions in whose formative conflicts we have forgotten, to embrace the sparkling array of gifts reflected in the many fragments of broken Christendom.

The Church as a Laboratory for Living

A church that hears its people recount their experiences in the world from which they come on Sunday and to which they return on Monday morning can be a kind of laboratory for living, "a place where you get to practice what it means to be human."[14] "A place to practice" is a subsidiary place off-stage, where you can warm up for the arena where the *real* action is. A church that believes it is here to serve the world empties itself. Like its Lord, it adopts the posture of servant and friend, while pointing to the transcendent. And also like its Lord, it begins with the specific worldly situations of its people: the twentieth-century equivalents of problems with sheep farming, spring planting, or orchard management; dealing with rebellious adolescents, disgruntled or dishonest employees, or even misplaced household articles.

In this training lab next door to where the action is, we can stop and reflect on what happens when the rubber hits the road at work, in our families, and in our local and global communities. We can pause and ponder — *identifying* specific experiences, *analyzing* the issues, using our religious symbols to help us *generalize* so that our learnings can be carried back out to enhance our ministry in situations and encounters that are very different from those we first identified in our "training lab." The church is thus like a bridge that links sacred symbols and secular situations, private yearnings and public duties, the worlds of procreation and production. It is a place where men and women can back off and gain perspective on the real world at home and work, a little distance from the "bottom lines" we encounter there.

Let us look at some of the dimensions of our lives in which the church as laboratory for living may help us gain insight and transformative power.

Loving Relationships

First, the church as laboratory can assist us as we attempt to enhance our capacity for loving relationships. It does so by being a place where we experience ourselves as God's "very good" creatures, by leading us to more helpful views of human sexuality, and by providing a vantage point for new perspectives on family life.

Exhortations don't transform us into caring people. We need to know that we are loved before we have much love to offer. And so the church will teach its most effective lessons in love when it conveys through people's experiences in the weekly round of meetings and classes the message "You are my beloved sons and daughters in whom I am well pleased." Complementing divine Father imagery with Mother imagery may provide stronger theological grounding for proclaiming the unconditional message "You are profoundly loved — no matter what." A powerful lived message of unconditional love can help lay to rest the persistent heresy that we have to earn our worth by what we do. Men need this message to lighten the burden of demands for performance; women need it for reassurance that they are equally valuable in creation and that a grown-up definition of "being good" means actively claiming their created, beloved selfhood.

Through its sacraments, the church has more than words to tell us that we, as living bodies, are "very good." The more clearly we see that the things we do in church serve everyday life, the more we can broaden our perception of sacrament beyond Sunday ceremonies. Holy bread, wine, and water are tokens of a physical world infused with the Holy. We can live out this knowledge in congregational life by relinquishing total dependence on words in worship and education and entering into the full human mystery beneath the words. We can also live more fully out of an understanding of ourselves as good creatures, sacramentally enfleshed, as we find ways to erase that persistent heretical equation flesh = sex = sin and to see "the resurrection of the body" as more than a phrase in a creed.

The congregation as a laboratory for loving relationships will celebrate fully the goodness of human sexuality, countering both the culture's obsessive hypersexualizing and the church's habit of putting sex in the corner, shaking a finger at it, and then ignoring it. Extending its sexual repertoire beyond control, the church can dare to explore the rich connections between eros and spirit, to speak about the erotic dimension of our love affair with God, and to acknowledge and manage more skillfully the tensions and energies men and women discover as they collaborate in ministry. We can then welcome the extra sparkle of energy that sometimes brightens our work together.

As a laboratory for loving, the congregation can provide us with some reflective space away from the heavy emotional freight of domestic life where we can gain a little perspective on our passions and return to our families wiser and stronger. A wide variety of intimate relationships in the church can be helpful both to people struggling in the isolated and idolized marriages that are so difficult to maintain in Western society and to single people who need opportunities for mutual self-revelation and companionship in action. Both single and married people can gain perspective from the Gospels' message that nuclear families are not appropriate objects of our ultimate hopes and loyalties and can regain an appreciation for the common humanity they share.

Daily Work

Second, in the church as a laboratory for living, we can also back off and gain needed perspective on our daily work. In a safe place at a little distance from the "bottom line" of the marketplace, workers can critique the structures of society that distort our lives and return to those structures with a renewed vision of justice. (Here it is important to emphasize that it is the *laity* who are in a position to carry out such a critique, while the clergy stand ready to assist the process with the useful tools they bring — their knowledge of tradition and their theological, educational, and liturgical expertise.) Church gives us a place where we can sit back a little and take time to supplement the marketplace question "What have you produced?" with the ministry question "How are we living?"

The church that combines reflective distance with attentive listening to the lives of its people will appreciate the variety of work in which those parishioners are engaged, and it will acknowledge fully the daily ministries of its women and men carried out both in public workplaces and at home. Out of its tradition it can affirm the importance of the work of love, so often eclipsed by society's promotion of the love of work.

Such a congregation will monitor its round of activities with care not to compete with members' work but to provide it with respectful support. A rigorous inventory of congregational activities will reveal not only what new initiatives need to be undertaken but which old projects need to be "laid down."

Leadership

Third, as the church attends to the tasks of welcoming people in to reflect on love and work in everyday life and sending them back empowered for more faithful ministry, it has many opportunities to serve as a laboratory for leadership. As it draws people in, it helps the self-sufficient to acknowledge their dependence (especially when its leaders are clear and open about their own dependence); as the church sends people back out it helps the diffident, trusting in their own center grounded in God, to claim their power to make a difference.

The church has sometimes had trouble seeing its task as empowering its people. So often the church as an institution, finding itself with very little influence, has snatched at the few shreds of power within reach. But as it follows a Master who gave up power in order to give it away to his followers, the church can discover that this lowly path is both faithful and effective. When a difference of opinion arose in his church, Larry Burton found an effective way of leading: he discovered that "the pastor can lift up both positions and wonder aloud how both things can be true?" He found that "refusing to be the expert can be as powerful as actually offering one's expertise."[15] Rob Elder learned he had the same kind of power as a teacher. He reported that one man wrote in his evaluation of a class that "for him, the times that I, as leader, was silent, were as powerful as the times when I spoke. He felt that the mild anxiety of a moment of silence helped encourage the thinking process for participants."[16] Religious leaders who can wonder aloud and be silent for a moment give the rest of us opportunity and permission to notice the places where our lives are out of control, those places that are so often openings to the power of God. They let us pause at those boundary places to discover our own meanings. Religious leaders who are bent on empowering the people they serve can work wisely with women who are struggling to acknowledge, to claim, and to redefine their power in this time of transition — both those women who are endeavoring to take on formal leadership in church and world and those women who see their informal, derivative power fading in the face of other women's direct exercise of power. Leaders with an agenda of empowerment can also help liberate male clergy who have found themselves in a crazy place in the church — sidelined from society's male power base, scripted as generic leaders in a feminized institution, often unable either to welcome feminine power or to exercise masculine resolve. Church leaders who live in the tension between defining themselves and working to empower others will find their authority and effectiveness enhanced.

An Open Moment in the Church's Life

We live today in a time between the no-longer and the not-yet. There is much to affirm in the steadfastness of those who have held firmly to the truth they knew and in the struggles of those who seek to break through to the truth that awaits them in the future. We need now to find ways of meeting and hearing one another with both challenge and compassion, ways of joining our strengths in new kinds of partnership. As members of the body of Christ, we are called to carry on his work — offering recovery of sight and setting at liberty those who are oppressed. Recovery of sight includes looking at the realities of women's and men's lives honestly. Liberation for men and women includes moving past contempt and revenge, oppression and collusion in oppression, toward forgiveness for the ways we have hurt others and been hurt, and a new beginning.

As men and women find ways to look honestly within ourselves and to listen openly to the other, we will discover the transforming energy that is generated when two different realities are held together, when we find the courage to give up the simple solutions of avoidance and escape, splitting and attack, and instead explore the contradictions and then move through them.

Many middle-aged men arrive at a turning point when they reach toward the feminine from which they have separated themselves, and in that turning they discover that their waning vitality is rejuvenated by new sources of energy. Our middle-aged, androcentric, mainline churches have been losing energy, too. They are just now beginning to consider including fully the feminine realities and strengths that have been pushed aside for centuries. Like our middle-aged male friends, the church is about to discover that embracing its hidden and rejected strengths will yield new wholeness and new vitality. The rediscovery of the feminine in the church means more than equal opportunities for women and inclusive language. Those are just the preparatory steps. After we have some women on hand as leaders and some language to talk about our experience, the time of transformation can begin.

What will this more whole church that includes the feminine look like? We find hints in the divine gifts at which feminine images traditionally hint: "God's immanence, perceived glory, and approachability."[17] In the image of those gifts we can observe feminine warmth and intimacy, energy and sparkle, concern for the reunion of the separated. As we look around our churches we can notice women's appreciation of creatureliness, context, and concreteness embodied in practical service and accessible theology. We will no longer discount or be embarrassed by the feminine strengths that the church already exercises. As we learn to appreciate fully both masculine and feminine gifts, the church will become more fully and energetically itself. The embracing of the feminine will lead us, not away from the truth in our tradition but more deeply into it, as we overcome the heresies that persist because of the imbalance between our masculine and feminine strengths. The incarnation, the goodness of creation and the resurrection of the body, justification by grace, and our membership in one another — these will no longer be lines for lip service but dimensions of a theology that informs our lives. This is "but the beginning of the birthpangs [Mark 13:8]." As our church becomes more fully itself, more receptive, and alive with new energy, it will be reborn as a new church in a new age.

Notes

Chapter 1

1. This point has been made by both Anne Wilson Schaef, in *Women's Reality* (Minneapolis: Winston Press, 1981), and Elizabeth Dodson Gray, in *Patriarchy as a Conceptual Trap* (Wellesley, Mass.: Roundtable Press, 1982).

2. Phyllis Trible, *God and the Rhetoric of Sexuality* (Philadelphia: Fortress Press, 1980), to whom this discussion owes much.

3. Philip Turner, *Sex, Money, and Power: An Essay on Christian Ethics* (Cambridge, Mass.: Cowley Publications, 1985), 47.

4. Parker Palmer, *The Promise of Paradox* (Notre Dame, Ind.: Ave Maria Press, 1980), 46.

5. Trible, *God and the Rhetoric of Sexuality*, 107–08: "both . . . are depicted as naked and not ashamed. The one flesh of sexuality (2:24) is defenseless flesh. . . . the two sexes that happened through the differentiation of the earth creature live precariously in the world. Their lives are solely dependent upon God. . . . In holy insecurity they live without shame or fear."

Chapter 2

1. Mark Gerzon, *A Choice of Heroes: Changing Images of American Manhood* (Boston: Houghton Mifflin, 1984), 14.

2. George Vaillant, *Adaptation to Life: How the Best and the Brightest Came of Age* (Boston: Little, Brown & Co., 1977), 299.

3. Carol Gilligan, *In a Different Voice* (Cambridge, Mass.: Harvard University Press, 1982), 159.

4. Susan Litwin, *The Postponed Generation* (New York: Morrow, 1986), 216.

5. Rosemary Ruether, *Sexism and God-Talk* (Boston: Beacon Press, 1983), 112. Footnote: Jeannette McGlore in *The Behavioral and Brain Sciences* 3 (1980).

6. V. Mary Stewart, "Cognitive Style, North American Values, and the Body of Christ," *Journal of Psychology and Theology* 2 (1974): 82–83.

7. Edwina Hunter, "Weaving Life's Experiences into Women's Preachings," *Christian Century*, Sept.–Oct. 1987, 67.

8. Roy M. Oswald, Dona Tamorria, and Michael Tamorria, (Research on clergy couples for the Alban Institute, Washington, D.C.).

9. Barbara Gilbert, *Who Ministers to Ministers* (Washington, D.C.: Alban Institute, 1987), 24.

10. Laura Deming and Jack Stubbs, *Men Married to Ministers* (Washington, D.C.: Alban Institute, 1986).

11. "Diane's Story," *Action Information*, Mar.–Apr. 1988.

12. Irene Claremont de Castillejo, *Knowing Women* (New York: Harper Colophon, 1973), 101.

13. James E. Dittes, *The Male Predicament* (New York: Harper & Row Publishers, 1985), 82.

14. Colette Dowling, *The Cinderella Complex* (New York: Pocket Books, 1981), 164.

15. Carol Pierce, "Power Equity and Groups" (Paper for New Dynamics, Laconia, N.H., 1986), 70.

16. *Illuminations of Hildegard of Bingen*, ed. Matthew Fox (Santa Fe, N.M.: Bear & Co., 1985), 8.

17. Ibid., 41.

18. Quoted in *The Living Reminder* by Henri Nouwen (New York: Seabury Press, 1977), 42.

19. Phyllis Trible, *God and The Rhetoric of Sexuality* (Philadelphia: Fortress Press, 1980), 86.

20. Ibid., 102

21. Jean Baker Miller, *Toward a New Psychology of Women* (Boston: Beacon Press, 1976), 119.

Chapter 3

1. Roy Oswald and Otto Kroeger, *Personality Type and Religious Leadership* (Washington, D.C.: Alban Institute, 1987).

2. Otto Kroeger (Lecture for the Alban Institute, MBTI Training Session, Washington, D.C.).

3. Anne Wilson Schaef, *Women's Reality* (Minneapolis: Winston Press, 1981), 131–32.

4. Mark Gerzon, *A Choice of Heroes: Changing Images of American Manhood* (Boston: Houghton Mifflin, 1984), 256.

5. Ibid., 172.

6. George Vaillant, *Adaptation to Life: How the Best and the Brightest Came of Age* (Boston: Little, Brown & Co., 1977), 54.

7. Ibid., 178.

8. David Keirsey and Marilyn Bates, *Please Understand Me* (Del Mar, Calif.: Prometheus Nemesis Book Co., 1984), 20–21.

9. Robert A. Johnson, *He: Understanding Masculine Psychology* (New York: Harper & Row Publishers, 1974), 43.

10. Schaef, *Women's Reality*, 118.

11. Sam Keen, *The Passionate Life: Stages of Loving* (New York: Harper & Row Publishers, 1983), 91.

12. John A. Sanford, *The Invisible Partners* (New York: Paulist Press, 1980), 45.

13. Elisabeth Schüssler Fiorenza's term, in *In Memory of Her: A Feminist Theological Reconstruction of Christian Origins* (New York: Crossroad, 1985).

14. Matthew Fox, commenting on John 17 in *On Becoming a Musical, Mystical Bear* (New York: Paulist Press, 1976), 56.

15. Schüssler Fiorenza, *In Memory of Her*, 149.

16. Dorothée Soelle, *The Strength of the Weak* (Philadelphia: Westminster Press, 1984), 119.

Chapter 4

1. James B. Nelson, *Embodiment* (Minneapolis: Augsburg, 1978).

2. I am indebted to Ruth Tiffany Barnhouse for many insights gained through her lectures. Many of these insights appear in her book *Identity* (Philadelphia: Westminster Press, 1984).

3. Irene Claremont de Castillejo, *Knowing Women* (New York: Harper & Row Publishers, 1973), 107.

4. Penelope Washburn, *Becoming Woman: The Quest for Wholeness in Female Experience* (New York: Harper & Row Publishers, 1977), 23.

5. Ruth Tiffany Barnhouse (Lecture for "Ordained Women in Ministry" conference, Alban Institute, Washington, D.C., 1984. See her book *Identity*.)

6. Judith Viorst, *Necessary Losses* (New York: Fawcett Book Group, 1986), 53.

7. Dorothy Dinnerstein, *The Mermaid and the Minotaur* (New York: Harper & Row Publishers, 1977), 135.

8. Ibid., 156.

9. Jean Baker Miller, *Toward a New Psychology of Women* (Boston: Beacon Press, 1976), 22.

10. Matthew Fox, *Original Blessing* (Santa Fe, N.M.: Bear & Co., 1983), 295.

11. Robert Hughes, *The Fatal Shore* (New York: Alfred A. Knopf, 1987), 248, 250.

12. Quoted in *Original Blessing* by Fox, 61.

13. Marjory Zoet Bankson, *Braided Streams: Esther and a Woman's Way of Growing* (San Diego, Calif.: LuraMedia, 1985).

14. Alan Richardson, *A Theological Word Book of the Bible* (New York: Macmillan, 1953), 84.

15. Elisabeth Schüssler Fiorenza, *In Memory of Her: A Feminist Theological Reconstruction of Christian Origins* (New York: Crossroad, 1985), 143.

16. The New Oxford Annotated Bible, Revised Standard Version, ed. Herbert G. May and Bruce M. Metzger (New York: Oxford University Press, 1973).

17. James B. Nelson, *Between Two Gardens* (New York: Pilgrim Press, 1983), 4.

18. Carol P. Christ, *Diving Deep and Surfacing: Women Writers on Spiritual Quest* (Boston: Beacon Press, 1980), 51–52.

19. Susan Walker, ed., *Speaking of Silence: Christians and Buddhists on the Contemplative Way* (Mahwah, N.J.: Paulist Press, 1987), 276.

20. Lecture. See Edwin H. Friedman, *Generation to Generation: Family Systems in Church and Synagogue* (New York: Guilford Press, 1985).

Chapter 5

1. David McClelland, *Power: The Inner Experience* (New York: Irvington Publishers, 1985), 84.

2. Richard A. Johnson, *He: Understanding Masculine Psychology* (New York: Harper & Row Publishers, 1974), 24.

3. George Vaillant, *Adaptation to Life: How the Best and the Brightest Came of Age* (Boston: Little, Brown & Co., 1977), 53.

4. Jean Baker Miller, "Women and Power" (Paper for Wellesley College, Stone Center for Developmental Services and Studies, 1982), 7.

5. Mark Gerzon, *A Choice of Heroes: Changing Images of American Manhood* (Boston: Houghton Mifflin, 1984), 3.

6. Jean Baker Miller, *Toward a New Psychology of Women* (Boston: Beacon Press, 1976), 32–33.

7. Herb Goldberg, *The Hazards of Being Male* (New York: New American Library, 1976), 32–33.

8. Ibid., 42.

9. Gerzon, *A Choice of Heroes*, 20.

10. References in this section from Stanley Breeden, "The First Australians," *National Geographic*, Feb. 1988.

11. Gerzon, *A Choice of Heroes*, 23.

12. Jean Baker Miller, "The Development of Women's Sense of Self," (Paper for Wellesley College, Stone Center for Developmental Services and Studies, 1984), 8.

13. Ann Belford Ulanov, *Receiving Woman* (Philadelphia: Westminster Press, 1981), 163.

14. Miller, "Woman and Power," 6, 4.

15. Susan Brownmiller, *Femininity* (New York: Simon & Schuster, 1984), 236.

16. Ibid., 212.

17. Goldberg, *Hazards*, 150.

18. Miller, "Women and Power," 23.

19. Ibid., 2.

20. McClelland, *Power*.

21. Miller, "Women's Sense of Self."

22. Robert Bly, "On Being a Man," interview by Keith Thompson, *Dromenon* 1982.

23. Matthew Fox, *Original Blessing* (Santa Fe, N.M.: Bear & Co., 1983), 145.

24. Elisabeth Schüssler Fiorenza, *In Memory of Her: A Feminist Theological Reconstruction of Christian Origins* (New York: Crossroad, 1985), 143.

25. Clyde Reid, quoted in *Who Ministers to Ministers* by Barbara Gilbert (Washington, D.C.: Alban Institute, 1987), 38.

26. *Action Information* 6:3.

27. Laura Mol, "Birthing the Common People of God," *Books & Religion* 15:5.

28. Gilbert, *Who Ministers to Ministers*, 44.

29. I owe this term to my colleague Speed B. Leas.

Chapter 6

1. *The Random House Dictionary*, 1980.

2. Daniel Levinson's phrase.

3. Gen. 2:16: "You may freely eat of every tree of the garden; but of the tree of the knowledge of good and evil you shall not eat, for in the day that you eat of it you shall die."

4. Quoted in "What Is the Nature of God's Power" by Lesley M. Adams (Senior essay, Harvard Divinity School, 1985).

5. John Nicholson, reported in *Washington Post*, 6 January 1985.

6. *Daughters of Sarah*, Sept.–Oct. 1986, 30.

7. Ruth Tiffany Barnhouse, *Identity* (Philadelphia: Westminster Press, 1984), 61.

8. Colette Dowling, *The Cinderella Complex* (New York: Pocket Books, 1981), 8.

9. Susan Brownmiller, *Femininity* (New York: Simon & Schuster, 1984), 212.

10. Irene Claremont de Castillejo, *Knowing Women* (New York: Harper & Row Publishers, 1973), 119.

11. Karl Menninger in Ruth Tiffany Barnhouse and Urban T. Holmes, eds., *Male and Female: Christian Approaches to Sexuality* (New York: Seabury Press, 1976), 193.

12. Penelope Washburn, *Becoming Woman: The Quest for Wholeness in Female Experience* (New York: Harper & Row Publishers, 1977), 101.

13. Carol P. Christ, *Diving Deep and Surfacing: Women Writers on Spiritual Quest* (Boston: Beacon Press, 1980), 80.

14. Elisabeth Schüssler Fiorenza, *In Memory of Her: A Feminist Theological Reconstruction of Christian Origins* (New York: Crossroad, 1985), p. xiii.

15. Book of Common Prayer (New York: Seabury Press, 1976), 264.

16. Susan Maybeck, "Threads of the Total Fabric," in *American Women in Ministry* (Valley Forge, Pa.: Judson Press, 1986).

17. Hymn 258, *The Hymnal* (Greenwich, Conn.: Seabury Press, 1940).

18. From *Julian*, a play by J. Janda, closely based on the writings of Julian of Norwich (New York: Seabury Press, 1984).

19. See Bruce Reed, *The Task of the Church and the Role of Its Members* (Washington, D.C.: Alban Institute, 1975).

20. Verna Dozier's phrase.

21. Book of Common Prayer, 308.

Chapter 7

1. *Life*, Martin Luther King Jr. issue, Spring 1988.

2. Carol Gilligan, *In a Different Voice* (Cambridge, Mass.: Harvard University Press, 1982), 152.

3. Dorothy Dinnerstein, *The Mermaid and the Minotaur* (New York: Harper & Row Publishers, 1977), 24.

4. *Washington Post*, 3 May 1988.

5. JoanMarie Smith, *Religious Education*, Fall 1985, 638.

6. Rosemary Ruether, *Sexism and God-Talk* (Boston: Beacon Press, 1983), 219; Mark Gerzon, *A Choice of Heroes: Changing Images of American Manhood* (Boston: Houghton Mifflin, 1984), 132.

7. Gerzon, *A Choice of Heroes*, 133.

8. Nancy Van Scoyoc, *Women, Change, and the Church* (Nashville: Abingdon Press, 1980).

9. Dinnerstein, *Mermaid and Minotaur*, 20–21.

10. Jean Baker Miller, *Toward a New Psychology of Women* (Boston: Beacon Press, 1976), 124.

11. David C. McClelland, *Power: The Inner Experience* (New York: Irvington Publishers, 1985), 91.

12. Jean Baker Miller, "Women and Power" (Wellesley College, Stone Center for Developmental Services and Studies, 1982), 1.

13. Colette Dowling, *The Cinderella Complex* (New York: Pocket Books, 1981), 33.

14. Richard P. Olson, *Changing Male Roles in Today's World* (Valley Forge, Pa.: Judson Press, 1982), 99.

15. Miller, *Toward a New Psychology*, 44.

16. McClelland, *Power*.

17. James B. Nelson, *Between Two Gardens* (New York: Pilgrim Press, 1983), 41.

18. Anne Wilson Schaef, *Women's Reality* (Minneapolis: Winston Press, 1981), 81.

19. Quoted in *The Seasons of a Man's Life*, by Daniel Levinson et al. (New York: Ballantine Books, 1978), 92–93.

20. Compare Richard P. Olson, *Changing Male Roles in Today's World* (Valley Forge, Pa.: Judson Press, 1982), 12.

21. Levinson et al., *Seasons of a Man's Life*, 92.

22. Ibid., 91.

23. Gerzon, *A Choice of Heroes*, 207.

24. Donald M. Joy, "Toward a Symbolic Revival: Creation Revisited," *Religious Education* 80, no .3 (Summer 1985), 408.

25. Gerzon, *A Choice of Heroes*, 135ff.

26. NBC News, 15 July 1987.

27. Levinson et al., *Seasons of a Man's Life*, 155.

28. Nelson, *Between Two Gardens*, 44.

29. James E. Dittes, *The Male Predicament* (New York: Harper & Row Publishers, 1985), 70.

30. Levinson et al., *Seasons of a Man's Life*, 60.

31. McClelland, *Power*, 100–01.

32. Gerzon, *A Choice of Heroes*, 244–45.

33. Ibid., 254.

34. Ibid., 261.

35. Cf. Miller, *Toward a New Psychology*, 124.

36. Phyllis Trible, *God and the Rhetoric of Sexuality*. (Philadelphia: Fortress Press, 1980), 85.

37. Ibid., 65.

38. Ibid., 130.

39. Brother Lawrence, *The Practice of the Presence of God*, newly translated, with an Introduction by John J. Delaney (Old Tappan, N.J.: Fleming H. Revell Co., 1977), 23.

40. Book of Common Prayer (New York: Seabury Press, 1976), 100.

41. *Practice of the Presence of God*, 28.

42. Book of Common Prayer, 366.

43. Quoted in *Growth Through Meditation and Journal Writing* by Maria L. Santa-Maria (Mahwah, N.J.: Paulist Press, 1983), 8.

44. *Meditations with Mechthild of Magdeburg*, ed. Sue Woodruff (Santa Fe, N.M.: Bear & Co., 1982), 47.

45. Douglas V. Steere, ed., *Quaker Spirituality* (Mahwah, N.J.: Paulist Press, 1984), 131.

46. James E. Dittes, *When Work Goes Sour* (Philadelphia: Westminster Press, 1987), 8.

47. Steere, *Quaker Spirituality*, 199.

48. Book of Common Prayer, 99.

49. See Bruce Reed, *The Task of the Church and the Role of Its Members* (Washington, D.C.: Alban Institute, 1976).

50. Schaef, *Women's Reality*, 159.

51. Barbara Osborn, Shalem Institute for Spiritual Formation.

Chapter 8

1. Mark Gerzon, *A Choice of Heroes: Changing Images of American Manhood* (Boston: Houghton Mifflin, 1984), 158.

2. Carol Tavris, *Anger: The Misunderstood Emotion* (New York: Simon & Schuster, 1982), 241–42.

3. Jean Baker Miller, *Toward a New Psychology of Women* (Boston: Beacon Press, 1976), 74.

4. Jean Baker Miller, "Women and Power" (Wellesley College, Stone Center for Developmental Services and Studies, 1982), 3.

5. Gerzon, *A Choice of Heroes*, 188.

6. Ibid., 210–11.

7. Ibid., 195.

8. Edwin H. Friedman (Lecture for the Alban Institute, Washington, D.C., 1985).

9. Dorothée Sölle, *The Strength of the Weak* (Philadelphia: Westminster Press, 1984), 36.

10. Dorothy Dinnerstein, *The Mermaid and the Minotaur* (New York: Harper & Row Publishers, 1977), 82.

11. *Washington Post*, 30 November 1985.

12. Elisabeth Schüssler Fiorenza, *In Memory of Her: A Feminist Theological Reconstruction of Christian Origins* (New York: Crossroad, 1985), 176.

13. Rosemary Rader, *Breaking Boundaries: Male/Female Friendship in Christian Communities* (Mahwah, N.J.: Paulist Press, 1983).

14. See Parker Palmer, *The Company of Strangers* (New York: Crossroad, 1981).

15. Patricia Washburn and Robert Gribbon, *Peacemaking Without Division* (Washington, D.C.: Alban Institute, 1986).

Chapter 9

1. Alfred T. Bamsey, review of *Reinventing the Corporation* by John Naisbitt and Patricia Aburdene (New York: Walker & Co., 1985) *Action Information* 13, (Nov.-Dec. 1986).

2. Important work on the dynamics of power, equity and groups has been done by Carol Pierce, New Dynamics, 21 Shore Drive, Laconia, N.H. 03246.

3. Donald M. Joy, "Toward a Symbolic Revival: Creation Revisited," *Religious Education* 80, no. 3 (Summer 1985): 401–02.

4. See Sallie McFague, *Metaphorical Theology* (Philadelphia: Fortress Press, 1982) for a helpful discussion of the need for many metaphors for God.

5. Elizabeth Dodson Gray, *Patriarchy as a Conceptual Trap* (Wellesley, Mass.: Roundtable Press, 1982).

6. Daniel J. Levinson et al., *The Seasons of a Man's Life* (New York: Ballantine Books, 1978), 249.

7. Helen R. Weingarten and Elizabeth Douvan, "Male and Female Visions of Mediation: An Exploration of Gender and Conflict Management" (Paper for University of Michigan, School of Social Work), 4.

8. C. Hahn, "A Family Systems Expert Talks About Congregational Leadership," interview with Edwin H. Friedman, *Action Information* 11:3–4.

9. From Dorothy McMahon, "Called to Be Human," in *Listen to the Spirit*, ed. Patricia Baker (Melbourne: Joint Board of Christian Education, 1986).

10. Diane Kessler, "Old Roles and New Symbols: Female Administrators in Transition," *Christian Century*, 11 Nov. 1981.

Chapter 10

1. Jerry Lewis quoted in *Clergy and the Sexual Revolution* by Ruth Tiffany Barnhouse (Washington, D.C.: Alban Institute, 1987), 36.

2. Research done by Roy M. Oswald and others.

3. Judith Viorst, *Necessary Losses* (New York: Fawcett Book Group, 1986), 193.

4. V. Glendinning, *Vita* (Santa Barbara, Calif.: Quill Publications, 1983).

5. Mark Gerzon, *A Choice of Heroes: Changing Images of American Manhood* (Boston: Houghton Mifflin, 1984), 2.

6. Irene Kassorla, *Nice Girls Do* (Los Angeles: Stratford Press, 1980), 187.

7. James B. Nelson, "Male Sexuality and Masculine Spirituality," *Siecus Report*, March 1985; Viorst, *Necessary Laws*, 194.

8. Viorst, *Necessary Laws*, 193.

9. Wendy M. Wright, "Reflections on Spiritual Friendship Between Men and Women," *Weavings* 2, no. 4: 18.

10. Ibid., 14.

11. Sallie McFague, *Metaphorical Theology* (Philadelphia: Fortress Press, 1982), 180.

12. Ibid., 183.

13. Peter Daly, "A Priest's First Noel," *Washington Post*, 20 Dec. 1987.

14. See Malcolm C. Burson et al., *Discerning the Call to Social Ministry* (Washington, D.C.: Alban Institute, 1989). Comments from participants are drawn from research for that book conducted by the author with Douglas A. Walrath.

15. Jay Lowery, short item in *Enablement* (Feb. 1990): 2.

Chapter 11

1. Ruth Tiffany Barnhouse, *Identity* (Philadelphia: Westminster Press, 1984).

2. Ibid.

3. Marjory Zoet Bankson, *Braided Streams: Esther and a Woman's Way of Growing* (San Diego, Calif.: LuraMedia, 1985).

4. Penelope Washburn, *Becoming Woman: The Quest for Wholeness in Female Experience* (New York: Harper & Row Publishers, 1977), 48.

5. Ibid., 49.

6. Dorothy Dinnerstein, *The Mermaid and the Minotaur* (New York: Harper & Row Publishers, 1977), 65.

7. Jean Baker Miller, "The Development of Women's Self" (Paper for Wellesley College, Stone Center for Developmental Services, 1984), 8.

8. Sam Keen, *The Passionate Life: Stages of Loving* (New York: Harper & Row Publishers, 1983), 183.

9. Mark Gerzon, *A Choice of Heroes: Changing Images of American Manhood* (Boston: Houghton Mifflin, 1984), 175–76.

10. Ruth Tiffany Barnhouse, *Clergy and the Sexual Revolution* (Washington, D.C.: Alban Institute, 1987), 9.

11. Gerzon, *A Choice of Heroes*, 2.

12. Barnhouse, *Clergy and the Sexual Revolution*, 11.

13. George Vaillant, *Adaptation to Life: How the Best and the Brightest Came of Age* (Boston: Little, Brown & Co., 1977), 326.

14. James B. Nelson, *Between Two Gardens* (New York: Pilgrim Press, 1983), 46–47.

15. Phyllis Trible, *God and the Rhetoric of Sexuality* (Philadelphia: Fortress Press, 1980), 80.

16. Howard Moody, "Pleasure too Is a Gift from God," *Christianity and Crisis*, 10 June 1985.

17. Richard J. Foster, *Money, Sex, and Power* (New York: Harper & Row Publishers, 1985), 95.

18. Linda Cusmack, Jewish scholar (Lecture at St. Mark's Church, Washington, D.C., 1987).

19. Martin Marty, "A Man of Grand Contradictions," *Christianity Today*, 21 October 1983, 8.

20. Rollo May, in *Becoming Woman* by Washburn, 45.

21. Quoted in *Original Blessing* by Matthew Fox (Santa Fe, N.M.: Bear & Co., 1983), 26.

22. Quoted in ibid., 63.

23. Keen, *The Passionate Life*, 156–57.

24. Fox, *Original Blessing*, 63.

25. Matthew Fox, *On Becoming a Musical, Mystical Bear* (New York: Paulist Press, 1972), 44–45.

26. Joann Wolski Conn, *Women's Spirituality* (Mahwah N.J.: Paulist Press, 1986), 239.

27. Tilden Edwards, *Living in the Presence* (New York: Harper & Row Publishers, 1987), 72.

28. Trible, *God and the Rhetorical Sexuality*, 159.

29. Fox, *Original Blessing*, 283.

30. See Barnhouse's discussion of this subject in *Clergy and the Sexual Revolution*.

31. James Hillman, *Insearch* (New York: Scribner, 1967), 114.

32. Mary Pellauer, "Sex, Power, and the Family of God," *Christianity and Crisis*, 16 Feb. 1987, 47.

33. *Episcopalian*, June 1987.

34. Dorothy McMahon et al., "Ministering with People in Grief and Loss" (Sydney: Uniting Church in Australia, Board of Education, 1987), 23.

Chapter 12

1. Dorothy Dinnerstein, *The Mermaid and the Minotaur* (New York: Harper & Row Publishers, 1977), a work to which this discussion owes much.

2. Nor Hall, *The Moon and the Virgin: Reflections on the Archetypal Feminine* (New York: Harper & Row Publishers, 1980), 150.

3. *Washington Post*, 16 Jan. 1984.

4. Dinnerstein, *Mermaid and Minotaur*, 51–52.

5. Laurel A. Burton, *Pastoral Paradigms* (Washington, D.C.: Alban Institute, 1988), 87.

6. Ann Belford Ulanov, *Receiving Woman* (Philadelphia: Westminster Press, 1981), 169.

7. Letter from Marianne Micks.

8. Matthew Fox, *Original Blessing*, 89.

9. Hall, *Moon and Virgin*, 84.

10. Diane Wolkstein and Samuel Noah Kramer, *Inanna, Queen of Heaven and Earth* (New York: Harper & Row Publishers, 1983), 172.

11. "Worst News for Working Women," *Washington Post*, 6 Jan. 1985.

Chapter 13

1. E.g. Carol Pierce, "Power Equity and Groups" (Paper for New Dynamics, Laconia, N.H., 1986); Carol Tavris, *Anger: The Misunderstood Emotion* (New York: Simon & Schuster, 1982); and Diane Neu of Women's Alliance for Theology, Ethics, and Ritual (WATER), in Silver Spring, Md.

2. Tavris, *Anger*, 245.

3. Pierce, "Power Equity and Groups," 17.

4. Tavris, *Anger*, 246.

5. Ibid., 253.

6. Pierce, "Power Equity and Groups," 36.

7. Ibid., 13.

8. Richard A. Johnson, *He: Understanding Masculine Psychology* (New York: Harper & Row Publishers, 1974), 33.

9. *Meditations with Meister Eckhart*, ed. Matthew Fox (Santa Fe, N.M.: Bear & Co., 1983), 15.

10. Pierce, "Power Equity and Groups," 1.

11. Carol Pierce, "The Stages of Awareness for Women and Men," *Moving Away from Role Stereotyping* (Laconia, N.H.: New Dynamics, 1983).

12. Daniel Levinson et al., *The Seasons of a Man's Life* (New York: Ballantine Books, 1978), 239.

13. Steve Brown, "Implementing Christian Ecology in the Local Church," *Action Information* 15 (Jan.–Feb. 1989): 6–7.

14. James R. Adams in "Ministry in the Church, Ministry in the World–What's the Connection?" by James R. Adams and Celia A. Hahn, *Action Information* 12 (July–Aug. 1986): 3.

15. Laurel Arthur Burton, *Pastoral Paradigms* (Washington, D.C.: Alban Institute, 1988), 87.

16. Rob Elder, "Tell Me That Story," 65.

17. Virginia Ramey Mollenkott, *The Divine Feminine* (New York: Crossroad, 1983), 40.